P9-ELF-690

PRAISE FOR PHILLIP BERMAN'S PREVIOUS ESSAY COLLECTION,

THE COURAGE OF CONVICTION

"Soars along on clear passages of profundity."

> Jack Smith
> *The Los Angeles Times*

"This collection of original essays on personal philosophy by such a diverse group of people avoids the Scylla of pretention and the Charybdis of self-righteousness . . . An impressive book."

> *The Saturday Review*

"Open it at random, and, without looking at the essayist's name at the head of the page, try to guess who he or she is by reading a random paragraph or two. You'll be disappointed to find out how poorly you do. But if you find, as I did, the commonalities of altruism and strength pervading all these essays, then your disappointment should be, as mine is, the cause for some small celebration."

> *The Humanist*

"There is no shortage of inspiration, and . . . anyone who isn't afraid to examine one's conviction may find it one of the most useful books of a troubled decade."

> Paul Craig
> *The Saturday Review*

ALSO EDITED BY PHILLIP L. BERMAN
PUBLISHED BY BALLANTINE BOOKS

The Courage of Conviction

The COURAGE *to* GROW OLD

EDITED WITH AN INTRODUCTION BY

Phillip L. Berman

BALLANTINE BOOKS • NEW YORK

All royalties from the sale of this book go to the Center for the Study of Contemporary Belief, the nonprofit organization established by Phillip Berman, M.T.S., to promote tolerance and intellectual and spiritual growth in society at large. Contributions to further this work are tax deductible and may be sent to the Center for the Study of Contemporary Belief, P.O. Box 300553, Denver, Colorado 80203. If you would like to learn more about the center's book projects or lecture programs, please write to the above address.

Copyright © 1989 by The Center for the Study of Contemporary Belief

Copyright © 1989 by Vera A. Cleaver, Margaret Cousins, Mary Francis Shura Craig, Judith Crist, Marion Pease Davis, Rosemary DeCamp, Prof. David Diamond, Charles Edward Eaton, Prof. Fritz Eichenberg, Albert Ellis, Ph.D., Dr. Margaret Coit Elwell, Dr. Frederick Franck, Dr. Henry J. Heimlich, Dame Hyacinthe Hill, Jerome Lawrence, Robert E. Lee, Cornel Lengyel, J. A. Livingston, Lee Loevinger, Leslie A. Marchand, Anne Marx, Arthur Marx, Sarah McClendon, Barrett McGurn, Dr. Gairdner Moment, William Nichols, Jules Olitski, Dr. Alfred Painter, Dr. Dan Q. Posin, Dr. Paul Schlipp, Harry Shaw, Leland Stowe, Dr. John Tebbel, Lawrence Treat, Ph.D., Ira Wallach, Phyllis A. Whitney, George Woodcock, Elizabeth Yates, Charlotte Zolotow.

All rights reserved under International and Pan-American Copyright Conventions. Published in the United States by Ballantine Books, a division of Random House, Inc., New York, and simultaneously in Canada by Random House of Canada Limited, Toronto.

The Malcolm Muggeridge Foundation: "The Prospect of Death" by Malcolm Muggeridge. Used by permission of the author and The Malcolm Muggeridge Foundation.

Page 318 constitutes an extension of the copyright page.

Library of Congress Catalog Card Number: 88-92348
ISBN: 0-345-35072-3
Designed by Ann Gold
Manufactured in the United States of America
First Edition: October 1989
10 9 8 7 6 5 4 3 2 1

I'm growing fonder of my staff;
I'm growing dimmer in the eyes;
I'm growing fainter in my laugh;
I'm growing deeper in my sighs;
I'm growing careless of my dress;
I'm growing frugal of my gold;
I'm growing wise; I'm growing—yes—
I'm growing old.

Robert Browning
Rabbi Ben Ezra

Contents

Acknowledgments

During the preparation of this book I was aided greatly by the assistance of Linda Dubroof, my lawyer and agent, and by Susan Smith, whose rapid-fire typing pulled me out of many a jam. I would also like to thank my supportive associates at the Center for the Study of Contemporary Belief, Dr. Wilbur Fridell, Dr. Douglas Brooks, Dr. Gregory Walters, and Dr. Robert Gordon-McCutchan. I have also benefited greatly from the editorial advice of Michelle Russell and Jane Bess, my editors at Ballantine Books. Finally, my greatest thanks must go to my wife, Anne Gordon, whose unwavering support and editorial advice added greatly to the quality of this book.

Introduction

When Joëlle Delbourgo of Ballantine Books approached me with the idea for this book, I reacted with both a measure of enthusiasm and anxiety. As a thirty-year-old, the prospect of collecting essays from men and women more than twice my age was appealing. Assuming there was truth to the saying that "with age comes wisdom," I instantly and rather selfishly concluded that editing this book might help prepare me for my own "sundown years." Still, I worried what elderly people might think of a young man editing such a book. What business does a young person have even tackling such a project? Doesn't one have to be old, as Elizabeth Yates suggests here, before one can talk about what it is like? It wasn't until I actually began to collect these essays that such doubts began to subside, for I was soon overcome by a quiet joy born from the knowledge that I was helping to assemble a rich, inspiring patchwork of wisdom drawn from more than three thousand years of collective human experience.

In the early stages of this project I received numerous rejection letters from potential contributors. One thing that struck me about these letters was the frequency with which people claimed it did not take courage to grow old. As one of them wrote: "Growing old is a natural phenomenon and nobody is doing it faster or slower than his neighbor. I therefore cannot understand that it takes courage." As these letters mounted, I began to wonder if I had made a mistake titling this book *The Courage to Grow Old*, and even considered retitling it. When these essays started to arrive, however, I saw that this too was an unwarranted doubt. I fell back upon my original conviction that it takes courage to live fully and vitally at any age, and that each stage in life presents us with different sets of challenges.

Of course, the need for and amount of courage we must muster depends entirely upon the circumstances in which we find ourselves.

Writing his contribution from the "apparently tranquil surface" of the retirement community in which he lives, John Tebbel sees that "to be aging and ill requires the greatest courage . . . to see someone taking care of a wife or husband with Alzheimer's disease, for example, opens the door to a particular kind of hell that must take extraordinary courage to confront every day."

Unless we are very lucky, aging inevitably entails increasing physical disabilities, whether it's the slow shift, as Henry Heimlich puts it, from "a cane, to a walker, then to a wheelchair," or the more rapid decline of an individual suffering from Alzheimer's. But whether we age slowly or rapidly, none of us can escape decline. The moment we are born we begin to die. It's simply a question of how and when. We can slow the process with right thinking and proper diet, but we can't stop it. What we can control is the way we choose to deal with our infirmities, and this is where courage—and a healthy dose of humor—works wonders.

Coping with the loss of one's lover demands yet another kind of courage, a courage evident throughout these pages. For William Nichols, who lost his wife, Mariethé, to Alzheimer's disease, the necessary adjustments have come, but not without recurrent sharp reaction and pain: "Where is she?" he asks himself. "Why isn't she here, and with me NOW?" To lessen the anxiety, he visits churches where the image of Saint Anthony can be found. Saint Anthony was Mariethé's favorite saint, and now, with her gone, he is compelled, "almost automatically," to "light my candle and, along with my prayer, actually feel as if I were talking to her—through him. With that comes a wonderful sense of calmness and strength."

While the loss of one's spouse may require the courage to face loneliness, it might also require the courage to love again. Marion Pease Davis, a widow since 1984, is attempting to start a new relationship with a man whose wife is dying of Alzheimer's. As she writes here: "The supportive, loving relationship I had with [my husband] has given me courage, as a great-grandmother, to risk a new relationship, to begin to build a new love. I have learned that one can grow through sadness . . . In the relationship with my new friend, the sadness of his wife's long, incurable illness . . . the horror of her no longer knowing him or their daughters as he faithfully visits her every week in the nursing home, and the happiness of our developing love are inextricably connected. The sadness has forced us to develop deeper resources of patience as well as the tolerance to accept uncertainty."

I could go on citing the many examples of courage to be found within these pages, but that would be a misrepresentation of this book, for it is not a collection of aging heroes. Rather, you will find here men and women sharing honestly their thoughts and feelings about growing old. Some of them have found that it takes extraordinary courage, while others have not. And so it should be, for the world is full of both the lucky and the unlucky, the courageous and the less than courageous. It was not my intention to create a Pollyannaish book of unbridled optimism at the expense of a balanced truth. George Burns may be chasing twenty-year-olds at the age of ninety, but I am aware that, as Paul Schilpp puts it here, "the frolic is not there for many . . . aging can be frightening and depressing."

"At eighty-three," writes Cornel Lengyel, "Jefferson composed his own epitaph and, celebrating his last Independence Day at Monticello, declared himself ready for the final adventure, 'untried by the living and unreported by the dead.'" Speculation about the nature of this "final adventure" is not uncommon with the elderly, and those writing here are no exception. Many, like Ira Wallach, see death as final and believe that "the aging person who selects a burial plot with a good northwest view of the Hudson River in an elevated spot on a grassy knoll is . . . avoiding acceptance of death." Malcolm Muggeridge, on the other hand, rather looks forward to it, "like a prisoner awaiting release, like a schoolboy when the end of term is near, like a migrant bird ready to fly south . . ." Others neither view death as a final end nor look to it so longingly, but rather await the prospect with curiosity, convinced, as is Robert E. Lee, that "the mystery sustains our optimism."

I assumed the majority of those who accepted my invitation would be optimists, but I wasn't opposed to the inclusion of a pessimist or two. Of the few here, composer David Diamond paints the gloomiest of pictures, for he has come to view his life with an "attitude of irony and pity," and feels that "there is no dignity in growing old." His essay, from start to finish, is a litany of woe. Yet I consider it one of the most important contributions to this book because he has shared his sadness with honesty and portrays what we all must fear, for who would wish to approach the end of his life believing, as he does, that "aging is torment in flux," where "only death can terminate the agonizing flow of deterioration"?

But there is more humor and lightness here than gloom. Surely the opposite extreme of David Diamond is Arthur Marx, who takes great pleasure sharing his father's favorite jokes about aging. "Middle age," said Groucho, "is when you go to bed at night and think you're going to feel better in the morning. Old age is when you go to bed at night and hope you wake up in the morning." Groucho especially loved the humor of Robert Benchley, who, upon being asked by Groucho how he felt after reaching fifty, replied, "I feel fine, except for an occasional heart attack."

Time, and what to do with what remains of it, is often on the minds of the aging. The "sound of time's winged chariot is louder in our ears," writes Charlotte Zolotow. "When the years ahead are fewer than those we've left behind, should we go on working even if it leaves unfinished books and music we have never had time for? Or should we plunge on as though our bones are not stiffening, and get through to the office, to the comfort of coffee in styrofoam cups thawing our arthritic fingers before we enter the turmoil and excitement of a day where we know we can give to other people . . ." It isn't an easy choice, deciding whether or not to retire. On the one hand, many here express a desire to cut back on commitments, to savor each step of the journey and to luxuriate in the liberation from, as D. Elton Trueblood puts it, "the hectic struggle to get ahead in life, to build a reputation, and to establish a home." On the other hand, most recognize that to pull back from work may be to pull back from life itself. Yet that need not be so. Many here have found retirement a wondrous blessing and have used the time to explore new ideas and to feel new feelings.

Since I've arranged these essays in chronological order, starting with the youngest contributors first, you will note as you read this book that the further you go, the more renunciation and contentment you will find. Those in their sixties and early seventies tend to reflect more on the questions of retirement and time, while those in their later seventies, eighties, and nineties tend to reflect more on the past and, as Malcolm Muggeridge puts it, "the prospect of death." However, if there is a single message in this book, a common wisdom that unites these men and women, it is surely their belief that one must continue to create, or at least live creatively, right up to the end. Indeed, the vast majority of these contributors are against mandatory retirement and urge the reader to enjoy not only, as Jerome Lawrence puts it, "the pursuit of happiness, but the happiness of pursuit." Journalist Barrett McGurn, whose essay is a study of the old people he has observed through life, concludes that "to live happily, to live at all, each of us needs a purpose . . . I am satisfied in my mind, however, that it is wrong to equate work with life and that after present labors cease, an avocation—painting, reading, travel, volunteer employment—should be able to fill the void caused by the end of life's second stage.''

If growth depends upon our ability to accept change, as I believe it does, then the elderly of our time have much to teach us. ''In 1913, when I was born,'' writes Ira Wallach, ''IBM could have paid the national debt out of its petty cash drawer, radio was a futuristic fantasy, television and space exploration the bread and butter of science fiction, and a bulky office adding machine was deemed technological sophistication.'' Who could deny that between World War I, which many here experienced, and World War II, which all of them did, these men and women saw more explosive social change in their lifetimes than any preceding generation? They witnessed the advent of the car, the plane, the Bomb, and the micro chip, the exploration of the moon, and the very eclipse of God himself in Hitler's and Stalin's concentration camps. For these men and women, the heroes and demons are quite different from those of my generation. I was surprised at how many of them have drawn their inspiration from the lives of Einstein and Schweitzer. When they write about these men it is as though they are still alive, so powerful were the impressions they left upon those of their time. Aside from the towering beneficence of Mother Teresa, I can't help but feel that mine is a generation impoverished for want of such paradigms of humanity.

During the year or so it has taken to complete this book I have been immersed with the thoughts and concerns of the aged. And while I doubt my publisher will be glad to learn this, the effect this has had upon me is to make me less ambitious, in search less of making my mark than in making sure that the time I spend on this planet brings joy to myself and others. For ''God does not read resumés,'' as Frederick Franck states here, and I am aware, more and more, not just as an abstract intellectual concept, but as a palpable fact close to my heart, that even the immortals are not immortal, and that the reclamation of our souls is surely the most important task we face. If this should bring one accolades, so be it; if not, so be that as well. I can only say that the gracious contributions of these men and women have helped me to appreciate the gift and beauty that is life and that I hope they can do the same for you.

PHILLIP L. BERMAN

The Courage
to Grow Old

Library Cable Network (LCN)

Mary Francis Shura Craig

B. 1923

🕱 🕱

Award-winning children's writer Mary Francis Shura Craig was born on a western Kansas cattle ranch near Dodge City but wasn't quite a year old when her family moved to the Pacific Northwest, where she lived until her teens. "Childhood to me," she says, "is the scent of summer dust on bedded pine needles." With a family steeped in oral traditions, where anecdotes of the living and the dead were spun around the dinner table, she grew up "thinking of time as a vast multicolored cord at one with the past and the future, of traits and oddities being bright strands that appear and reappear, changed only by the environment of the current age."

Now the proud author of over twenty-five best-selling children's books, including *The Simple Spigott* (on the 100 Best List World Book Encyclopedia, 1960), *The Search for Grissi* (Carl Sandburg Award, 1985), and *The Josie Gambit* (ALA Notable Book, 1986), Ms. Craig admits that the great joy of writing for children is that they are still in the process of becoming and are therefore "satisfied, and sometimes delighted, with the small triumphs that fall their way."

Ms. Craig has also authored numerous adult mysteries, as well as several short stories, and contributed poetry to both popular and scholarly magazines.

A MOSAIC OF MINUTES

I need to say at once that age has always seemed relatively immaterial to me. I don't know whether I have an extraordinary quota of endorphins or a mood pendulum that is weighted toward joy, but I am no less happy now than I have been most of my life.

Let me also add that it has never occurred to me to consider "growing old" as a process separate from the continuum of my life. At no time do I remember defining myself by the category of age. I was not consciously young, nor middle-aged. I was simply alive and busy.

To isolate old age in my mind is to summon a battery of negative stereotypes, all linked to loss—of delight, of beauty, of strength. Then the uninvited calamities—loneliness, illness, and death. However, if I shift that consideration only a little, to consider other human beings whom I have known in their great age, the stereotypes disappear, the losses are redefined, and my mind glows with memories of some of the most important people in my personal world.

The day may well come when I reread these words with astonishment at my own shallow perceptions of my future. Be that as it may, I can only express how I feel about growing older from the perspective of this hour.

To date I live with undiminished pleasure. In a way, I credit this to my complete fascination with the process of writing. I have always known where I was going in terms of my working life. The presence of a long-term, conscious goal has helped me to maintain stability through the ubiquitous changes of over half a century. Whatever else was going on in the world, my country, or within the smaller circle of family and friends, the language was always there, as inevitably accessible as it was impervious to catastrophe.

I liken this stabilizing force to the stout rope threaded through metal eyelets on the fence between the house and barn on our family ranch. Western Kansas is infamous for weather powerful enough to bring a man to his knees, unremitting blizzards, blinding pillars of dust, and funnel-shaped gale winds howling out of the southwest. It is almost impossible to drive a man to his knees when his hand grips a solid strand leading to where he wants to go.

Many times I have pulled myself along only on the strength of that rope. I fully expect to do so many times again. I cannot imagine the

5

words failing to delight and sustain me, but if they do, I am surrounded by the words of other minds that I will delight in returning to. Take the sadder case that I cannot read. Then I will listen. Take the bleaker case that I cannot hear. I can remember. The most dire case of all is that one's body should house a mind that cannot think. At that point, though, the consciousness of loss is gone as well.

Because of this distraction with my mind, I have been only moderately conscious of the effect of aging on my physical appearance. Once in a while I am startled to catch an oblique reflection of myself and see some old woman walking along wearing my clothes. So far I have been able to laugh. It isn't that I lack natural human vanity but rather that my self-identity has always been rooted in different earth. The same obtains for the people I treasure. I cannot think of a single human being whom I have ever cherished whose appeal to me was based on youthful cosmetic attractiveness alone. As a matter of fact, I often turn in a crowded city to stare at a face on which experience has written a pattern of celebration.

Blessed with good health and superabundant energy, I have dealt with the inevitable final stages of entropy only vicariously. The thought of failing strength alone is not painful to me. The prospect of being a physical burden, with its accompanying loss of privacy, is. But here we see through a glass darkly. I build what defenses I can against that humiliation, remembering that the landscapes of the world are dotted with fortresses that have never been stormed.

My work and my life are both solitary. Being accustomed to my own company, I don't dread loneliness in its ordinary sense. It is important to realize that being alone is not the same as being lonely, and that your own company is preferable to that of many companions.

My favorite entertainment comes from inside my own head. I have lived with it full of growing stories about fictional people all my life. But books have last chapters. It is the responsibility of the writer to devise that last chapter with such care that the reader's thoughts can flow back over the story as if it were a varied terrain under flood water. The trivial is inundated and the high ground visible.

Lives have last chapters too. The very process of approaching that last segment of work gives me pause. For heaven's sake! Must I review a work that I will have neither the time nor the strength to revise? But we flow our minds back anyway, whether we want to or not. The picayune disappears and the significant rises to glow in the light.

Each of us will see a different mountain. Our individual perceptions dictate the relative magnitude of factors in that backward view. We have defined right and wrong, beautiful and hideous so many times that, by the defining, we have defined ourselves. We can deal with this cumulative data any way we choose. Perversely enough, the losses of age often provide gains in time for contemplation. Like the writer who catches his dangling thread of story and tucks it in neatly so that it not fray the reader's patience, we can bring closure to unfinished business. One sometimes even discovers an opportunity for some minimal revisions.

But in any case, we are defined. We are free to accept ourselves for what we have made of ourselves. We are past a lot of affectations. We need not assume roles or spout precept to preach, or teach, or even to convince anyone else. We are what we believe and our convictions are the ground on which we stand as human beings.

There is something wonderfully wholesome about accepting yourself at last, the good and the bad, the raucous and the humble, all tumbled in together.

So I ask myself where am I standing, after all this time?

The answer for me is that I balance myself uneasily on shifting ground. I know that the single constancy in life is change. After that first resounding slap brings us, gasping and screaming, into expression, we deal with remnants.

All we ever have is what is left. Even the remnants change.

Loss of innocence comes early. You are not the sun of any other human's universe. You wear no magic armor against your own human frailty, pain, or defeat. Your dreams do not come true.

Loss of trust follows hard on its heels. Almost every human head carries its own hidden agenda. Rare is the man who will not willingly sacrifice you for his own reasons. You are indispensable to no one but yourself.

Strangely enough, this hard-won knowledge can bring us the perverse and exhilarating pleasure of taking risks at an age when hanggliding is not an option. We know the name of the game and the price of the candle. Since we only fear what we do not understand, once we are stripped of blinding illusions, we can love, and trust, and depend without reservations as long as we are ready to pay the possible price— one more time.

There is a heady pleasure in always leaving the door off the latch for the unheralded return of prodigal sons.

Living teaches you that time is neither healer nor enemy. It is neutral and seamless and of steadily diminishing quantity. You alone are in charge of quality control. One accepts this transient tenancy, grateful that the conditions of the lease include blazing sunsets, the spinning grandeur of seasons, and the company of other species as well as your own. And laughter.

Since time is not the enemy, we need to identify what threatens us. We each know our enemies and they are not the same for any of us.

The fire that burns away my reason is anger. Yet I know that anger comes from the same fire that fuels other passions. Deliver me from the sterility of a passionless life! But if this energy does erupt in anger, let your fury be righteous and in a cause other than your own desire or welfare. This is the anger that keeps your own life bright. The world has been vastly enriched by the articulated indignation of mature and respected minds speaking from the wisdom of age into the inexperience of their times.

For me, the most alienating habit of mind is judging. One can't judge without sooner or later turning one's face away from those whom one has named guilty. I have to turn to judge myself for arrogance and remind myself that no man dictates the circumstances of his life. Neither can anyone honestly determine his own behavior and responses to another person's life circumstances. Like the tracery of underground root structure that supports a tree, a man's hidden tangled experiences shape his growth. The battle against judging is the challenge of mentally living more life than one.

I was slow to learn that fiction becomes quick with life through minutiae. Life, being a mosaic of minutes that pattern into hours, should be lived that way, a minute, an hour at a time. And I would run up a flag for all small pleasures, a favorite tree tracked through its seasons, an apple peeled in a single curling strip, and I'd stay with those pleasures until the cat's nap is finished. Such leisurely indulgences are reserved for us who have earned our time.

But if it were all to do over, I would study Greek.

In fact, I may anyway.

© Peter A. Weissenstein 1987

Judith Crist

B. 1922

Judith Crist has been advising Americans on which movies to watch or avoid for more than a quarter of a century. Known as a gutsy writer who keeps her "built-in bunk detector, zap-the-producer gun, parody-the-plot knife, and other critical weapons in fine condition," she gears her criticism toward the middle of the intellectual road, which in part accounts for her tremendous popularity.

After earning a master's degree in journalism from Columbia University in 1945, Ms. Crist joined the now defunct *New York Herald Tribune* as a reporter and served subsequently as an editor for the arts and as a film and drama critic. She was film and theater critic for NBC's "Today Show" from 1963 to 1973. She has also served as critic for *TV Guide, New York* magazine, *Saturday Review, The Washingtonian*, the *New York Post*, and several other publications, and has done reviews for local, network, and public television. Since 1959 she has served as an adjunct professor at Columbia's Graduate School of Journalism. Her books include *The Private Eye, the Cowboy and the Very Naked Girl* (1968),

Judith Crist's TV Guide to the Movies (1974), and *Take 22: Moviemakers on Moviemaking* (1984).

Widely honored for her work, Ms. Crist has received the George Polk Award (1952), the Page One Award (1955), a Columbia Graduate School of Journalism Alumni Award (1961), the Centennial President's Medal from Hunter College (1970), and several New York Newswomen's Club Awards.

In 1970 she organized the Judith Crist Film Weekends in Tarrytown, New York, which enable actors, producers, writers, and directors to exchange views with fans and scholars on the creative and business aspects of filmmaking.

PASSING THE TORCH

There is a particular aspect of the "courage" to grow old that I encountered in 1952. A general assignment reporter for the *New York Herald Tribune*, I was called into the managing editor's office one spring day and given a professional dream-fulfillment: I was to join the Washington bureau in its coverage of both the Republican and Democratic national conventions in Chicago that summer. I remember the chill of delight, the quickened heartbeat, the thrill of achievement in being the one city-side reporter selected to go. We talked at length and then I asked, "What about Emma? Does she know?"

Emma Bugbee was the sweet grande dame of the staff, a by then motherly-looking white-haired woman who had joined the *Tribune* staff in 1912 and was a veteran of every political convention since. The quadrennial conventions were her plums, for beyond the sheer zest of the journalistic game in those pre-television-saturated days, there was, for the city staffer, a residue of topnotch contacts, a pipeline to the capital beyond the purlieu of the Washington bureau and all the advantages of having been "in" on the beginning of a new national administration. Emma had made the most of it all; she was, in fact, the only one on the paper to have all of Eleanor Roosevelt's private numbers.

No, Emma had not been told, the editor informed me, and I should not talk of my assignment until she was. Sharing my secret only with my husband, I literally skulked past Emma's desk in the city room, avoiding her eyes and offering only a brief "hi" in passing. My own rejoicing was tinged with guilt.

About ten days later I saw Emma emerge from the managing editor's office. I ducked my head, concentrated on my typewriter, and suddenly was aware of her approach. "Judy, what wonderful news!" I rose and she threw her arms around me. "I'm so happy that it's you. I can't wait to tell you what to expect—and I'll alert the people you should know . . ."

It was, of course, sportsmanship, generosity, friendship, magnanimity. But I grew to realize through the years that it was also a part of the courage to grow old—the courage to let go, to pass the torch.

The conventions—with Eisenhower and Stevenson the nominees—were a once-in-a-lifetime experience: I was "too pregnant" to go in

1956; by 1960 I was the editor for the arts and by 1964 a film critic. Beyond the excitement, the hard work, the personal and professional enrichments of those weeks, however, what has stayed in the forefront of memory is the sendoff that Emma gave me, the advice, the contact lists, the hugs. And I have watched her "courage" become part of my own aging process.

For achievers like myself, those of us dedicated to the continuing pursuit of professional success, there is the tendency to hold on to all gains, keeping one eye on the competition and—a neat ophthalmic trick—the other on the climbers on the lower rungs of the ladder. But slowly, as the years pass, the eyes relax, the grip loosens, and a hand is offered to the climbers. What was once simply, "Sorry, I'm too busy for that" when a new outlet is offered becomes, "I'm too busy, but I know a bright young person who could do it," and that becomes, "Why me? There's a talented newcomer you should think of."

It isn't altruism: there's the reflected glory of "making" another's career, the nostalgia and empathy in observing professional growth, the satisfaction of having a share in someone's success. I see this too in my role as teacher, a parental (after thirty years, grandparental?) approach to my graduate students, a more objective and somehow more appreciative attitude toward their work, a greater interest in their potential and talents than in their immediate flaws and failures. My rewards are no longer in the "evaluations" they make of me and the course at term's end but in the keeping-in-touch afterwards, in those who let me know that a mark was made on their minds.

What it is—and it becomes more evident closer to home—is the courage to surrender, to loosen the grip in deed and attitude, whether it's in having one's own way or having the last word. It's also, of course, a matter of facing present and generational realities. The ego shock when the first person said, "Oh, Judith Crist—are you Steven Crist's mother?" has now become a flush of pride in being associated with the name of my-son-the-journalist.

My brother-the-sociologist once needled me by noting that professionals "peak" in their mid-fifties. Actually, I have been at my busiest and most involved a decade later. For me, "peaking"—whether it happens in your fifties, sixties, or seventies—means the realization that you have already proven your worth and that you can accept, with no twinge of conscience, the fact that you are becoming bored with your daily routines, that indeed what goes around does come around, and that—to pursue the jargon—you have already been where it's at. It means allowing oneself to slow down, to reduce the race to a walk, even a stroll, as obligations decrease and the false sense of responsibility declines. I no longer consider it a major sin to refuse to read galleys of a forthcoming book (sent in hope of a dustjacket quote) if the subject doesn't appeal to me; to miss a movie or a play that I don't "have" to see—I who have spent decades addicted to anything that moves on a screen or a stage, free at last to make personal choices, to be selective. I remember well the widow on an early "Newhart" episode bemoaning the fact that her husband had never taken time "to smell the roses"— and he had been a florist. But I find myself taking guiltless time to watch the squirrels attack my latest squirrel-proof feeder or even, delight of delights, to stare into space, instead of watching an "important" television show; to reread a classic instead of forcing myself to read a bestseller; to enjoy a dinner with friends instead of dashing to see an "interesting" little play. I have finally become too old for trash and for trivia that take two hours or an evening from my lifetime.

The prizes, awards, and rewards of the past are treasured and their more recent recipients respected. But the competition is almost, if not quite, over, in attitude at very least, and the achieving is for self-testing and pleasure rather than self-aggrandizement. These years are for personal pleasure. I long ago eschewed the "social ramble" attendant on success; always clear in memory is the bedraggled autograph-seeker outside Sardi's who would demand of anyone, short of Bette Davis, "Are you anybody?"

We let our intergenerational circle of friends fluctuate, expanding with interesting newcomers, contracting with our growing intolerance for bores and boors and hypochondriacs. But at the center of that circle is a tight-knit group of friends from our newspaper days. Some years ago we all vowed to stay put in and around New York City so long as we were physically and economically able to do so, never to move off to retirement homes or communities in soggy or arid warmer climes. There, we agreed, we'd be just some more golden agers from somewhere. But if we all stuck together we'd always have around us people who knew us as something other than senior citizens, as achievers, blowing our bubbles of reputation, as "somebodies" who were damn good at what we did and accomplished.

To let go of that, we guessed rightly, would take more courage than any of us could muster.

© Helen Miljakovich 1985, All Rights Reserved

Jules Olitski

B. *1922*

❦ ❦

The Russian-born painter Jules Olitski is probably best known for his "color field" paintings of the 1960s, achieved by the technique of spraying paint directly onto unprimed canvas. He continues to enjoy an international reputation; his work is included in many major museums and significant collections in the United States and abroad. He is also a sculptor of note: an exhibition of his sculptures at the Metropolitan Museum in New York City earned him the distinction of becoming the first living American artist to be given a one-man show at that venerable institution. Mr. Olitski not only has created art but also has taught it at Bennington College and at New York University, where he earned a master of fine arts degree in 1955.

He has written that the events that shaped him, "some welcomed, others endured," have been the "decision to be an artist, made upon the death of my grandmother; art studies at the National Academy of Design; life in the U.S. Army; living in Paris on the GI Bill; first marriage and first child; second marriage and second child; dozen years of teaching in colleges and universities; third marriage to Kristina." A rejuvenating event occurred in 1984 after he

15

entered a rehabilitation treatment center for alcoholism. He left it with, he has written, "a new life of health, sobriety, and, I feel, spiritual awakening." Since then he has been able to do his creative work with "a sense of joy, excitement, hope, and a good measure of awe. I can hardly imagine a happier life than mine at this moment."

In the summers he and Kristina make their home in Meredith, New Hampshire. In the winters they travel south to Islamorada, Florida.

A LETTER TO KRISTINA

Dear Kristina,

I wish you were here. I'm having the dickens of a time trying to write an essay on the courage to grow old. I've all but given up. I just can't find the center; the piece needs a center—something to which I can relate my day-to-day experience. I keep seeing a bicycle wheel: the hub, the spokes radiating from it, and finally the round completeness of its shape. Right now I feel only edges and fragments. I guess I'm simply not aware of myself as old, or, for that matter, needing courage. Sure, I notice delivery boys now call me "sir." And sure, I can no longer run as fast as I used to or work as many hours at a stretch—and must I mention my bald head, gray beard, and a belly that escapes my belt? And where, I wonder, is that sense of wholeness, that benign wisdom old age is supposed to bring? Even so, I can't think of an age when I felt more alive and happier than now. Why is that? It's not that I feel fulfilled, as if I had accomplished something I'd set out to do a long time ago. Not at all. It's more a feeling that everything is still there to do, or to do better. I certainly feel that about my work and I feel that more and more about my life (although, as you know, I don't really know how to separate the two).

Nicolas Poussin said that the goal of art is delight. It sure is—and shouldn't that be the goal of life? Why not delight? Why not pleasure? Why not the joy of life? Is life to be lived solemnly? I wish when I was a kid growing up that someone told me that the goal of life is delight. My poor, dear mother; when she was young she had a wonderful girlish laugh and with a bit of wine she danced a lovely jig. But the older she got, the more she sighed. She sighed and sighed until she died.

I'm reminded now of that late night TV war movie I saw when a soldier talks about a buddy of his who'd just been killed: "Don't feel bad about him, Sarge. Joe had a terrific philosophy. He never worried about anything!" Now, wouldn't that make life easier? "What, me worry?" Sounds like *Mad* magazine's Alfred E. Newman. Still, I'd rather that than be like our friend Jocko, who acts as if he has all the answers about life, as if he has everything all worked out. Phooey!

Do you remember that I told you once that as a kid growing up I always felt there was some secret about life; some secret that everyone

17

but me had figured out? So I read and read looking for the answer on every page. I know now I'm no more in the dark than most people. But you know that I still read that way, hoping that this something, whatever it is, will reveal itself to me on the very next page. It just occurred to me—that's the attitude I have about going to my work: something will be revealed—and I must follow. Picasso's remark comes to mind, the one where he pointed to a painting he'd just completed and said: "It's not what I was searching for—it's what I found." I like that. Maybe that's the attitude to take about growing old—it's what I found. There is always the pull toward the expected—and giving into that can be deadening. I guess what I am trying to say is that this thing that appears under our hand while we were looking elsewhere is more real, more right than the expected thing, the known thing, the recognized thing. No one can say for me what old age is like. I must find it out for myself. That's where the adventure is. Cicero said: "It is weariness of all pursuits that creates weariness of life."

Maybe I should be, but I don't find myself concerned about time and how precious it is and how it's running out and that I must make every moment count. I dawdle a lot. I let things take their course. One thing leads to another. I have a good time. It's out of necessity that I do most anything. It's curiosity and anticipation that usually gets me going. I lie in bed thinking: What would it look like if I did this, that, and such and such in a painting or a sculpture—what would it look like? I begin to see it in my mind's eye and I get excited. My God, it seems a beautiful thing! I must get to the studio. That will get me out of bed.

I've been thinking about death these past few days. And I've been crying. The news from the vet about Caro is awful. A month at most, he said. I walked down to the dock this afternoon and the cat walked alongside me, the way he does—how old is he, anyway? Eighteen? Seventeen? I forgot. Suddenly it was unbearable. I haven't felt that way since Whiskey died. I just looked at the drawing I did of him moments after he died in my arms: the sixth of September, 1981. Seven years since we buried that dog near the bridge on the way to my studio. I remember that night. It was a terrible night. The wind howled and there were torrents of rain. Standing by the grave I howled myself. We piled up stones and built a cairn over his grave. You know, I speak to him every time I cross that bridge. I call to him, I tell him how good he was and how much I love him. I tell him to sleep. It hurts. And now the cat. We must not bury Caro next to Whiskey. Caro never cared for

Whiskey. Remember the time Whiskey was caught in the fence and Caro went after Whiskey's rear end? Let's bury Caro on the rocky knoll above the cairn. That way he can look down on Whiskey and on everything else. Cats like high places. My God, how I love that cat. I'll try to do a drawing of him while he still is with us.

How to deal with loss? Suppose it was you, God forbid!—could I go on? I don't think so. Is it cowardly of me that I can't imagine a life without you?

The only time I think about my own death is when I remind myself that I could die at any moment. This is what I try to remind myself of when I am lacking courage. Usually it's when I'm being cautious, afraid to try something out. Risk. Somehow, telling myself that I could die at any moment frees me. Everything seems of a sudden to fall into place. Paradoxically, it's as if, literally, I have nothing to lose. I can go ahead and do, or say, whatever needs saying or doing.

I once said to an artist friend who was feeling blocked in his work: "You can do anything in art, so long as it's not you doing it." What I meant had to do with giving one's self over to what William James called a greater self. Well, I find this letting go is good for living too. I must write my friend and share with him something I just came upon that Schiller said: "Man is wholly himself only when he plays."

I love you,

Jules

William Kirk

Arthur Marx

B. *1921*

❈ ❈

Arthur Marx, the son of the famous comedian, has written several successful biographies, among them *Life with Groucho* (1954), *Goldwyn* (1976), *Red Skelton* (1979), and *The Nine Lives of Mickey Rooney* (1986). He has also written television scripts for "All in the Family," "Maude," and "The Jeffersons," and has contributed scores of articles to popular magazines, including the *New York Times Magazine, Sports Illustrated,* and *Parade.*

In collaboration with Robert Fisher, Marx has written a number of plays, including *The Impossible Years* (which starred Alan King and ran for 645 performances on Broadway), *Minnie's Boys* (the story of the young Marx Brothers, starring Shelley Winters), and *My Daughter's Rated X* (a comedy that won the Straw Hat Award in 1970 for the best play of the summer stock season in the U.S.). Most recently, Marx and Fisher wrote the off-Broadway hit, *Groucho,* which opened in New York in 1986, to unanimous rave reviews, and in London in 1987, where it was nominated for the Lawrence Olivier Award as Best Comedy of the Year.

When not in front of his typewriter or directing a play, Marx can usually be found playing tennis at the Beverly Hills Tennis Club, where, as far as he is concerned, "I am still the best player at the club."

STILL THE
BEST PLAYER AT THE CLUB

When you consider the alternative, it doesn't take a great deal of courage to grow old. The way I look at it, old age is actually a reward for not getting run over by a truck or dying of a terminal illness.

Reward or not, there are things about growing old that are bound to change your life. The realization that I was no longer the stripling I thought happened to me almost overnight. One day I was rolling along under the illusion that I was still a young man in the prime of life. I was still active professionally, turning out a book or play a year, and staging the latter. I was playing fairly strenuous tennis four or five days a week, and was still considered one of the top players at the Beverly Hills Tennis Club, as I had been since the age of fifteen. My wife, Lois, and I still had a very active sex life (we had to buy a new mattress and box spring), I could still read normal-size print without glasses, and I could still eat Mexican food without having to reach for the Maalox bottle. I still had all my teeth. And, oh, yes, I even had hair—although most of it was on my chest.

Prior to that there may have been minor indications that I wasn't quite as young as I thought I was. Stairs seemed a little steeper. Newsprint seemed a little smaller. And when I tried to get into a movie theater on the senior citizen's discount the girl at the box office never even asked to look at my ID card before selling me a ticket. But I just attributed that to laziness, or to the fact that I had an honest face, not an old one.

Then one day I received a letter asking me to contribute to this publication. Suddenly, I realized I was fooling no one. I had to face it: I was a senior citizen whether I admitted it or not.

Not that I was deliberately trying to mislead anybody. I simply figured that if I didn't dwell on the fact that I now had more years behind me than I could possibly have ahead of me that I'd somehow slow down the aging process—which, after all, is really all we can do. It's probably that very denial of advancing years that has sustained me and kept me healthy and active professionally at a time of my life when so many of my contemporaries have chosen to retire. What's more, I have noticed that a lot of my retired friends have given up on life. They are eager to say, "I've quit tennis because every time I play something hurts me," or "I've stopped trying to get a picture or a play produced because there are so many young people out there to compete against." As a result, they either look older than Methuselah or else are dropping like flies every day.

Yet, and without trying to sound like a braggart, I've recently had one of the biggest successes of my playwriting career. This in spite of the fact that even my collaborator, Robert Fisher, was over sixty when we wrote *Groucho*. This play about my father has been a huge hit in both New York and London and has received the kinds of rave reviews from the critics that I only wish I could have had with my first play, which was produced, and flopped badly, when I was thirty-five.

This seems to belie Somerset Maugham's contention that "creative people do their best work before forty," and it proves, if not for the first time, that "it's never too late."

There was a time, I admit, when I would have agreed with Maugham. That's when I was thirteen and considered anyone past thirty a doddering old man. I remember, for example, going to the Beverly Hills Tennis Club when I was a junior tournament player and wondering why most of the people I saw running around the courts, some of whom were parents of kids my age, weren't home on their front porches in rocking chairs. One day I met a fifty-year-old named Elmer Harris (the playwright), with a white handlebar mustache and a potbelly. I couldn't believe that a man of his years would dare go out on the court and play singles. He had to be asking for a heart attack. I remember saying to myself that when I was his age I wouldn't step on a tennis court, except maybe to teach my grandchildren. But I later discovered, after he beat the tar out of me, that he could play singles with the verve and stamina of a young man and was recognized as one of the best players at the club.

My father, a hacker but an enthusiastic one, was around fifty when he hung up his tennis racket for good. One day when coming off the court, he said to me, "You know, Art, I think I'm getting too old for this game. From now on I'll get my exercise taking the dogs for a walk." Though he was in perfect health, I agreed it was the smart thing to do. I didn't want the world to lose such a funny man, nor me my father, just because he wanted to look young enough to play such a violent sport.

When Groucho was in his fifties, and about to marry for the third time, I thought to myself, is Father crazy? How could anyone his age possibly think of getting married again, and to a twenty-one-year-old at that? How could he have any interest in sex? And even if he did, could he possibly hope to satisfy a wife nearly forty years his junior? And how could she want him for anything but his money?

Today I'm just a little bit older than he was then. From this plateau I have revised my opinion of what's "too old" for sex, romance, and marriage. I'm fortunate in that I'm happily married and have been for twenty-nine years. But if I were in my father's position—meaning sixty and single—I'm sure I'd see nothing wrong with taking a young bride. Not too young, of course. She should be at least twenty.

I'm joking, in case you haven't guessed. But kidding about age is something I learned from my father. Groucho may have hung up his tennis racket at fifty, but he was still cracking jokes about age and death when he was eighty-seven. That's what sustained him. I remember asking him once, when he was in his seventies, what he would do if he had a chance to live his whole life over again. "I think I'd shoot myself," he said, without batting an eye.

But he didn't really mean that. He was actually a sentimentalist (though he hated to admit it) and thoroughly enjoyed life up until the very end. As a matter of fact, though his career had its ups and downs, he had the greatest success of his career—the TV show "You Bet Your Life"—after he was sixty. The show stayed on the air for fourteen years and made him more money than he'd ever earned on Broadway or in pictures.

Having spent most of my formative years around Groucho, it's only natural that a great deal of his wit, wisdom, and philosophy about growing old would rub off on me.

Although my father remained in relatively good health almost until the day he died, he never complained about what, if anything, was ailing him. But he did love to kid about what happens to the body after Old Man Time takes his licks. One of my favorite remarks of his is: "Middle age is when you go to bed at night and think you're going to feel better in the morning. Old age is when you go to bed at night and hope you wake up in the morning."

One of my father's favorite remarks about old age sneaking up on you came from the late great humorist, Will Rogers, a close friend of his. When Groucho and Rogers were relatively young men—Groucho in his thirties, Rogers about ten years older—they traveled the same vaudeville circuit together. In those days, each vaudeville act had its own baseball team, which they pitted against each other during their off afternoons. One afternoon while Groucho's team was playing Rogers and his team, Groucho, who was on first base, was forced to run to second when the batter hit what should have been a sure double-play ball. But when the shortstop threw the ball to Rogers, who was playing second, he was standing twenty feet away from the bag, allowing Groucho to safely reach second standing up. Nevertheless, Rogers insisted that Groucho was out.

"What are you talking about?" complained my father. "You were nowhere near second base when you caught the ball."

Rogers gave this mustachioed upstart a contemptuous look and said, "Listen, Groucho, when you get to be my age, any place you stand is second base."

My father considered that one of the all-time great lines about advancing age. His second favorite line on the subject came from the mouth of his other humorist friend, the late Robert Benchley. Groucho called him up on his birthday and asked, "How do you feel, Bob, now that you've reached fifty?" "I feel fine," replied Benchley, "except for an occasional heart attack."

Joking about the inevitable is, I admit, another form of denial. It's putting your head in the sand and refusing to face reality. That may not be growing old with courage, but it certainly helps make the trip a more pleasant one.

I am also aware, as it is said in Ecclesiastes, that there's a time to be born and a time to die. And I'm certainly not looking forward to the latter as long as I'm in good mental and physical health, able to turn out a good day's work, to make love to my wife and enjoy her cooking, to appreciate my family, and to play good tennis.

As a former junior tennis star, it came as quite a shock to me the day I discovered I was over the hill as a tennis player and ought to give up tournament play while I was still proud of my game. I remember the time exactly. I was twenty-nine years old and playing in the semifinals of the Santa Monica Open, an important tournament that I had won twice previously, against a young college player from UCLA named Glen Bassett. He had the legs of a marathon runner but he wasn't much of a stylist, and I looked down my nose at him while we were warming up. I figured I'd polish him off in straight sets and reach the finals for the third time in as many tries.

Things were going my way until I had him 5–2 in the first set. At that point I discovered that it was becoming harder and harder to put the ball away. Balls I thought I had put away were being run down by Bassett, who put them away himself on the next shot. Eventually, I lost my lead and the match to Bassett's youth, speed, and stamina. Still I refused to acknowledge that my young opponent was the better player just because he was twenty and never got tired. I blamed the loss on the fact that I was having difficulty seeing fast passing shots when I was up at the net. As a result, I had my eyes examined, and sure enough I had a slight weakness in one of them, which called for prescription lenses. It had nothing to do with age; young men wore glasses too, I told myself.

The following year, in the same round of the Santa Monica Open, I played Glen Bassett again, and this time I wore glasses. And again I had him 5–2 in the first set and again wound up losing in straight sets, for the same reason. He was running down my put-aways and putting them away himself. It was then that I realized that advancing years had something to do with my loss, and that if I didn't wish to be humiliated by old age in the future I should stick to "club" tennis. I'd patrol the courts at the good old Beverly Hills Tennis Club where I was still the champ and could enjoy myself. No disgrace about that. Don Budge hung it up in his thirties too.

For about twenty years I remained the top player at our club. And I felt pretty good about it too. Somehow I believed I'd found the fountain of youth. Then I noticed that some of the young club players were beginning to give me a hard time on the court. Not only was I having to work hard to beat them, but suddenly, for no reason at all, I was beginning to acquire physical infirmities. One afternoon, while attempting to serve an ace to a younger opponent, I threw my back out. I blamed it on the five-gallon Arrowhead Spring water bottle that I had to lift onto the cooler once a week. I took care of that problem neatly. I let the gardener change the bottle when the old one was empty. If he wasn't around I'd drink Scotch instead. My back was cured and I felt as strong as ever—so long as I wore the back brace my orthopedist prescribed.

On another afternoon I was playing a college player who, though he gave me a good battle, usually faded in the crucial stages of the match. He'd get what we in tennis circles refer to as "the elbow," meaning he choked under pressure. This time, however, before he got the elbow I got "the ankle." Things were going quite well, 4–3, my favor in the first set, when I stretched to reach a wide forehand shot a man of my age had no business trying to get. Losing my balance, I fell down hard on the cement and sprained my ankle. It was the first time I'd ever sprained an ankle in all my years of playing, and it was painful as hell. To make things worse, this happened the day before my wife and I were leaving for a vacation in Europe. I had to spend the next six weeks hobbling through châteaux and cathedrals with an ankle so swollen I could hardly get my shoe on. Lois was too diplomatic to tell me outright that a man of sixty had no business playing singles with a twenty-year-old tournament hopeful. She let me come to that realization myself by buying me a cane to get me through the trip.

When we were back home, and I was finally able to walk normally again, I came to one of the wisest decisions of my life. I decided that if I hoped to remain the best player at our club, there was only one way to do it: Never play singles with anyone younger than I. Now, when any of the young lions challenge me, I simply tell them, "Get lost, kid. Come back when you have a reputation." When I can no longer put them off with that, I tell them I have a hangover or a business engagement. And I leave, and won't return to the club until I am sure that all the younger players have gone home to do their homework or to study their bar mitzvah speeches.

I've stuck to this premise for the last few years, and it works. I haven't had a bad back or sprained my ankle (or even had a heart attack) since. Of course, the young punks who challenge me daily are beginning to get the idea that I'm afraid of them. But what do I care what they think? As far as I'm concerned, until one of them beats me, I'm still the best player at the club. And in my heart I always will be.

I don't even mind that the young players are beginning to make snide remarks about my reluctance to accept their challenges. I'm perfectly content to pick my spots and play only opponents I know I can handle without even having to rush the net or serve very hard. Preferably old ladies and kids under ten.

That's the kind of courage, combined with a little craftiness, it takes to grow old—at least at the Beverly Hills Tennis Club.

Dr. Henry J. Heimlich

B. *1920*

❦ ❦

In August 1986, five-year-old Brent Meldrum of Lynn, Massachusetts, saved a playmate from choking by applying the "Heimlich maneuver" after seeing it performed on "Benson," a popular TV series. While few may know who Henry J. Heimlich is, the professor of advanced clinical sciences and president of the Heimlich Institute at Xavier University in Cincinnati, Ohio, can certainly take a share of the credit for this rescue, as well as for the fifteen thousand lives his method has saved in the United States over the last fifteen years. Indeed, he is credited with having saved more lives than anyone in history.

Heimlich's career of medical innovations goes beyond the Heimlich maneuver, however, and spans more than three decades. His contributions have included a surgical method for building a new esophagus (the first time a body organ was replaced), a product for life-saving chest drainage (Heimlich valve), and a method for enabling stroke patients to relearn the swallowing process. He has developed a portable oxygen system (Heimlich micro-trach) for patients suffering from emphysema, cystic fibrosis, and other chronic lung diseases. In recent years, his attention has been focused on finding cures for cancer and

AIDS, and in promoting his Patriots for Peace program, through which he seeks to find a solution to the danger of war.

"I have never been satisfied with existing methods and seek to simplify and improve them. After devising an operation for the replacement of the esophagus, I became aware that one such discovery helps more people than is possible in a lifetime in the operating room . . . My ultimate goal is to prevent death and promote well-being for the largest number of people by establishing a philosophy that will eliminate war."

BEFORE IT'S TOO LATE

As a physician, I have treated hundreds of elderly patients from the time I was a twenty-year-old medical student to the present. Yet, it was only in the year and a half that my father lived with me prior to his death that I truly learned about aging. That was the best year of my life. Here was a man I knew and loved longer than any other person, but we only became true equal friends during that last year.

The sad truth is that, barring sudden death, growing old means a series of increasing disabilities. As a doctor friend says, "After sixty, it's patch, patch, patch." Seeing an elderly patient in a wheelchair is a still picture, a cameo that leads to accepting the handicap as his usual status. In contrast, observing the anguish of a strong and independent will reacting to each retrogressing limitation from the acceptance of a cane, to a walker, then to a wheelchair, is a lesson that all of us should be privileged to witness and prepare for. Progressive disabilities include diminishing eyesight and hearing, as well as the impaired function of vital organs—heart, lungs, and kidneys.

As Pop's mobility diminished, I once tried to console him by saying, "Dad, I know it's difficult for you, but today I saw a fifteen-year-old boy who has been in a wheelchair most of his life." With the honesty only an old person is privileged to express, this man, who had always been totally unselfish, answered, "But that doesn't help me." From that conversation I learned to respect the reality of a disability, not to try to camouflage it.

Increasing disabilities are a visible reminder of approaching death. Many people say they would rather die suddenly from a heart attack or accident. African tribes at one time put old individuals out in the jungle to be eaten by lions; Eskimos placed them in the cold; aging American Indians tied themselves to a stake in a battle and fought until killed. Those actions were essential in societies that could not provide for extra mouths. Today, developed countries can afford to maintain the elderly and utilize their productivity; yet, there is an ever increasing suicide rate among the elderly because their needs are not being met due to present-day society's lack of compassion.

After all the niceties about eternity are expressed, the reality is that survival is most important. Study pictures of surviving concentration

31

camp victims and you will understand that there is a desire and tenacity for living. Consider the victims of accidents or disease who prefer to live with disabilities most humans cannot conceive of enduring. Or how the young child with a chronic disease that will be fatal in ten or fifteen years struggles to hold onto life. Similarly, the "brave" general who sends his soldiers to die by the thousands invariably secures his own long life. The reason we have not had nuclear war is not the threat of destruction to vast numbers of citizens—we have always been disposable; rather, it is that the political leaders and military chieftains who so readily send others to die are themselves threatened. "But see how the Muslim fundamentalists, even children, march out to die for the Ayatollah Khomeini in Iran," you may respond. "Isn't death more acceptable in less developed civilizations?" Regardless of the culture, leaders, political and religious, have always used nationalism, religion, and hate to maintain their power; and their people, the victims, always follow. In our own wars young men have landed on foreign beaches going to certain death or entered jungles or fought against fellow Americans in our Civil War. None of them really wanted to die. Whether in the U.S. or in developing countries, sick people I treated always wanted to live, and their families grieved if they died. There is a limit, however, to pain and to prolonged dying which has resulted from medical "advances"—mechanical gadgets, drugs, and tubes. The desire to be left to die in these circumstances should be respected.

During World War II, I was in a U.S. Navy guerilla army—12 American marines and sailors and 250 Chinese soldiers based in northwest China, in the Gobi Desert in Inner Mongolia. What a wonderful life I would have missed if I had been killed at age twenty-four in another of the senseless wars brought on by incompetent political leaders and military "heroes."

The opportunity to learn from the Chinese culture served me well more than forty years later. In 1986, a Chinese physician spent several weeks as a fellow at the Heimlich Institute. Dr. Hua lived in my home and spent his evenings with Pop and me. He applied Chinese traditional medical techniques of massage to Pop's legs which caused swelling to completely disappear although it had been present for months despite the usual medications. Several months after Pop died, I saw Dr. Hua in Los Angeles and he said, "You are the only American I know who treated his parent as we do in China." My time in China had not been wasted.

I feel sorry for those who consider their elderly parents a burden, rather than a privilege. I hope one of my children will want to live with me when my physical limitations increase. Not just for my sake, but for the knowledge of aging he or she will gain, the love that is engendered by proximity when a child is older, and the gratification that comes as they later reminisce. If this desire is considered an imposition or selfishness, so be it. I know that the rewards are unlimited and can be duplicated for both parent and child in no other way.

I now play tennis three or four times a week, whereas twice a month sufficed in years past. My former one to two weeks of skiing each winter has increased to three or four weeks. I realize that I could have enjoyed sports more frequently through much of my life and sometimes wonder if I should have regrets. But I know such activity would have been boring in the past when there were more interesting goals. Succeeding in the physical challenge of winning the game—my tennis game and skiing have improved markedly—leaves me with great exaltation after each victory or new hill conquered. It is a sign that I am still young. Yet, I now am conscious of the fact that one day I will have to cut back and eventually eliminate both sports and will be taking the steps to the cane, walker, and wheelchair.

At this time, I am more productive than ever before in my life. I have several new and exciting research projects: treatments for cancer, AIDS, emphysema, and cystic fibrosis. I am certain they all will be successful. My program, Patriots for Peace, a plan for world peace, is as practical as the well-established Heimlich maneuver, Heimlich chest valve, and Heimlich operation. Growing old threatens the opportunity to complete ongoing projects. Other than that fact, I am prepared to go, I hope, as my father did—gradually, with independence and creativity to the end.

A short time ago a reporter interviewed me at home and had lunch with Pop and me. I asked Pop to talk about some of the concepts for rehabilitating young criminals that he had developed more than fifty years ago. Those methods are still being used and are still ahead of the times. The resulting article said that Pop had a better recall of the past than of the present. The reporter had neglected to ask what Pop thought about President Reagan's latest economic policy—he'd have gotten an inspired, clear, dynamic, and logical explanation of a present problem based on more than ninety-nine years of experience. Instead, his conclusion was subjective and stereotyped. What a loss for the reporter!

For the elderly, it is more important than ever to respect and admire the unique contribution they can make to society by listening to the experiences they have tolerated as well as those they enjoyed. Sharing thoughts about past successes or failures of the elderly may propel the young into action that enables them to achieve the same successes or avoid similar failures. We can all learn not only from what the elderly say but, more important, from what they feel. I shall never forget the lessons I learned from the thoughts Pop shared with me, and I now make an effort to share my thoughts and fears openly with my own children. The youth of today have a valuable resource available in the increasing numbers of old people. They would be wise to excavate this treasure.

Pop died December 30, 1986, four months before his hundredth birthday. In the last year with him our friendship developed and matured. We always had a good relationship as father and son, but not as equals—not as friends. I have come to realize that for our generation a father and son cannot be real friends until the son reaches sixty and has lived his own lifetime of family and personal experiences. Few fathers and sons have that opportunity.

There was no man more loved and highly respected than Pop, but in my youth I resented every adult telling me how wonderful my parents were. In the envious eyes of a child it seemed to take something away from their relationship to me. Dad had become a social worker seventy years ago "because people had helped me when I was young," he said, "and I wanted to help others." His work resulted in many reforms for adult prisoners and youths, but it paid very little—he had to carry a second job to support the family. Several times a year he visited New York State prisons; his purpose was to help prisoners retain ties to their families. I was twelve and my sister an attractive sixteen-year-old when he took us on the first of several visits to the prisons. My sister and I were guided through Attica, Sing Sing, and Auburn prisons by trustee prisoners, and we visited and chatted with the inmates. Guards opened each gate with a huge key and greeted us as we approached, and the gates slammed shut behind us with a loud clang. One day, I overheard a man say to the warden, "How can you let these children wander through the prison?" "All the men know they're Phil Heimlich's kids," he replied.

Twelve years ago Pop left his lifetime home, New York City, to live here in Cincinnati. "It's time to move," he said, when his last grandchild left the city. Only after his death did I appreciate that when he changed his life and left his two sisters and friends he was eighty-seven years old. Four months after he arrived, I was out to dinner with my wife, Jane, Pop, and a woman, perhaps fifteen years younger than he, who asked, "Phil, how do you like Cincinnati?" He replied passively, "Oh, I like it all right." His seeming lack of enthusiasm stirred her homegrown loyalty and she said assuredly, "You'll like it better when you're here longer." "I like anywhere I am," he responded without hesitation. It was the first time I was consciously aware that I learned something important from and about Pop.

Pop lived in his own apartment until his last year and a half, when he moved into our home. At that time, I started coming home to have lunch with him and looked forward to our talks after dinner. It was great to have a live-in male friend, and I began asking questions and saying things that I had avoided for so many years. In one wonderful moment I said, "Dad, men of our generation are ashamed to say 'I love you.' But our kids taught me to say it. Pop, I love you." "I love you too," he responded warmly, and we hugged and kissed as never before. Thereafter, this ninety-nine-year-old closed every conversation on the phone or with visitors by saying with an expression of discovery in his voice, "You know what—I love you."

"Pop, you graduated from City College in 1909 when few boys went to college," I said one evening. "Do you ever regret not making a lot of money? You could have used it for your social work." "What would I have done with more money, Hank?" he answered. "I had everything I wanted."

I hope I don't have to wait until my children reach sixty before we become "equal" friends. But I think we are beginning to understand each other better than Pop and I did at a younger age. One day I said to my daughter, "Pop is the most successful man I know." "But I thought you said he never had any . . ." Then her quizzical expression relaxed, she smiled, and didn't finish the sentence.

In the last six months his disabilities gradually worsened. Personal and medical care needs required increasing time and assistance each week. Fortunately, a friend had told me she had been frequently annoyed by the time and effort she had to spend with her aging mother, but that she missed those tasks after her mother died. Knowing this, I took pleasure in being able to spend more time caring for Pop. We sometimes had a role reversal, which psychologists tell me is not unusual. I would carry out the medical rituals, tuck him into bed, and give him a hug and kiss. Sometimes I'd say, without being conscious of it, "Good night, my son." At other times, Pop would say he thought of me as his father.

I knew we had reached a point of complete understanding when he said, matter of factly, "Hank, I don't want to live any longer. I'm just a burden now. I won't ask you to do anything because you're a doctor and it would be on your conscience." A few months earlier I would have stammered through a denial of his impending demise. Instead, I could say honestly, "I can accept your decision, Pop, and won't prolong your life unnecessarily." And I didn't.

Dame Hyacinthe Hill

B. *1920*

❦ ❦

Although best known in America for her syndicated astrological column, "In the Stars," Hyacinthe Hill's global reputation rests primarily on her prodigious output of poetry, which has been translated into more than ten languages.

Widely honored for her work, she was awarded the title of Dame by the Knights of Malta, named Daughter of Mark Twain, and Poet Meritissimus by the International Academy of Leadership. She has also won the coveted Keats and York Society Awards of England, the Leonardo da Vinci Award of Italy, and a Poetry Society of America Annual Award, and was selected as International Woman of the Year in 1985 with Laureate Honors in the International Hall of Fame of Woman of Distinction.

MINNIE MOUSE FUN GLASSES

We were shopping. We couldn't help but notice the most outrageous sunglasses possible. They had a huge, green palm tree with cerise balls glowing in its fronds on the left frame. On the right frame was Minnie Mouse, dressed to kill, in eye-blinding brilliance. In the center, above the nose-curve, was a rosebud. We both burst out laughing, and then my husband stopped: "You wouldn't! They are not dignified!" I answered, opening my purse, "They aren't meant to dignify. They're meant for fun. They're fun glasses."

How is the courage to grow old different from the courage we have had to use throughout life? I think one major difference is an increased need for, and use of, humor. We need more fun and games as we age. It is a way of both hiding sorrow and pain and helping ourselves and others support a bravery which may begin lagging under life's blows.

Why old people need courage is obvious. It requires tenacious pluck to keep fighting against an overwhelming tide: man's destruction of the world environment through waste and greed; youngsters physically and spiritually weakened by drugs; a morally lax culture; corruption of, and by, politicians and church leaders; and a whole economic system that seems to be crashing about our heads. Many old people, who have done their best to build their own protection against poverty, have seen their life's savings taxed away from them by their own government. We all have seen the poor, the ill, and the mentally incompetent forced to live in the streets or in degrading conditions. It takes courageous self-denial for grandparents to think about such conditions and be able to do so little about the planetary woes we are leaving our children. In fact, much of our plucky humor stems from our faith that those coming after us will be able to handle them. Such humor is a proof of faith.

It also takes valor to face the world using canes, wheelchairs, and walkers, to be confined to one room or one bed, to be stuck with needles, probed, and cut up, to stick heads into CAT scan machines, and to wear life-support systems. It takes gameness to suffer pain silently so as not to cause anguish to others.

The fortitude of seniors is not just a whistling in the dark; although, sometimes it is that too, for the fear is there. More often, it is a blessed, creative act, such as Yeats describes in "Sailing to Byzantium":

An aged man is but a paltry thing,
A tattered coat upon a stick, unless
Soul clap its hands and sing, and louder sing
For every tatter in its mortal dress.

People who are born or plagued with disabilities early in life have had to develop courage in order to survive. Perhaps it is easier for them to accept bravely the disintegration of age than it is for great beauties or macho sportsmen, who sometimes see suicide as the only answer to facing the accruing infirmities of age. Survivors learn the benefits of laughter.

The humor of healthy old people tends to have certain characteristics. It is almost always benign. It makes use of the creative imagination, of delightful incongruities, wildly lovable fantasies, and a generous dollop of braggadocio. If you listen, you will note that it rarely involves negative ethnic slaps, or stories about people with handicaps. Senior citizens, for the most part, are sensitive to the hurts such so-called humor can cause.

The humor of older people also tends to be gentle and self-effacing because they have lived through or are suffering great sorrows and want to spare others even the smallest pain. One ninety-year-old man, seeing the embarrassment his great-granddaughter experienced when she accidentally farted in public, took the blame on himself by saying: "Oops, excuse Grandpa!" Perhaps that well-meaning man wasn't trying to teach the young girl how to take life's little lumps, but he certainly taught her that we can make light of trivialities.

Some of the plucky humor of seniors involves wish-fulfillment. A poet-friend, who was overworked supporting herself and her ninety-year-old mother, had two cats who were companions to one another and to the older woman. One of the cats was so jealous for my friend's affection that it learned to jump on top of a bookcase and reach way out to dangle precariously the lamp chain over her head whenever she was on the phone. One day, observing how successful the kitten was in its undertaking, my friend's mother, who was very heavy, unable to walk, and confined to bed and chair, said, laughing at the incongruity of her situation, "I wonder if I can learn to leap up on the bookcase!" She got the hug she was angling for.

Much of the humor of the elderly has a ring of truth hidden behind the comic mask. When one old woman we know saw someone about to shake her hand, she would say very flirtatiously, "These cheeks were meant for kissing." After the laughter and the kiss, she would say, "That's a good, socially acceptable way of eliciting affection which we older folk need lots of." What she didn't say was that arthritic fingers are not only painful, but fragile. She was worried that some hearty handshaker might break one of her frail digits in his enthusiasm. Being careful of her legs on entering cars, she would sing an old folksong:

> 'Cause my legs is little and long
> and they might get broke in two.

Humor is often a gallant way for an elder to save his own face. One ancient gentleman had grown so old that he no longer knew which women were his daughters and which his nurses. When one of them asked him, "Who am I?" he would answer, "Have you forgotten your name?" If she persisted, he would answer, with a dismissing gesture of his hands and a twinkle in his eye: "You are one of my many adoring and adorable girls."

Many times, I have heard Americans accused of being superficial, fun-seeking, spoiled brats, a mixture of Annie Oakley, Paul Bunyan, Mae West, Diamond Jim Brady, and P. T. Barnum. We are told that exaggeration and putting on a happy face is typically American. Perhaps. But I think a better generalization of us would be that we are about largeness and largess, generosity of spirit, magnanimity, and wild boasting. These are some of the forms our bravery takes, and the need for, and use of them, tends to increase as we age, as we learn to make proper use of our freedom and relearn how to play.

The responsibilities, the sorrows, the pains are there for us, but they can be worked out, or, at least, sublimated. It is much better for seniors to accept the privileges and pleasures of growing old, the freedom we have to do, say, and act almost any way we choose with fewer restrictions. A major characteristic of play is, in fact, freedom.

Now, at last, if we wish, we can get rid of the corsets, brassieres, business suits, hair dyes, and painted nails; or we can dress up like the most slapstick clowns. It's our choice. We are free to fancy ourselves fairy godmothers, or patriarchs, and can dress up according to our pretension. We no longer desire the part of the younger hero or ingenue. There are many dramatic roles suitable for the older person: an ancient pirate one day, or sea-battered Ulysses the next. Although there are

fewer roles for women, we still have the majestic old queens, the ma-
triarchs to emulate. Someday, we may become the models just for being
our own brave selves. In the meantime, loose, flowing garb is a costume
that covers a multitude of sins, liver spots, dewlaps, spare tires, mars,
and scars, when the body has gone to fat or exposes scrawny bones.
Hats with big brims, or wigs, cover up hair problems and add to the
dramatic mystery of the playacting. "Today, I am Mata Hari, or the
Sheik of Araby."

When I was much younger, I was so impressed with a team of clowns
that I wrote a poem about them entitled "Through a Flaming Hoop."
Part of it goes like this:

> I cannot give you sun or moon, but I
> can show you clowns who make the vasty sky
> become a circus ring; stars digestible
> as sugar spun to light; the milky way,
> a rope for children's play
> . . . .
> children watching them remember heaven,
> and laugh their way through clouds. Laughter's
> a leaven
> that lifts man up and puts the devil down.
> When I grow young I want to be a clown.

Well, I have grown young. I embrace my second childhood with
open arms and think there is nothing nicer than to be a clown. Make-
believe can help us rise to such heights of beauty as to leave stodgy
seriousness floundering behind in the mud. Now that I can enjoy pre-
tending to be the Pied Piper in my motley clothes, I recall the time when
I visited the Emily Dickinson Home in Amherst, Massachusetts. While
there, I attended a lecture in a local library, where I was startled to see
that almost all the women present wore blue dresses and white sweat-
ers, and all had their hair cut and styled in a similar fashion. They looked
at me coldly as though I were a creature from outer space. No doubt
that was an unusual day and an unusually synchronous event, but I
remember thinking: "No wonder poor Emily Dickinson retired from
society." All play has a tendency to be beautiful. That group of women
were playing their own game and were beautiful in a strictly patterned
way. But I was outstanding, like an O. Henry heroine, "an onion in a

sea of frangipani." Standing outside the situation, I saw that I made that group beautiful, because I kept them from being monotonous. I was the red spot on the white canvas. Sobersides try to exclude playful people, but the joyous ones draw circles that include the serious. The cut-out paper doll syndrome doesn't work for the elderly. Variety is a much more important aesthetic quality to them—or at least it ought to be!

The rebellion against the ordinary, through a bravely joyous embracing of the comic spirit, is more than just an interlude, a relaxation. It is an integral part of the living process. Because it augments, adorns, and amplifies vitality, it is necessary to the individual and to society as a life-enhancing, culture-enriching function. It contributes to the well-being of both the actor and the audience. The brave old actors are like the brightly colored autumn leaves, the last, grand show before the deathlike silence of winter, the gorgeous display of sunset. Spoilsports may see our bravery as only make-believe designed to sustain the fiction of our personal value, a means of restoring energy, or just a covering up of flaws; but our heroism becomes, in its intensity, a death-defying sacred act, a sacrament, high, holy, and mystical. We are marching into the valley of death wearing nothing but the perfume of our joy. We do not go raging against the dying of the light. We do not go with a bang, or a whisper, but like dear old Cyrano we go flaunting our plumes. Our audacious way of aging is one of the gifts we leave to those who follow.

My husband has chided me many times for seeing life through rose-colored glasses. I am all too aware that the old computer under my scalp has blown fuses; that the television, through which I look out at life, has loose screws; that all my machinery is breaking down. If I were to cry over it, the parts would only rust sooner. It wouldn't do any good. What does do good is trying to make other people happy.

The Blofeld edition of the I Ching states:

> When joyously led, the people forget their burdens;
> in wrestling joyously with difficulties, they even
> forget that they must die. Joy's greatest quality is
> in the encouragement it affords the people.

When I said that I wanted the Minnie Mouse Fun Glasses, my husband at first replied: "I'll pay for them if you want a toy, but I won't walk with you when you wear them." Later, when he saw how much delight they caused, when he saw people ask me where they could buy them, and when he saw others examine them carefully to see if they could make something similar, he relented. I even saw him surreptitiously trying them on himself. Since then, I have worn them to hospitals and nursing homes and always had a positive reaction.

Now, when weighed down by the woes of the world, I don my brightest, most clowning outfit. I hide my tearful eyes behind my Minnie Mouse Fun Glasses and gaily sally out upon the stage of the world quoting, "If she had a broomstraw stuck in her hat, we'd think it was a feather. She's like that."

Yes, "there's a dance in the old dame yet."

William Potthast

Vera A. Cleaver

B. *1919*

❧ ❧

Vera Cleaver, in partnership with her late husband, Bill Cleaver, has authored many of the most highly regarded children's books of the past three decades, among them *Where the Lilies Bloom* (1969), *Grover* (1970), *The Whys and Where-fores of Littabelle Lee* (1973), and *Queen of Hearts* (1978), all of which were National Book Award nominees.

Since the death of her husband in 1981 she has continued the writing life, authoring *Sugar Blue* (1984), *Sweetly Sings the Donkey* (1985), *Moon Lake Angel* (1987), and *Belle Pruitt* (1988). Of her work, she has said that "I cannot believe that at some exciting future time my literary art, if that is what it may be termed, will be dug from a ruin and used again in the shaping of opinions and tastes. Yet the creation of it now, this awful and wonderful endeavor with its inherent interests and concerns and mysteries growing from every corner, brings me my own kind of peace and I thank God for it."

Although living alone in Florida, Ms. Cleaver sees herself as a "widowed-single but still married," and has "learned how to install a new ribbon in my

45

typewriter, how to change the chimes on my grandfather clock, found out that there are two kinds of screws and screwdrivers, what it means when the little light in the circuit breaker glows red." She has also "discovered that galvanized gutter systems will rust, while aluminum ones will not."

IF IT IS NOT GOOD,
MAKE IT SO

A land shapes its people, I think. I come from the Prairie Plains of South Dakota where, according to some musical poet of the time, "Fewer hearts in despair were aching." The tune was pleasant enough. Growing up, I didn't know what the word *despair* meant. Neither did I know the true meaning of *happy*. It was not given to my parents or to my brother and sisters and me to be happy. We laughed, we had our antics, we reveled in the ceremonies of family, but we never got the habit of happiness as others know it. It was always as if we were waiting for something better or worse to happen.

My childhood world was prairie, and my family and I were as it was. In trust we planted our fields, tended our orchards and our livestock and fowl, painted our barns, baked our bread. Save that of our own creation, there was little social life. We had a car and about twice a month went to town. Everything—town, school, churches, neighbors—was miles away. Our closest neighbors, a family of German-Russians, came at harvest time, and when all of our grains were in we went to help them. They ate black bread and clabber.

We did and did not forgive drought, blizzards, and grasshopper raids. A prairie is revengeful; it will fight back. So did we. During winters we slept at night in unheated rooms with layers of blankets over us and with warmed, flannel-wrapped rocks at our feet. We smelled a little, I think, because when nothing thawed there was only meltwater. To my mother, who had a passion for cleanliness, this must have been a torment. Her wealthy aunts sent boxes of closet-overflow clothing from Omaha and Kansas City, so there were times when we were unnaturally stylish.

The rules of our religion were simple: Don't cuss or lie. Be envious of no one. Work for what you expect to receive. Be honest. If you have any, remember that good looks are not a personal achievement. If you would have a friend, be one. Believe in tomorrow.

I am a human being and so have a sense of tomorrow. I know that my right to live will one day end. The man in the pulpit says that we must prepare for this. I have been to hear his threats and his promises and have come away freshly unconvinced. I cannot hold to a faith without logic, and my logic argues that when I die I shall neither descend nor ascend. I believe that my soul is my mind and that when it stops all of me will stop, that I will have had my turn, some of it funny and fun, much of it clumsy and riddled with mistakes. I shouldn't like to be again that person who made all those youthful mistakes. I prefer my aging intellect which has settled me into a nice rut. Out of practice now, it has stopped asking questions: Why have I been here? Why must I now be as I am? What's ahead of me? My rut is comfortable. I can't think there is danger in it, that I should be preparing for something.

I believe that if the man in the pulpit did not promise the solace of life after death there would be fewer suicides among the young who must surely regard themselves and their tortures, whatever they might be, as complete. If they did not believe so, they would put the gun or the poison away and wait for a wiser time, wait for a reform of their painful philosophies.

I don't know if the man in the pulpit would listen to this reasoning. Probably he wouldn't. Probably he would give me a tender look and a pat and offer to come and talk with me any lonely afternoon.

The good people of my community assume that the elderly need tender attention: the comfort of conversation, hot tea, special foods, a pot of geraniums to remind us about nature, maybe a cat or a dog unless we live where cats and dogs are prohibited.

I live in a free-standing home, and when something in it needs repair I fix it myself or pay to have it fixed. Since the death of my husband I have learned how to install a new ribbon in my typewriter, how to change the chimes of my grandfather clock, found out that there are two kinds of screws and screwdrivers, what it means when the little light in the circuit breaker glows red. I have discovered that galvanized gutter systems will rust, while aluminum ones will not.

My cat and dog know my habits. Each morning, after breakfast, all of us go out for the newspaper and for our first look at the day. I like the dawn, the emptiness of it, but then its colors come, and I am reminded of the unfinished manuscript on my desk. Until noon the cat roars around outside. The dog doesn't budge from his snooze place under my desk.

A woman who lives across the lake from my place told me that I should attend group meetings, that I should learn how to play, take dancing lessons, take a cruise. Cruises, she said, were great for single ladies. Lonely widowers took cruises, she said. I told her I wasn't interested in meeting a lonely widower, that I am widowed-single but still married. This is true, but not morbidly so. I am not morbid about anything. My life is still good. I work at making it so. I see that it is so when, in the afternoons, I take my pets for an outing. They tear around investigating everything and I sit at the table under the trees. There is an abundance of plant and wildlife on my lakefront. Recently a newspaper report had it that the wild yellow asters in this region are extinct. They are not extinct. There are stands of them on my lakefront, and I would be glad to show them to anyone who is interested enough to look, but I don't want people with cameras and other recording paraphernalia nosing around here. They would step on the snails and scare the herons. The herons mostly come in the spring and summer, but sometimes in the fall I see them stalking around among the reeds, such magnificent birds. The asters are fall and winter bloomers, and I have a mental association with them. They will become extinct when the time for that comes. There was an especially good crop of them last year during the days of the Christmas season.

For me, Christmas is not the painful time it is for some. I ignore it. I tell my friends that I forgot it was Christmas, and that I am senile. They laugh and I laugh. They leave cookies or books and go away. I don't accept their invitations to Christmas dinner. It is easier to stay alone and remain quiet. There is a strength in solitude. For some reason, on Christmas day, my plants always look a little wan. So, after my stint at the typewriter, I feed them.

Not all of this is as brave as I make it sound. I have days when I think that there is no meaning anywhere to anything, and I haven't found any quick cure for this kind of thinking save to recognize its danger and turn it around. Of making gravy, one of my cookbooks advises: "If it is not good, make it so." I have found that rule may be applied not only to gravy but to thinking as well.

I know how to play, but I prefer work because it puts some shine into my life and gives me a sense of self-custody. Work is cleansing. It's a healer.

In association with the elderly we hear much about dignity these days. It is as if the word and what it means is newly discovered, like a cure for an immigrant disease. We are told that the aged, whatever our conditions, must be permitted to live out our last years or months or days in dignity, that the government should supply it, that the men and women of medicine should write prescriptions for it and police their prescriptions. That is well and good. For the infirm, for those who have lost their way, the miracles wrought in Washington and those that come from the doctors' prescription pads are, sometimes, most admirable. The lawmakers in Washington have an easier time with their miracles than do the internists and surgeons, I think. Patients may be constituents, but in a hospital or a nursing home the role of patient comes first. If this is resented, the patient might hurl things, might refuse the needle and the pill. Most unadmirably, he might even insist on dying.

I think about dying, not because I am ill, but because I am old and, by nature, an orderly person. Being so, I make mental lists of the things I will and will not do.

I will not have my physical appearance altered by ways of plastic surgery. No face-lift, no restructuring, no tucking of this sag or that one. It is all right with me if others want to indulge in this. I don't and won't, just as I won't fall into the twenty-third-hour trap of estate building. I see those who do this, elderly men and women who rush to accumulate more so that they may bequeath more. I am through with collecting things and I am done with money-making, a recent and fascinating revelation. My work produces income, but my interest in the money it produces has stopped.

Several years ago I lost interest in my physical appearance. I remember precisely the way I was brought out of that trap, the woman who did it and the impact she had on me. She and I talked the way people in doctors waiting rooms do. I thought we might be of about the same age. We spoke of the weather, the high cost of living, the difficulties of widowhood and aging. Manicured, well dressed and coiffed, this woman looked nourished. The whites of her eyes, so white that they were almost blue, told me that if she had a liquor cabinet she opened it only when her friends came. Solemnly, her eyes told me what she thought of me. So, after hearing the doctor say that I didn't eat enough, I came home, discarded all my old sloppy clothes, brought those I had been hoarding from their closets, and made an appointment for a professional manicure and haircut. I cooked and ate what I cooked, not standing up, not from the stove as had been my habit, but from my dining table properly set with fresh cloth and napkin. I had a drink before dinner—an ounce of scotch and three ounces of water.

It was December then. It is February now, cold and brown. But soon the brownness will go and the green will come back. The turtles will waddle up from the lake to lay their eggs, and I will have to mark where they have been laid so that my lawn maintenance man doesn't run over them when he mows.

The thought that there will come a spring when I will not be here to see again the greenness of it does not disturb me. These days I decline to be disturbed by anything for more than an hour at a time, two hours at most. I have grown tolerant of the world and its errors, many of them transient, some of them silly. My age has done that for me.

To recognize the silliness takes a seasoned head. Mine is that, and so I let the silliness pass. I am not afraid of what remains.

Newburyport Daily News, Newbury, Mass.

Margaret Coit Elwell

B. 1919

※ ※

With the publication of her Pulitzer Prize–winning biography, *John C. Calhoun: American Portrait* (1950), Margaret Coit Elwell established herself as one of America's foremost historians and biographers. She is the author of several highly praised books, including the Thomas Edison Award–winning *The Fight for Union* (1961), *Andrew Jackson* (1965), and *Massachusetts* (1968), and has contributed articles to *Look*, the *New York Times Magazine*, and *Saturday Review*. In 1958 she was awarded an honorary doctorate by her alma mater, the University of North Carolina.

In the early 1940s Mrs. Elwell served as a correspondent for the Lawrence, Massachusetts, *Daily Eagle*, the Newburyport *Daily News*, and the *Haverhill Gazette*. In 1955 she was invited to serve as author-in-residence at Fairleigh Dickinson University. Thirty years later, as professor of history, she left Fairleigh Dickinson to live in Massachusetts. In 1985 she accepted an appointment as professor of history at Bunker Hill Community College in Charlestown.

Currently working on a book to be titled *The South Joins the Union*, Mrs. Elwell says that her eleven-year marriage to Albert Elwell, Massachusetts legislator and farmer, has been "the most fascinating, wearing, challenging experience I have had in my life."

GROWING OLD—
A HOW-TO-DO-IT MANUAL

They were sitting on the deacon's bench on the porch: my husband in his undershirt, the hired man without a shirt, and Eric, aged ten, the hired man's son. As I came out, Eric jumped to his feet.

"Take my seat, Mrs. Elwell," he said.

"Why, Eric," I said, "your mother taught you good manners."

"Yes," said Eric. "My mother taught me to always give up my seat to old ladies."

That did it! I realized where I was; I realized what I had become. Two years ago, before the fall downstairs that broke my left leg, I had still fancied myself a "Cosmo girl." After all, Helen Gurley Brown and I are contemporaries, and she posed for a cheesecake photo in *Cosmopolitan* this past June.

But it was over thirty years ago that a young Massachusetts senator, fated to become president of the United States, told me that I had beautiful legs. Now, as I write these words, a heavy brace hobbles the crippled and atrophied left leg, and the right leg is bunched with muscles grown in compensation for the weakness of the left. My waist has grown, too, by about six inches, and my right arm is restrained by splints and a sling. (In April of this year I fell again and shattered my right shoulder.) And I had been an athlete, flexible and strong muscled. I built my muscles. Like the poet William Butler Yeats, I thought you could hold off old age by diet and the lifting of weights. But God gave me the bones that are now irrevocably and irreversibly turning to powder. Calcium? Estrogen? No. I am "too old." I never thought all this could happen to me.

My husband said, "Margaret, you act as though you had a special dispensation from God that nothing that happens to other people could ever happen to you. This is a mighty dangerous, difficult, dirty world. Hardly anyone ever gets out of it alive." I wanted to be one who got out alive. I had worked to prevent osteoporosis, to protect myself from becoming a statistic, one of the fifty-five thousand women a year who suffer "permanent crippling" from that disease. I had eaten right and worked out for over thirty years, walked for two miles a day. I had looked forward to growing old. I had thought it would be a ball.

The trouble was, I had had such great role models. There was my German "Aunt Baba," who was keeping house and working in her garden and running a girls' private school in her seventies. There was my Russian-born "Aunt Olga," also in her seventies, the favorite party guest and the most popular hostess in Charlottesville, Virginia, acting like a queen in her dark, tiny house near the railroad track. Then there was Dr. Nan Dyer, who, after spending forty years in China as a medical missionary, retired to the old brick house from where her father had ridden out in 1861 to join his saddle mate Rooney Lee in the Army of the Southern Confederacy. She lived on coffee and doughnuts, bourbon and books, and was found dead in bed at the age of 107!

And, of course, there is my greatest role model of all, my own husband, Albert. Now pushing ninety, Albert served several terms in the Massachusetts legislature when he was already in his seventies. He can do nearly everything he ever did in his life—in bed or out. He still has the sharpest mind I ever saw. He can still jump over the side of the truck or throw in eighty-pound bags. During the great heat wave of 1988, I tried to follow my usual routine while he followed his. After three weeks, I keeled over with a heat stroke; he kept working his ten or twelve hours on the farm. I, twenty years younger, had to learn that I could never measure myself by him.

I draw courage to grow old from the inspiration of our friend Nackey Loeb. Only a few years ago, Mrs. Loeb would have seemed the woman who had everything; a husband who adored her, children, a beautiful home on the ocean in the North Shore section of Massachusetts, all the trappings of wealth and privilege. Then, while the couple was on vacation in Nevada, their car went off the road. Mr. Loeb escaped serious injury. Mrs. Loeb emerged from the acccident a paraplegic, fated to spend the rest of her life in a wheelchair. Then, a few years afterwards, Mr. Loeb developed cancer and died.

What was Nackey going to do? She closed and sold their beautiful house and moved into a smaller house in southeastern New Hampshire near her grandchildren. Finally, she took over publication of her late husband's newspaper, *The Manchester Union Leader*, and was soon able to write editorials as slashing and invective-laden as his were. When I congratulated Nackey for her courage in finding a whole new life for herself, she looked at me and said quietly, "But, Margaret, what was the alternative?" The alternative was, of course, stagnation and death. Nackey chose life.

And yet, as in all of life's crises, there is always a turning point. For me, it came last spring as I was lying crippled on that same deacon's bench on the porch. My husband was sitting opposite, his solid form blotting out the sun. Suddenly, I heard the call of a bird. It was as if I had never heard a bird song before. I looked and I saw a streak of a birch, white against the green. I looked at my husband. For all his aliveness and strength, he could not have heard the bird; his hearing is almost gone. He could scarcely have seen the birch; he has only twenty percent vision. And suddenly I knew that I could choose to live or choose to die, that I could give up or go on. So I chose life, even with all its limitations. For as you age the world is still out there, beckoning you with all its pleasures and treasures, but continually, there are less and less for you. The world goes on; it does not stop, but it wants you to get off. And if older people tend to live among their memories, it is because the past is there for them. The future may not be.

Until two years ago, crippling illness was something that happened to other people. Death was something that occasionally happened to people you might know. Then in one month's time last year, I lost my sister, my "other mother," and my dearest friend. Yes, it does take courage to grow old. I had known that this would happen, but I had never dreamed that it would all happen in two years' time.

One factor in finding the courage to grow old is to realize that death may come as a friend, not an enemy. Faced with the pains, the losses, the limitations of old age, the individual begins to lose his or her fear of death. One faces its inevitability. One wonders, in this damned and doomed and polluted world, why anyone would want to live into the twenty-first century. I have had a great life, but that is part of the trouble. I know what the quality of life used to be.

It would be comforting to those seeking the courage to grow old to think that ageism is gone now. Sometimes it is, but if you are a woman, you have to stay sexy and beautiful. And if you are a man? When author Clayton Hoagland's wife died, he began to seek smaller quarters. He found the perfect apartment only a few blocks away, but they did not want a "single man" as occupant. How many wild parties they thought an eighty-year-old was going to throw is not clear.

But ageism is for the aged to find the courage to conquer. One who tried was Congresswoman Millicent Fenwick. Through the 1970s, even compared with such senators as Bill Bradley and Clifford Case, Ms.

Fenwick was a distinguished member of the New Jersey congressional delegation. When Senator Case retired, Ms. Fenwick sought his seat. A beautiful woman and a single mother, Ms. Fenwick supported her two children on her earnings as a Powers model before entering politics. Rapidly becoming known as a rampant individualist, she soon emerged as a character in Garry Trudeau's "Doonesbury" cartoon, defiantly smoking her little pipe. She ran a good campaign for the senate. She might have made it were it not for outside interference. *The New York Times* (a paper across the Hudson from New Jersey) came out against her for the alleged reason that at her age what future did she have? The argument that a man running for president of the United States was approximately the same age as Ms. Fenwick was of no weight. In 1980 what kind of future did Ronald Reagan have? So I wrote the *Times*: "You are ageist, sexist, and full of the old you-know-what." Ms. Fenwick was narrowly defeated by a man who had millions of dollars to spend, but what a role model she could have been! And I'm not sure Ms. Fenwick's mistake was in being a Republican. I think it was in growing old.

Not all believe that late life belongs to the old. Former Colorado Governor Richard Lamm believes that if you have had a successful and satisfying life span, and particularly if you are ill and miserable, you perhaps should be painlessly "put to sleep." Just who is to decide; who, in particular, is to decide who might be an exception, whose life is valuable enough to be worth saving, is not clear. What if someone had decided that Pablo Picasso, Pablo Casals, or Michelangelo, still producing and creating in their eighties and nineties, had "no future" when they became seventy years old?

On the other hand, many people might prefer death to having to accept a slower but equally sure death sentence—confinement in a nursing home. I hope I will have the courage to stand up against this being done to me. You must find the courage to be a little selfish; never go into a nursing home for the sake of your family. Never, never let anyone put you in a nursing home!

Certainly the late Helen Hooven Santmyer deserved better than a nursing home when she published her lifelong effort, *And Ladies of The Club*, the greatest best-seller since *Gone with the Wind*. She should have had TV interviews and cocktail parties, a radio show and autograph sessions at bookstores. All this would have killed the old girl, but she would have had fun! Isn't fun what we are told life is all about? She deserved the rewards of publication, but she died at eighty-seven, within a year, in the nursing home anyway.

For myself, I would never want to live out my life with a lot of other old crocks, continually getting ill and dying. I have been fortunate all my life to live in a more or less extended family situation; the fights, if nothing else, keep you alive.

So where do we find the courage to grow old? We find it in the good fight. "Fight," says Senator Claude Pepper. "Do not go gentle into that good night," urged poet Dylan Thomas. To find housing for our old age is a challenge that will help give us courage. Housing for all, not "elderly housing," not "affordable" housing, or housing segregated by age or class or color, but good housing for all will be one of the great battle grounds of the 1990s. Maggie Kuhn's concept of "shared housing," where the young, the middle-aged, and the old share living together is one possibility.

Many seek the courage to grow old in loving their wives or husbands. But when tragedy strikes, as in the form of a crippling stroke which renders the mate a vegetable, it always hits and separates the most tender, the most devoted, the most loving couples, particularly those who need each other the most. This is a very high price to pay, particularly if the couple have only each other, no children or grandchildren. But the price is worth it.

Divorce is one of the greatest evils of our time and we must find the courage to fight it. Divorce is bad for children and other living things. No one has ever made a convincing argument that divorce is good for children, aside from the rationalization that children are happier when all the strife and fighting are over. Nonsense! Strife and fighting are a part of any normal marriage, and if kids don't get it at home, they can always tune it in on television. The idea that marriage is a peaceful idyll is a myth that shatters so many marriages at the first jolt. The children are taught to run from problems, not to solve them.

More important, divorce tears down one of the two major props of a child's life. A child needs two parents. This is where the grandparents come in. In recent years, grandparents have been battling, sometimes even through the courts, often successfully, for the right to visit their grandchildren. But important as it is to the grandparents to see their grandchildren, it is even more important to the grandchildren. Grandparents have to find the courage to assert their direct participation in their grandchildren's lives, not run away into segregation in Florida or

Arizona. Often, only they can provide the positive roles as to what a good marriage means.

Divorce is bad for other people besides children; it may not even be healthy for the person wanting the divorce. For the elderly, either the male or the female, rejected late in life, a divorce can be devastating, emotionally and financially. A lost love cannot be regained; this has to be accepted. And despite all the alleged joys of the "singles" scene, it is hard to be a swinging single at age seventy. A spouse, male or female, abandoned at sixty or seventy after thirty or forty years of marriage is a pitiable sight.

Is it inevitable that the elderly become the "elderly frail"? Or, as a Tufts University scientist suggests, is aging the penalty for a faulted lifestyle? In any event, by fighting the battles of life, you find the courage to grow old. If you are healthy and strong, these battles against enforced confinement, against segregation by sex or age, against divorce, will challenge your energies. If you are part of the "elderly frail," the need to fight the good fight will help keep your mind off yourself.

The difference between being old and being young is that when you are young, you know things will get better. If you wait. Sometime. But if you are old, you know they may not get better. As the Carolinian John C. Calhoun put it, the "reward is in the struggle, not in the victory itself." Life is a battle in which we all lose in the end.

On a lighter note, folk singer Kenny Rogers turned fifty this year. He found the milestone "traumatic," until his eighty-five-year-old mother-in-law pointed out that the alternative to growing old is to die young. This fortified his courage. After all, with an income of $30 million a year, even being eighty-five would not matter very much. And what woman would mind becoming fifty-seven if she looked like Angie Dickinson?

As for getting old and finding the courage to grow old, I am not sure I would advise anyone else to try it. It can be a rough trip. But if I had to do it again, I would demand a return ticket.

Eugene L. Corey

Marion Pease Davis

B. *1918*

✖✖

In May 1957, Marion Pease Davis's husband, Paul, fell unconscious while working at the family sawmill. He spent three weeks in a hospital, mostly in a coma, and was later diagnosed as having encephalitis, the medical term for "sleeping sickness." The doctors decided that Mr. Davis needed lighter work than that of operating his sawmill and lumber business, and that he needed to work under constant supervision. Because of his chronic condition, they also recommended that Mrs. Davis become the major wage earner of the family. Soon thereafter, she became the head of the household.

Feeling that she must complete her college education to support the family, Mrs. Davis worked from 8:00 A.M. to 5:00 P.M. at a secretarial job, then attended night school until 9:00 P.M., until she was accepted at the local university. While in school she delivered newspapers from 3:30 to 7:30 A.M., after which she attended classes and did homework from 8:00 P.M. often until midnight, until she made the Dean's List, at which time she was eligible for grants and student loans. In 1965 she was awarded a bachelor's degree in psychology with honors from the University of Bridgeport. Four years later she graduated with a master's degree in social work from the University of Connecticut.

In the years that followed, Mrs. Davis served the Connecticut State Welfare Department as a caseworker and supervisor of the Protective Service Unit, directed the psychiatric social work department of the Greater Bridgeport Community Mental Health Center, and was chair of the Center Housing Committee. In 1982 she retired from her position as psychiatric social work chief of the Greater Bridgeport Community Mental Health Center. She currently operates a private psychological counseling service from her home in Connecticut.

In 1984, after twenty-seven years of slowly deteriorating health, Paul Davis died.

THE COURAGE TO LOVE AGAIN

In July 1984, my husband, Paul Davis, suffered a brain seizure while in the shower and died one month later from his scalding burns. I mourned Paul's passing for the next two and a half years, wondering, in lonely moments, if any love could ever replace the love I'd felt for him. I still miss (and will no doubt always miss) Paul's witty stories, his classical-music playing, his frequent courtship of me with flowers gathered from our garden, and his unexpected hugs as I worked around the kitchen. He was a sensitive, intelligent man who taught me to respect and communicate my feelings; his constant courtship of me added greatly to my self-esteem as a woman. We learned together the importance of loving and trusting each other and sharing hard work as a basis for our successful, forty-seven-year marriage.

Now that Paul is no longer with me to share the work around the house, my day varies considerably. I generally start each day with a meditation, or the "practice of the presence of God" (something I have maintained for the past thirty years). I then do a few household chores, go outdoors to mow the lawn or tend to the garden, carry in firewood, or shovel snow off the paths. After a shower I attend to correspondence or read. Meanwhile, I receive calls from prospective psychotherapy clients. I keep my appointments with them in the afternoon and early evening, generally for one- or two-hour sessions. Twice a week I lead a prayer and meditation study group. I might freeze peaches from the orchard that Paul and I planted, or can fruit and vegetables from my organic garden. Seasonal chores include summer mowing of the outer parts of my two and a half acres with my 1940 John Deere farm tractor. I might attend a workshop to keep my therapeutic skills updated, preside over our local League of Women Voters board meeting, or present a program to a local group on some aspect of "Aging with Creativity and Power." At present I serve on five community boards and an assortment of committees.

But staying busy and active, especially when you have lost a loving, trusting husband, just isn't enough. I finally recognized that the period of mourning was over when I said to a friend, another widow, "I think if I'm ever going to meet any eligible men, I'll have to attend something besides women's groups." She recommended that I join the local senior citizens group working to organize a senior center here in our town.

Soon thereafter I became secretary of the executive council, and things began to change: the man who became vice-chairman of the council and I developed a mutual attraction for each other.

The supportive, loving relationship that I had with Paul has given me courage, as a great-grandmother, to risk a new relationship, to begin to build a new love. I have learned that one *can* grow through sadness. In the relationship with my new friend, whom I shall call Allen, the sadness of his wife's long, incurable illness, Alzheimer's disease, the horror of her no longer knowing him or their daughters as he faithfully visits her every week in the nursing home, and the happiness of our developing love are inextricably connected. The sadness has forced us to develop deeper resources of patience as well as the tolerance to accept uncertainty. It has also enabled us to deal successfully with the dominant, although generally unspoken, perception in our culture that the relationship we share is somehow sinful.

Some people during the past year have asked if I feel a conflict within myself between my present love for Allen and my old love for Paul. Others wonder if I feel a moral conflict since I'm having a long-term, loving relationship with a married man. But for me, there is no conflict, for Allen's doctor has told him repeatedly that his wife will never come home to live again. How can one break up a marriage that has, for all practical purposes, ended? However, Allen continues bearing his financial responsibilities for her and expects to as long as he is able.

True love looks beyond death. About five years before Paul died, at a time when I was quite sick, I became concerned about what would happen to him if I were to die first. He was still a handsome man, attractive in many ways and sexually potent; but, due to his repeated "brain seizures," he was unable to keep track of many details, such as checkbooks, appointments, etc. I suggested to him then that if I died before he did he should not feel guilty about looking for another wife as soon as it felt right for him. He then said that I should feel free to find another husband should he pass away. And so, five years before his death, we began to release each other and prepare ourselves for the possibility of loving someone else.

As with grass, new love naturally fills the empty spaces left by a lost partner. This does not diminish the first love, but rather honors it by saying: "My life with you was so great that, now that it is over, I need another strong love with which to fill the emptiness that losing you has left within me."

When I was young I thought sex and romance were only for the young. Certainly when one has had a romantic, long-term marriage, ending only in death, one might legitimately have conflicting feelings about starting another such relationship, especially at seventy. Could another love ever be as great as the one already lived? Could anyone really love this aging body with its fair share of wrinkles, a bit of unwanted fat, and other evidences of the passage of time? Could two mature people learn to accommodate the differences bound to have developed as they grew in the varying environments of separate marriages? Would grown children accept the possibility of a stepmother or stepfather and all the ramifications of changed financial or other benefits that might go with a marriage late in life? These are the sorts of questions that hold most of us back, create conflicts within ourselves that are difficult to tackle. But the God-given need for love is ageless and essential, and something for which one may be proud to fight. The surprising, breathtaking attraction that two mature people may feel for one another would not have been recognized by me when I was younger. But when it occurs, it can conquer most of one's lingering doubts and unwanted fears.

Men and women who have had satisfying sex in a long-term marriage have likely learned to satisfy each other in many ways besides traditional intercourse. Now that I am older I know that those who dare to love again in a caring, thoughtful way are apt to find great comfort in a tender embrace, a great sense of support from being loved again by another mature person for whom one also has a great love and respect.

Throughout my life, my thinking on aging has evolved as my experiences have changed. When I was an impudent youngster of eighteen, I thought my mother at forty-five was "old." Now that I'm seventy I don't feel "old," just wiser. In spite of occasional stiffness and a few minor aches I have surprising energy. My own feeling of well-being and stamina was validated two months ago when I went to my internist for a checkup. I cautiously asked him if he thought I were doing too much, as my many friends sometimes imply. He answered, "You don't look seventy, you don't act seventy; whatever you're doing, keep doing it." So I will try, as I grow older, to continue to be the whole person I encourage my clients to become, physically, mentally, emotionally, and spiritually.

In the midst of Allen's despair over his hopelessly ill wife's lingering death, we continue to make plans for our marriage, if and when it becomes possible. His favorite quote from the Bible is: "Where there is no vision, the people perish." Meanwhile, we enjoy the hours we have together. We look forward to living, but we are not afraid to die. If the fates are kind, we may have a few happy years ahead in marriage together. If the fates are unkind, his wife will linger, having already lived on past her own happiness. Or one of us may die too soon. If we were able to get married now, we would, for we'd like to respect the mores of our culture. But whatever happens, at least we have made the end of our lives more comfortable, more exciting, more fun, more filled with love. Jesus said to his disciples: "Love one another." And this is what we have done. So I say, where's the conflict?

POSTSCRIPT: On March 24, 1989 "Allen" died of multiple myeloma, peacefully, holding Marion with one hand and his second daughter with the other.

Robert E. Lee

B. *1918*

With collaborator Jerome Lawrence, Robert E. Lee's place in American theater history is assured by a prodigious volume of work, including the contemporary classics *Inherit the Wind, First Monday in October, The Night Thoreau Spent in Jail, Auntie Mame*, and thirty other major productions.

Co-founder of Armed Forces Radio Service, American Playwrights Theatre, and the Margo Jones Award, Lee stays actively involved in both the academic and professional theater scene as dramatist, director, and teacher. He has received an honorary doctor of literature degree from Ohio Wesleyan, a doctor of letters degree from the College of Wooster, and a doctor of humanities degree from Ohio State University. For twenty years he has taught advanced playwriting at UCLA, where he is an adjunct professor.

In partnership with Jerome Lawrence, Lee has been the recipient of many of the most prestigious awards in the theater, including the Donaldson Award, Variety Critics Poll (both in New York and London), two Peabody Awards for Distinguished Achievement in Broadcasting, and the Lifetime Achievement Award from the American Theatre Association.

"Naturally, we are doomed," says Lee blithely. "All of us are absolutely doomed on this planet. A few months, a few years, and where will we be? Yet we're infected with this totally irrational optimism! We dare to wake up every morning, dare to get out of bed. We dare to put things on the stage. We dare, as playwrights, to pretend we are gods. Arrogantly flying in the face of such dangers, writers play the greatest sport in the world."

CONSIDERING
THE ALTERNATIVE

Nobody consulted me about the Big Bang. I was rather young at the time—in fact, about as young as anyone can be, since I wasn't even born yet. Of course, nobody else had been born yet, either. Oh, there are two possible exceptions, since the Scriptures don't bother to tell us where they came from. One is Cain's fiancée, who hasn't been seen since Genesis 4:17. If she was of voting age when the Lord lit the fuse, that would make her at least two generations older than her hairy husband. Maybe Cain had a thing about older women. Then there was a shadowy chap whom Abraham bumped into while trekking from Ur to Canaan. His name was Melchizedek, and the Bible doesn't give us any clues on his origin. But what credentials he has don't certify him as much of an authority on creations generally.

My own feeling is that the Creator cooked up the universe pretty much on His own. In a number of ways, He seems to have botched the job rather badly. Take planned obsolescence, for example. I always thought this sleazy gimmick had been dreamed up in some shiny corporate boardroom: a scheme whereby a product is designed to go on the fritz just after the warranty runs out. But no! God invented it. We call it "old age," and it's something which could have been very nicely scratched from the blueprint—unless you consider the alternative.

God gives us a rather flimsy guarantee of three-score years and ten, plus a high-price ten-year extension with lots of small print. In biblical times, they were a little short on vitamins and antibiotics, but freeway traffic wasn't as bad then. From an actuary's viewpoint, the deal's about the same as it was in the Pentateuch.

Before the Big Bang, the world was without form, and void. But have you taken a good look at the Milky Way lately? Not from amid the glare of city lights, but from a desert or mountaintop? It's a mess! If that's the Lord's idea of "order out of chaos," I hope He never helps me straighten out my files or document my tax return.

It all moves and changes. Nothing lasts. And there really isn't a damned thing we can do about it. We can theorize, but who has the gall to claim that he really understands it all?

What we are is coiled up in the DNA helices imbedded in the maternal womb. We have no control over our own sex, or that of our children, the color of eyes or hair, or any of our physical attributes. God gave us a few choices: what we could have for breakfast, whether we could vote Republican or Democratic—or stay at home. Two things always happen to every one of us, but only once. We are each born. We each die.

In the days before the U.S. got into World War II, I happened to be living with a French family up in Westchester. They were deeply involved in the work of the Alliance Française. On one occasion I was drafted into service to raise and lower the curtain in a theater where an illustrious visitor from Paris was about to make a speech. My knowledge of French is not nonexistent; "sparse" perhaps, is *le mot juste*. Anyhow, I raised the curtain. A distinguished gentleman came forward and spoke almost interminably in French. He relinquished the podium, and I promptly lowered the curtain. It turned out that the long-winded preamble had actually been the introduction to the principal speaker, whom I had amputated from his audience with the backside of the curtain. I shall never forget his surprise and the look of Gallic indignation he threw at me. Quickly, I yanked the other line and brought back his audience. (It was, however, the best laugh of the evening.)

If you'll excuse a rather tacky oxymoron, Death is the supreme fact of Life. It is a little like the drawing of a curtain. Every play must end. But you can't yank the curtain up again as easily as I rectified my blunder with the French orator.

There are dissimilarities on other counts too. In theater, the action ends, the houselights come up, the audience is cut off from the play. But the end of a life is more like the closing of a scrim, the intercession of a veil which allows a continuation of contact. The remembered words, actions, convictions of an individual are not severed from those who follow him. No knifelike curtain really falls. We still see and enjoy those who have gone before us, as others may be influenced by what we have said and done. Perhaps those who follow will see us more clearly than we see ourselves.

The poets grasped the crux of it: what we don't know saves us. The certainty of an ultimate ending persists, but the mystery sustains our optimism. It is only knowing the "when" that causes dismay.

Some years ago, when our son Jonathan was about five, he started asking questions about death. I explained it as well as I could, i.e., not at all. Suddenly his eyes lit up. "I've got it!" he said as I sat on the edge of his bed. "God's saving it for a surprise!"

Can you think of any better explanation?

"Grow old along with me," says Browning's Rabbi Ben Ezra. "The best is yet to be." Well, I'll go along with that. Do I have any choice? I only know that I can wring every droplet of fun out of my life by brooding over the end of it!

The capriciousness of the life-death balance is what makes the entire thing an adventure of the highest order. I believe that God has a marvelous sense of humor. Honestly, I think He is playing with us, and He wants us to play with Him. The zest is the rattle of the dice in the cup, not throwing them out on the green velvet. Snake eyes or lucky seven— the anticipation is over. I enjoy the doubt, the uncertainty, the magnificent issue of the game.

Again, to recall that old sourpuss Browning: he speaks of someone's death as "a sunset-touch . . . enough for fifty hopes and fears, as old and new at once as Nature's self." And he urges us to "take hands and dance there, a fantastic ring, around the ancient idol, on his base again: THE GRAND PERHAPS!"

What gives me the Courage to Grow Old? The same thing. The Grand Perhaps.

I enjoy a very fortunate and happy life. I have a glorious wife, two dazzling children, and two grandchildren who are polishing up to dazzle on their own.

Oh, it's not all honeydew and bliss. I've had more Broadway flops than hits, survived a plane crash, spent more than my share of weeks in hospitals. I also love chocolate, but life can't be all Cadbury. You need an occasional tweak of bitterness.

I'm no masochist. I try to pretend that my really painful adventures are happening to somebody else—preferably to a person I don't much like. (I have a list of several Broadway producers and critics on whom I am prepared to visit these hapless speculations.)

I also nourish an insatiable curiosity which makes me eager to learn, even as they're sticking the endoscope down my gullet. I hate anesthetics. I want to know what's going on. The doctors will often rig up a TV screen so I can see what they're doing to me. Who knows? Maybe I can make a suggestion!

It hurts? Sure, but it's like hitting your head with a hammer; it feels so great when you stop.

I am Jamesian to the core, a hopeless meliorist. I think nothing stands still. Everything is constantly getting better or getting worse. I think the good is getting better faster than the corrosive negatives are creeping up on us.

I swear, I think God put me here to further that process of improvement. And, imperfect though I am, I refuse to let those imperfections impede me in pursuing that purpose.

Celebrating or bemoaning birthdays has, I think, nothing to do with it. Louis Untermeyer was composing outrageous limericks and assembling monumental anthologies for ninety years. George Abbott, who directed our first play on Broadway, has a hundred years behind him and is still working like a beaver slapping together his first dam. And is any acting teacher younger in spirit than Stella Adler? She far outshines the be-blue-jeaned kids, fifty years her junior, who clamor to get into her classes.

Vast reaches lie out there to be touched, explored, interpreted, reinterpreted. The world has acquired more new information in the years of my lifetime than all mankind has assembled throughout the millennia since the first Ice Age. And we're only starting.

I'm not a young man. So? Should I disqualify myself because I have fewer hours to see and breathe and think than my daughter has? Or my son? My wife's father, well past eighty, was working in his backyard the week before his heart stopped. Pointing to a row of fruit trees he had just planted, he said: "In twenty years, these will yield more than we can possibly eat!" He was right. Those trees now give magnificent pears and peaches and apples. Though he's not here to savor the taste, others do. Or perhaps he's enjoying vicariously through the tingle of a latter-day tongue. Can anyone say that planting those trees wasn't a thousand times more useful than dwelling on his age and infirmities? Emerson says everything has its compensations. Salty-saccharine Lord Tennyson swears, "Though much is taken, much abides. It is not too late to seek a newer world!"

It is a fine ego that leads me to pinch off this pseudo-essay, fraught with snatches from so many great poets, with a bit of doggerel from my own pen. (Pen, hell! I write on a word processor!) But I caught a glimpse of myself in the mirror a few days ago. I don't do it often, because I don't believe what I see. I feel about twenty-two—and I think there's more truth in my feelings than in my reflections. But here's the poem:

My nose isn't Grecian,
My brow isn't granite.
I'm near the completion
Of years on this planet.

I enjoy a fairly
Anonymous fame;
They quote me, but rarely
Remember my name.

My eyesight is grand
When my glasses are clean.
I'm overly tanned,
I'm lined, but I'm lean.

I can usually hear
Somewhat more than I'd like to.
If it's down-hill and near,
It's a place I can bike to.

My nails are a sight
That would sicken a leper.
My hair isn't white—
But there's salt in the pepper.

The enzymes still mix,
The colon still works,
The glottis still clicks.
The patella still jerks.

I'm not yet a ghost,
Nor planning to rot—
And I'm making the most
Of the years that I've got!

Lance Richardson

Charles Edward Eaton

B. *1916*

꘎꘎

Born in Winston-Salem, North Carolina, where his businessman poetry-loving father served as mayor for twenty years, Charles Eaton was encouraged, from his "earliest scribblings" at the age of seven or eight, to become a poet and writer. Years later, while working toward a master's degree at Harvard, he met Robert Frost. There began a lifelong friendship which served to stimulate and reinforce his literary ambitions.

Since the publication of his first book of poetry, *The Bright Plain* (1942), Eaton has written in a number of verse forms and has composed lyrical as well as dramatic poetry. Well studied in philosophy, his writings exhibit a strong intellectual content, although landscapes and nature have also played an important role in his work. He does not belong to any school and is neither a traditionalist nor an extreme experimentalist. He believes in balance in his poetry and has sought to speak in a contemporary voice about matters of enduring interest.

Over the years Eaton has taught English at several universities both in the United States and abroad, served as vice-counsel for the American embassy in

Rio de Janeiro, and has contributed several thousand poems and short stories to journals and magazines around the world, among them *Harper's*, *Saturday Review*, *Atlantic Monthly*, and *New Statesman*. His work regularly appears in anthologies featuring the best American short stories and poetry.

He has won numerous awards for his work, including the Alice Fay di Castagnola Award from the Poetry Society of America, one of the highest awards in American poetry. Recordings of his poems are in the permanent collections of Yale University, Fairleigh Dickinson University, and the Library of Congress, and his literary papers are being collected by Boston University and the University of North Carolina at Chapel Hill.

A firm believer in the spirituality of swimming, Eaton's love for the sport has inspired an entire collection of his poems, *The Shadow of the Swimmer* (1951).

RIPENING PAST DESPAIR

I was fortunate to start my career, and indeed my life, with a positive outlook that stays with me to this day. It was modified, of course, by disillusion as wryly expressed by William James when a student asked him the meaning of life: "On my bad days it is just one damn thing after another." For me, however, there have been enough good days so that my "chain of being" has an underlying tensile strength which, nevertheless, has to be frequently and briskly rubbed to remove the tarnish.

This affirmative attitude is perhaps best represented by the title poem of my first collection of poetry, which was published by the University of North Carolina Press in 1942 when I was in my twenties. Quoted in its entirety below, perhaps it will suggest the love of life that has remained with me, though in a more complex way, over the years:

THE BRIGHT PLAIN

This has been a day
  luxurious and lilting and spun
  like a long-linked spool of brightness from the sun.

This has been a day
  like the first stanza: beginning rhyme
  of the song drift (da capo: da capo) of importunate time.

This has been a day
  when life-long travelers through the glistening world
  found air lavish: prodigal: the landscape hurled

In glinting rock:
  sun-lake and long legato green.
  Joy was the way breath leaned

Like a fresh wind
  into day, barely ruffling the grass, the landscape's ease,
  leaving desire unhorizoned: the bright plain between
    distant trees.

Biography, as well as temperament, played a part in my outlook, for I was fortunate to have a father who, though a businessman and mayor of Winston-Salem, North Carolina, for twenty years, knew more poetry by heart than any professor I have ever had at the four universities I attended as an undergraduate and graduate. My mother was a painter, and I was, so to speak, brought up at the easel. Both parents encouraged me to be a poet from my earliest scribblings at the age of seven or eight. Added to their belief was the encouragement along the way from many teachers, including Robert Frost, who was already "a grand old man" when I met him at Harvard and who managed to remain green at the top into his eighties.

Such support and reinforcement can help to generate confidence that will last a lifetime. Indeed, it may be that the courage to grow old has its seed in early experience. This is not to suggest that I was an unqualified optimist—far from it. I soon realized, and the knowledge has increased with the years, that the world is a place of unceasing competition. There are always some who will have been able to deal with the conditions around them better than you, and all but a few of us must inevitably fall into the category of second best. In spite of what some of our athletic entrepreneurs have advised us, winning, in the worldly sense, is not everything. An early awareness of this fact enables the old to take the measure of life's tensions, oppositions, and ambiguities, and, in my case, to develop the talent for reconciliation which is the mark of the artist. Still, the view of the possibilities of life as "a bright plain" was, and remains, the ideal. I still agree with Van Gogh, who said that the task of the artist, ultimately, is "to try to say something comforting."

Having written for over fifty years, I will confess, however, that this basic philosophy has encountered many difficulties and met with many more tests than I realized would be the case when I wrote my ecstatic poem. Any philosophy that is too simplistic, either narrowly affirmative or pessimistic, fails in the face of contradictory events. In fact, one must undergo a constant and vigilant discipline, particularly in our increasingly complicated and often distressing world, to maintain any kind of steadfast point of view. Consequently, from the beginning, I have sensed that this cannot be accomplished and sustained without a structured life to combat the alienation that often surrounds us.

In this respect, the time element is of the essence. In youth we feel we can keep on asking questions, but in old age we think we should be able to come up with at least *some* answers, only to find that nearly all "solutions" are temporary and bring new and unexpected problems. The longer we live, the more we realize that there is not a single answer to life, but many. When we are young, we say that if only we could have this or that, achieve this goal or another, have money and fame, we could be happy. The list moves on into old age, and, having been fortunate to achieve one or two of these, we find that complete happiness is a many-splendored illusion. Moreover, in a youth-oriented society the old are daily bombarded in the media by images of the young, a soft drink and chewing gum version of life which seems to have little to do with their own condition and which makes some of us, at least intermittently, feel adrift in an alien culture and subject to "television blues."

My own effort to confront such alienation has involved a lifelong dedication to health as well as endeavor. One must, of course, give oneself to experience or there will be no life in your work, but it takes some doing to survive its depredations. One must understand one's limits, both physical and mental, and, at the same time, not be afraid to test and, wherever possible, extend these limits, for even the most studious and perceptive student of the self cannot rigidly predict its elasticity and vitality. In asserting as fundamental tenets "know thyself" and "the unexamined life is not worth living," Socrates surely meant to suggest that examination implies exploration of character and possibilities throughout a lifetime.

Grow old gracefully with courage, yes, but not too gracefully if that means stagnation, blandness, a complacent contemplation of past accomplishments. Grow old gracefully only if grace can accommodate passion and persistence. I do not believe in retirement as long as one keeps one's health and faculties. I have worked on well past the usual retirement age and intend to keep going as long as I have anything to say. Each of my books has explored another area of my experience and imagination, and I continue to have a rich landscape, still "unhorizoned," whose far reaches I have never traveled. This means, on a typical day, getting up early for a brisk walk with my dog, a Samoyed named Natasha, while I munch on raw carrots. After a more substantial breakfast, I work at my desk, sometimes in bed to conserve energy, until noon, knock off for a walk with my wife and Natasha, and then a twenty-minute swim. Afternoons are devoted to revisions, correspondence, business matters, and then another walk and swim. I am, as Robert Frost told me he was, "essentially a walker and a reader," but I would add to these activities swimming, the cleanest and most "spiritual" of sports, which has inspired an entire collection of poems.

A Spartan existence? Decidedly not—how many works of art do you remember having come out of Sparta? Evenings and weekends are devoted to pleasure. In fact, I have been called a hedonist, but an epicurean would be nearer to the mark when you remember that the philosopher advised us to enjoy today in moderation so that we can enjoy tomorrow as well. Savored, long-drawn-out pleasures—my wife and I love music, plays, paintings, evenings with friends, and, of course, good food where, alas, desire has had to heed moderation somewhat more than I would like.

Frankly, though I understand and appreciate the title of this anthology, I do not think much about growing old. Preparedness, yes, practicalities, attention to the underlying stabilities necessary for a successful old age, but not the daily morbid preoccupation with, and saturation in, the fact that I am over seventy. I agree with E.M. Forster, who said that he liked best those who "acted as if they were immortal and time eternal." I do not, any longer, even believe in the sentimental ideal that old people are automatically entitled to "golden" years—a life on "golden pond." Though appealing as a projection of desire, I suspect that for me mellow indolence would soon deteriorate into boredom and depression. I have found that "God laughs at the man who says to his soul: Take thy rest," and that the notion of challenge and response seems to be one of the laws of a vital life until its end. Among the joys of old age is that the mind, though scarred with embattled memories, is also stocked with some splendid shibboleths, and that one knows that sometimes a war cry is better than a whimper.

Nevertheless, anyone who has lived to the age of seventy has endured some setbacks and blows that put the greatest strain on his courage, and the mechanism that regulates challenge and response grows tired. Depression comes more readily to the old, and only a disciplined will and intellect can give us the strength to rise to the occasion. For example, a few years ago, out of the blue, I was struck by a severe case of shingles, one of the most painful and nerve-racking of illnesses, that lasted over three months. No wonder the legend arose that if the "girdle" of inflammation that surrounds the body ever entirely meets it will kill you. For several weeks I felt that the "missing link" would be forged by one more day of pain. What to do? I decided that instead of passively enduring the sleepless nights and difficult days, I must somehow rally and turn negative energy into positive. Consequently, I fell back upon my greatest strength and forced myself to write a poem almost every day in the late afternoon. Miraculously, the psychological release had a beneficial effect, and I could sleep from then on with little or no medication almost every night. Moreover, I wrote some of my best work as compensation for my illness. I believe that particularly the old must make a determined effort to turn things around, to be combative, if you will.

This insistence on courage and the need to keep one's zest goes to the very heart of my thinking about old age. One can *practice* to be a qualified optimist as well as an unremitting pessimist. Along with fidelity to the job at hand, a kind of natural ebullience is necessary to carry us through life. Nothing can quite take the place of sheer animal spirits, not only in adversity, but in spurring and inspiring us to sing our "hymn to joy."

Nothing in life, however, should be taken as too cut-and-dried. People are various and need to express themselves variously. Any theory of self, no matter how well integrated, contains hidden in it several other selves that would think differently and propose otherwise. Looked at in one way, we are shapely creatures, and, in another, of uncertain and ambiguous form. Nevertheless, the best we can do is to maintain some dominant sense of the self that is workable and productive, but has, however, a gift for flexibility and crossover. We recognize this in the familiar expression "Pull yourself together" and are continually having to rescue the self from destruction just as we must continually retrieve, and revivify, many parts of the world around us. One of the rewards of old age is that the strategies for preservation have had so much practice that the affirmation of one's choices seems more secure and stable than in youth. One can entertain all the things one did not do or did not become with increased equanimity, grateful for what did succeed.

How to end a meditation on growing old except perhaps to call once more on the voice of the dominant self for a coda. I like to remind myself that in our haste to explore outer space and be the most powerful and prosperous nation, which of course has its thrilling aspects, we should not forget the long, troubled, but essentially beautiful story of the earth, nor, by discounting human values, count ourselves out of the universe. Chaucer spoke long ago and with much affection of this "little green earth." As often as possible when I get up in the morning and am at my freshest, I take some time to remember this early delight in the world which has lived all these years in the bloodstream of English poetry and has sooner or later triumphed over the infections that would reduce the health of the spirit below survival point. Though we can honor the honest grief that made Hölderlin cry out at one point: "In such spiritless times why to be poet at all?," nevertheless are we not called upon to remember that nature, the most joyous of companions, is, in one sense, entirely hard-hearted unless we ripen past despair?

Much has been said lately about the "graying" of America, and, though veneration for the old may never reach the heights that it has in China, it is clear that those of my generation, both somewhat older and younger, will have a greater influence on our society. It is paramount, therefore, that old people do think about their condition, respond vigorously to our culture, share their long adventure with the young, and join hands in the affirmation of the total human experience. The courage to grow old is more than a personal quality to be desired. It is at the very heart of the dream that, though men have many faces and many faculties, they must stand up to Destiny together, and prevail upon it to acknowledge the bravery and persistence inherent in the very name of Man.

© Jack Mitchell 1988

David Diamond

B. *1915*

❧ ❧

David Diamond, whose nine symphonies, eleven string quartets, and many art songs have been praised by Leonard Bernstein for retaining "the most lasting aesthetic values," is one of America's most distinguished composers. Over a long and often controversial career, frequently plagued by financial hardship, he has never been the prisoner of fashionable avant-garde movements and has remained one of the world's most unremittingly serious and dedicated composers, known for his professionalism, integrity, and independence of judgment.

From 1934 to 1935, while living at the New York City YMHA, Diamond mopped floors and jerked sodas to sustain himself while studying composition with Roger Sessions at the New Music School and Dalcroze Institute. In 1935 he was awarded the Elfrida Whiteman Fellowship for his "Sinfonietta," a work based on one of the poems in Carl Sandburg's *Good Morning, America*. In 1936 he left for Paris to compose the music for E. E. Cummings's ballet scenario TOM. In Paris he met Maurice Ravel, as well as Albert Roussel and André Gide, all of whom encouraged the young composer. The following summer he returned to Paris to study with Nadia Boulanger. With the suggestions of Stravinsky, Diamond's orchestral "Psalm" secured for him, in 1937, the Juilliard Publication Award. The following year he won the first of his three Guggenheim Fellowships and his career was securely launched. He went on to win several New York Critics Circle awards, the Prix de Rome (1942), the Paderewski Prize (1943), the Rheta Sosland Award for Chamber Music (1965), the ASCAP–Stravinsky Award (1965), and, most recently, the William Schuman Award (1985). In 1966 he was elected to the American Academy National Institute of Arts and Letters.

He has taught in Salzburg, Austria, at the State University of New York at Buffalo, the University of Colorado at Boulder, the University of Denver, and, since 1973, has been a professor of composition at the Juilliard School. His works have been performed in every major concert hall in the United States and Europe.

DARK YEARS AND
DIFFICULT QUESTIONS

I have come to approach the last years of my life with an attitude of irony and pity, for to me, there is no dignity in growing old. We are born, we mature. We feel sadness and happiness. We praise and we mourn. We age, sicken, and die. Is that worth a lifetime on earth?

An uncertain world has made life a misery for me. How can I age with decency in an indecent society whose culture is constantly being sullied by the most fraudulent self-seeking? Excess and insolence are pounding our world into sludge. More and more, day by day, I am made aware of the evil men do in the name of religious faith and politics. Great technological achievements notwithstanding, the purpose of humanity seems to have been its baffling history of trial and error, comedy and tragedy, with ignorance and superstition leading the way from darkness to horror, and the ever threatening final abyss staring up at us with beckoning eyes of greed and destruction. There will be no more heroes in war, only corpses.

The fate of man depends on his good sense and his sense of what is good. But that fate is now in the hands of semantic distortionists. And how does one rest firm in this world of constantly shifting trivialities? Even the imaginative idiocies of TV commercials antagonize more than attract. Whatever youthful idealism I held disappeared fast as the wear and tear of living in this world took its toll. If man could make life such a hell on earth, I am sure he could make no heaven elsewhere.

I have a kind of medieval religious consciousness. Its very naiveté prevents me from becoming an atheist. I am too full of questions about the universe and can only probe and postulate and drive myself into dead ends of the spirit by doing so. For the first twenty years or so of my life I had been instructed to believe God was a positive force for good. In recent decades that belief seems to have become a positive force for violence. Consequently, I have come to believe that life is inexplicable and man even more so. Perhaps Voltaire was right when he said that the world cares very little whether you are well or sick, and might have added, since it cares so little about itself.

There are always the pretenses of still being youthful and energetic-geriatric delusions. I have always been loyal to my youth even though youth does not always accommodate old age. A special sensibility and wisdom must accompany it, and the time of our youth has insufficient wisdom to make us prescient. It is easier for old age to memorialize youth. As a result, obsessive thoughts and a reactive depression overwhelm me daily.

For me, aging is as much an affliction as was my adolesence. I was most fulfilled during my middle years. Then as now, music alone will carry me through safely to the end.

Neither deafness nor blindness threatens me, but chronic fatigue and somnolence are debilitating and paralyzing at times. What really matters is endurance. I am never bored. But illness has made me taciturn and morose.

As I have advanced into old age, hope and praise have become less important, while recollection has become stronger. As I age I remember more vividly, because the anticipation of death brings the past into sharper focus. I have noted, too, that I remember best when I am melancholy.

And everything I remember from my childhood is sad. I force myself to recall the happier, more amusing things from childhood, like the idiotic happenings in early youth, as well as the destructive things in my mature years. But today, everything that I recall from the past is tinged with sorrow or regret. "Why is my pain perpetual, my wound incurable?" I ask with Jeremiah.

My chronic melancholia is the result of many childhood traumas, among them the shock of loneliness. I knew sadness from my earliest years, and that sadness has never left me. By the age of twenty I was convinced that I had been born melancholy. In all probability, for all the strife and stress and despair, by nature I was a contemplative—a disquieting state, unless you are a saint. Memory and truth lead me on a dark procession toward eternity—"a circle whose center is everywhere and circumference nowhere" (Timaeus of Locris).

I have in my head only music and childhood. They are refractory forces, mysterious and inexplicable in old age. I learned early that there was no end to the rainbow, and that the pot of gold was more likely empty than full. Music is all that I have left to beat down my despair. Under its influence, death seems incomprehensible.

I live alone in order to get my music composed, and because I cannot accept people as they are. The best part of living alone is the conservation of energy, since there is no one to converse with. When alone, some sing out of fear of the night, or to cheer themselves up. I do not. I embrace the night, call out to an owl, a bat, a stray cat or dog.

In youth I walked a lot and talked little. In old age I walk very little and talk too much.

I have lived hard enough and long enough to forgive myself for many of my errors, although remorse still torments me. I continue to speak out with disturbing candor. Insolent retorts are returned at once. People, those celebrated others who are our daily hell, even when they are in the wrong, want to hear only what they think is right, and reserve the right to brook no criticism. So I criticize them vituperatively and add a few more enemies to an already long list. My anger, though unpredictable, is almost always justifiable. "Anger is an impulse attended with pain to avenge an undeserved slight openly manifested toward ourselves," said Aristotle. Society, certain individuals, the cruel indifferences shown me by the majority of interpreters in music, have produced so many obstacles over the decades that I am constantly under stress or duress. Overt anger often extricates me from the quagmire of depression. I am often the victim of other people's cool indifference, which to me seems a kind of cultural cruelty, even madness. Only in fearless confession can you judge someone who stands in your way, or who has offended you. Truth has many entrances and exits. But I recognize that anger is too often a dead end; it does more harm than good. But no matter. "When you are angry," I was once told, "your natural modesty leaves you." Modesty be damned! I thought. It is one of the most suspect of virtues and ought to be lumped in the same bucket of sludge with false humility. In old age it can become outright senility. It is raw emotion that I live with now.

Aging is torment in flux. And only death can terminate the agonizing flow of deterioration. I have been complex and melancholy. I remain so. This has made me uncertain of the future. The dead populate my memory's vast land of suffering and have therefore helped me to live. But personal loss can also poison the soul. We gain little from losing those we have loved. We are made sorrowful. We are not ennobled by our suffering. It extemporizes old age.

So approaching the end of life is prolonged agony for me. In private I shuffle about, moan and groan mutedly. But my conscience interferes, informs me that my music is what matters most, and my youthful energy returns with stunning impact. The notes flow, the critical acumen returns, I become young again and eat and drink with gusto. I teach with conviction. I do not let my students down.

But then I let myself down by facing the inevitable truth that I am old. And I know that there soon will come a time when I will say: I have heard all the world has to say, and I want no more of it.

Stathis Orphanos

Jerome Lawrence

B. *1915*

❧ ❧

The honored playwright-director has created, in partnership with Robert E. Lee, enduring works of the American theater. His work has ranged broadly from the timeless magic of both *Auntie Mame* and *Mame* to the impassioned defense of intellectual freedom in *Inherit the Wind* and the revelation of the precious quality of human intellect and courage in *The Night Thoreau Spent in Jail*. Lawrence & Lee plays have been translated and performed in thirty-three languages.

Born in Ohio, Lawrence has served on the boards of directors of the American Conservatory Theatre, Plumstead Theatre Society, the Stella Adler Theatre, the Dramatists Guild, the Writers Guild of America, and the Authors League of America. Committed to excellence in theater, he is cofounder of American Playwrights Theatre and cofounder and judge of the Margo Jones Award. He has received honorary doctorates from Villanova, the College of Wooster, Fairleigh Dickinson University, and Ohio State University, his alma mater, from which he graduated cum laude in 1937. He was master playwright at New York University, Baylor, and the Salzburg Seminar in American Studies and is currently adjunct professor in the Graduate School at the University of Southern California.

Lawrence still considers himself a young playwright. "A cop stopped me once for making a wrong turn, and he said, 'Have you ever been arrested?' and I said, 'Only emotionally.'" Believing that he "froze at eighteen," Lawrence says that "you don't need drugs or booze or tobacco or artificial stimulants to turn on. The things that really give me a high are sunsets and music and people—people especially. And travel and seeing the world and the Pacific Ocean every day. What turns me on is when Bob and I are working together and we get a line that gives us both goosebumps. That turns me on."

THE JOYS OF MENSCHHOOD

Paul Muni, one of the great stage and film actors of this century, taught us how to grow old. And how to grow young.

It was a privilege and joy to have Muni as the Broadway star of *Inherit the Wind*. Later I wrote his biography, *Actor: The Life and Times of Paul Muni*, as a labor of pure love. Most of the book concerns the three hundred roles Muni played in the fabled Yiddish theater between the ages of twelve and thirty-two, almost all of them bearded patriarchs, good gray wise men or fools (even once or twice an old, old lady).

Muni's work on the Yiddish stage served him well when he moved on to the English-speaking stages of Broadway and then onto the motion-picture screens of the world in the Academy Award–winning roles of Louis Pasteur, Émile Zola, Juárez, and many others. But in Pearl Buck's *The Good Earth* Muni performed the switch of his life. At age forty-one, he was asked by Irving Thalberg to play Wang Lung as a nineteen-year-old for the first third of the film. He was terrified. "I've been able to pile on makeup, stoop a little, quiver my hands, and be the oldest alte-cocker you ever saw, even when I was twelve, even with roller skates under my long rabbi's robe. But who the hell can play a teenager when you're past forty, and a Chinese kid in the bargain?" Talked into doing the part, Muni was totally convincing as the open-faced young Wang, acting youthful with body language, with a youthful spirit bubbling inside, with naiveté, with innocence, with tenderness, wonder, incredulity, and a joyful, giggling charm. It was the most effective portion of the landmark film.

Almost thirty years later, on Muni's seventieth birthday, we drove up to Santa Barbara to give him a copy of a newly published dictionary that contained an entry defining him simply as *actor*, which pleased him mightily, as he was a collector and respecter of dictionaries. He strode erectly around the house, brandishing the volume like an athletic weight lifter, and declaring: "Look at me. According to the IRS or the Department of Motor Vehicles, today I'm seventy. But you can't fool me. I'm not stooped over. I don't have a high, thin, trembling voice. My hands don't shake like jelly. But when I was a kid, that's how I played seventy-year-olds. Frankly, boychicks, I was a more convincing seventy-year-old when I was twelve."

We've all heard the near-cliché admonition, "Act your age!" from our seniors. What age? What stage? Of whose life? Another rebuke of children by the average American parent made Muni shake his head: "Be good!" That, he felt, had a puritanical, moralistic ring to it: an instant impulse for the youngster to declare war. The French have a more apt phrase: "Sois sage!" Be wise! But Jewish parents say: "Be a mensch!" Like most Yiddish it's really untranslatable. Mensch doesn't mean simply "man," being muscularly masculine, with hair on your chest. The phrase means: "Be a person, a courageous human being with individuality and dignity and guts; have a distinctive place in the universe." Perhaps that's the role we should all try to master at every stage, on every stage of our lives.

A woman can be a mensch too. The German title of Brecht's famous play, *Der Gute Mensch Von Sezuan*, is usually translated into English as "The Good Woman of Setzuan." A Yiddish eye would translate it more appropriately as the good person, the good human being, the good essence of humanity. So whether you are a young man or an old man, a young woman or an old woman (all a matter of opinion: don't believe statistics), you can be a *mensch* all of your life.

I'm against mandatory retirement. Why do we dump men and women of surpassing skills and wisdom and understanding and continuing creativity into the concentration camp of "old age" simply because they have reached the arbitrary fencepost of sixty-five? I don't believe your chronological age has anything to do with the newness of your ideas, the freshness of your conceptions. I realize retirement from the literary life is somewhat different from the imposed cancellation of a job in the average workplace. You can't continue to drive a bus in your living room, or build a skyscraper in your bathroom. But there are always new avenues to explore, new horizons still unimagined.

As for myself, I have always preferred not merely the Pursuit of Happiness, but the Happiness of Pursuit. Unless the next play is in our typewriters or word processors, unless I am witness to student-minds opening to the wonder of the intelligence and creativity all around us, I can't sleep at night. If there is not a journey-of-the-mind awaiting me tomorrow morning, why go to sleep? Why get up? Why have any more birthdays?

There's a legend in the land that past a certain age, your sexual drives slow down, atrophy, or disappear completely. Mine, though often sublimated, have not diminished a whit, nor has the joy of foreplay and the subsequent consummating orgasm of fathering a literary child.

A Lawrence & Lee play, *The Crocodile Smile*, is a poetic polemic against the wasteful practice of retirement. It opens in Paris a couple of generations ago as a doctor examines a depressed and near-suicidal patient he thinks he has never seen before. He finds the man's body sound, nothing wrong organically. He advises his melancholy patient to go to the theater, to see Bocador, the incomparable laugh-maker, perform. "Now there's a fellow who can make anybody forget his troubles." Slowly, the doctor realizes his patient *is* Bocador.

Probing Bocador's past, the doctor inquires if he had a happy childhood. "Oh, childhood is always happy," Bocador replies, "for everyone except children." The actor's life in retrospect parades across the stage: his failed marriage, the untimely death of his lifelong performing partner, his inability to pass on his genius as a laugh-maker to his bumbling son, his dedication then despair for a living theater which has been his life.

At the end of Bocador's saga, the doctor has only one prescription: retirement. But this is a strange word to Bocador, unknown territory.

DOCTOR. Could you sell your theatre?

BOCADOR. They would make it into a department store, and sell bicycles and plumbing and women's corsets.

DOCTOR. What do you care, as long as you get a good price for it? Go to Deauville, lie in the sun. Take the leisure to enjoy life. A vacation, Monsieur Bocador, a perpetual vacation!

BOCADOR. What does one do on a vacation?

DOCTOR. Oh, sleep until noon . . .

BOCADOR. I do that now.

DOCTOR. Forget the theatre. Sell it, let yourself live!

BOCADOR. And what am I? A closing? An ending?

DOCTOR. (*Persuasively.*) It's a circle, my friend. I've seen this happen with hundreds of men. Stockbrokers, shopkeepers. People who have worked too hard, worried too much. A time comes when the way of life must change. Rest, Monsieur Bocador. Rest.

BOCADOR (*Nodding.*) Rest.

Bocador wearily drags himself back to his silent, empty theater, prepared to close it. He tries to warm his cold hands over the now-dark footlights. Then he seems to hear remembered laughter, feels the presence of an audience out front.

BOCADOR. (*Shouting, suddenly, urgently.*) Lights! Bring up the lights. You can't play comedy in the bottom of a well!! (*As the lights slowly rise.*) The Doctor says shopkeepers, stockbrokers must slow down. Close the circle. Give up their businesses and retire. Go bury themselves in the sand at Deauville. (*As if embracing the stage.*) But this is not a shop! Not the Bank of France! This is a THEATRE! There are doctors enough to tell us to give up. It's our business to show people how to laugh and be strong! (*Bocador has thrown off all his melancholy and speaks with the power of new stature.*) We shall, all of us, stand on this stage and spit at death. And we shall make them laugh— until the tears come!

So the theater can be life-enhancing, despite the frequent attempts by the commercial theater to disembowel itself like some mad practitioner of hara-kiri. And the metaphor of the stage goes on all of our lives, each of us trying to give a continuum of peak performances, the sign of a true professional in our art and trade. We realize this most when two-thirds of a century has slipped by as personal-historical drama, including, we hope, quite a bit of high comedy.

The most annoying question I get is: "Are you still writing?"

"Yes! And I'm still breathing."

"What was your last play?"

"I haven't written it yet. If you mean my most recent play, I'll be happy to discuss it with you."

And the most frequent question-accusation: "Oh, you're one of those atheist-agnostic fellas who wrote *Inherit the Wind*—and you're giving Jerry Falwell and all the rest of the Fundamentalists conniption fits. Whatsamatter with you? Don't you believe in God?"

You're goddam right I believe in God, or more rationally a Supreme Intelligence, the creative mind of the universe of which we are all a part. Constantly. Even as "senior citizens." We have been created by that Intelligence to create and re-create.

Let's use some literal, fundamental Fundamentalism: Genesis 1:1. God—or that Intelligence—created the universe (with the willing help of the creative evolutionary process). But please note that He—or possibly She—didn't rest on the second day or the fourth day. He kept going, and then rested (see Genesis 1:2) on the seventh day. And any

Creator who could turn out a hunk of work like the universe, with great starring roles like the stars, is damn well going to get up the morning of the eighth day and go to a universal Selectric or word processor and KEEP RIGHT ON CREATING.

I challenge my play writing students: "You want to be God-like? Go thou and do likewise. The happy habit of a writing discipline, every day of your life, makes you get up and get to work on that eighth day, and that eight-hundredth day, and that eight-thousandth day. And when you are eighty."

Is all this a religion? I'm not sure. Actually, I am a theological mongrel: a Deist, a Transcendentalist, a Jewish Scientist, who would certainly be labeled by the religious right what they think is a degrading insult: a Secular Humanist. Daily rituals? I try to exercise my mind, my body, my soul, and my writing muscles, particularly in what may be my sunset years, or—who knows?—sunrise time.

My morning regimen includes a spiritual vitamin in the form of a page of Unity's "Daily Word," plus some capsule-size vitamins A, B, lots of C, E, and one aspirin. I try to write five pages a day, and then about 4:00 P.M. swim fifty laps of a good-sized pool, wherever I happen to be: New York, Malibu, the People's Republic of China, the Soviet Union, or in the chill waters of Lake Dal in Srinagar in the Vale of Kashmir. And every day a read: some subject, some author, new or ancient, I've never touched before, and a few pages of a reread, books I loved half a century ago, mostly to see if they still belong in a corner of my mind (most of the time, yes—and I try to make more room).

The play goes on. I'm too busy to worry about any final curtain. But shall I rage, rage (in Dylan Thomas's words) against the dying of the light? Yes. Not my own, but the unfair and untimely deaths of young men and women, with only a shred of their lifetimes lived, from AIDS, from cancer, from bullets and bombs and missiles in trumped-up wars against our self-invented "enemies." Mostly I shall continue to rage against the death of planet earth.

Muni's whispered final words were a challenge to himself: "Munya, be a MENSCH!"

I hope when that moment comes for me, I shall have the courage to say the same, to try to be the same.

Photo by Roberta Long

Cornel Lengyel

B. *1915*

꒰ ꒱

The poet of the forest finds not only rhyme but reason in the simple life he has chosen to live on his homestead, "Adam's Acres," situated in northern California's El Dorado National Forest. He lives here a solitary life with his wife, Teresa, and an assortment of animals. "Contemplating nature in its more elemental setting" provides him, he says, "with a taste for the simple and the sublime. Since I need few things for mere survival I am better able to separate what is important from what is nonessential."

Lengyel's books include *Four Days in July* (1958), a widely acclaimed re-creation of the men and events behind the Declaration of Independence; *I, Benedict Arnold: The Anatomy of Treason* (1960); *American Presidents: From George Washington to John F. Kennedy* (1961); and, *The Creative Self: Aspects of Man's Quest for Self-Knowledge and the Springs of Creativity* (1971). His most important work, however, is his poetry, for which he has received numerous awards, including the Maxwell Anderson Award for Poetic Drama, the Maritime Poetry Award, the Poetry Society of Virginia Award, the Di Castagnola Award from the Poetry Society of America, and a National Endowment for the Arts award.

Upon reading Lengyel's sonnet sequence, *The Lookout's Letter* (1971), the late philosopher George Santayana wrote to tell him that "you have invented, as far as I know, a new form of verse, the blank-verse sonnet; and from the beginning you have made it seem a natural and powerful instrument. The steady sure way in which you carry it through, without a hitch or any faltering in force or clearness, shows that it can be made to serve, as the traditional sonnet did in its day, almost any form of discursive poetry . . . You write these single lines, almost without a lapse in tone or quality, like Shakespeare in his early plays."

RUMINATIONS ON
SENESCENCE

E verybody wants to live long, but nobody wants to grow old,"
Benjamin Franklin remarked some two hundred years ago. The
talent for aging, like the talent for youth itself, seems a part of everyman's endowment. Whether one treats it with courage or cosmetics, it
is a universal process and no one holds a patent on it. Given enough
time, almost any young clown may become a white-haired philosopher.

It takes a degree of courage no doubt to breathe the air and survive
in the twentieth century, a century during which more than fifty million
men, women, and children have met with violent deaths at the hands
of their fellowmen. Yet the courage we may need more is perhaps the
courage to grow; and rather than to grow old, the courage to grow
young. A survivor's last challenge may be to recover the once-promising
child he used to be; to press forward into futurity with wonder, delight,
and curiosity; to renew his capacity for self-transformation; to share
his measure of freedom and his sense of fellowship with all living creatures, despite his diminishing time and increasing limitations. "Unless
you become like a child again, you cannot enter the kingdom of
heaven," said Jesus.

Compared to the life span of a bristlecone pine, my own span seems
brief. Yet already I have lived longer than a majority of my contemporaries. In Shakespeare's England, the average span was under fifty;
in India, it remains under forty. In modern Africa, one-fourth of the
black children, numbering millions, die before the age of six. According
to Desmond Morris, author of *The Naked Ape*, man's natural biological
span is between forty and fifty. Medical science has extended this to
seventy plus; Peter Medawar, another prominent English zoologist, pre-
dicts the extension to between one hundred and one hundred and fifty
years.

Living longer doesn't necessarily make a man wiser or happier. It
does give him more time to digest his experience. With his extended
learning time, a senior citizen should have acquired more information,

less misinformation, and so formed more accurate views of himself and the world he lives in. Yet we all have met elders who cling to the collective delusions of the past. More than one, despite his season (when he could afford to be truthful and disinterested), will subscribe to old lies or newly packaged superstitions, whether scientific, religious, or political. More than one would promote an oligarchy of octogenarians, with senility wielding the chairman's gavel.

But the obverse should also be noted. In spite of the encroachments of age, men past sixty and seventy have accomplished memorable things. Consider Michelangelo painting the *The Last Judgment*; Voltaire producing *Candide*; Goethe finishing *Faust*; Verdi composing *Falstaff*; Freud developing his last controversial study, *Moses and Monotheism*. Consider the late contributions of Edison, Frank Lloyd Wright, Buckminster Fuller.

Within my own small range I have had friends who retained a creative outlook on life in old age. A namesake, Melchior Lengyel, was a Hungarian playwright who had written successful scripts in Hollywood, including *Ninotchka* for Greta Garbo. He was in his middle eighties when I saw him off on his last journey to Italy. Referring to his age, he told me with a smile of delight as we parted: "This is the most suspenseful and exciting time in my life."

Another cherished friend in his late eighties, Mr. A. C. Berg, had spent much of his earlier life as a lumberjack in the redwoods in Mendocino County. Later, he planted a six-hundred-acre apple orchard. A small, nimble white-haired gnome, he called at our homestead one morning with his ancient Ford truck and said he wanted to help us get our winter supply of wood. We spent the day together in a remote part of El Dorado National Forest sawing up rounds of seasoned timber with a two-man saw. Hour after hour, Mr. Berg pulled at his end of the long saw, I on the other, back and forth, till we had cut enough wood to fill the truck. Mr. Berg had a great fund of ballads and pioneer stories which he loved to recite. A Paul Bunyan of the western woods, he retained great zest in living and took a childlike pleasure in the natural world. Though he had spent many years in rough and dangerous toil in the wilderness, he had a sweet and amiable nature, and it was always a pleasure to share his company.

Another friend, Jack Lyman, had been a teacher of mine during the Great Depression. A graduate of Harvard and Oxford, he retired to his family ranch in Saint Helena in Napa Valley. At ninety-six, he wrote that he would like to visit me. He made the long and circuitous trip by bus from Saint Helena to Auburn, then to our homestead in El Dorado Forest, and we spent a memorable evening reminiscing, sipping from his homegrown vintage wine, reading from his own book of poems. A tall, slender poet-scholar, with long shoulder-length white hair and beard, he resembled Walt Whitman. At ninety-six, he had retained all his faculties. He told me that, after a lifetime of studying and teaching literature, his favorite poet remained Shelley.

I wish that Dr. Lyman and Mr. Berg could have lived longer, for time, I believe, is too short for everyone. Inaudible whistlers are forever interrupting or calling off the game. The generations are forever coming on or going off the fields of high or low enterprise, passing each other as in a perpetual carnival, in changing masks and costumes, in a medley of hails and farewells, sneers, hiccups, or stuttering valedictories.

All the crowds of young men and women we see in the streets of the world, laughing, singing, shouting, raging, pursuing each other, pursuing their bright or dismal illusions, all will have left the scene in less than a century. All our contemporaries are transients. Our vast assemblies are, in a sense, a supernatural crowd. And the present instant, alive in myself as the writer of these lines and in you as their reader, is a vanishing point. We both are engaged in a ghostly enterprise. All that we boast as our works or revelations, all that we build and launch for the stars, all that we will, scheme, dare and dream, all that we do is perishable. The labor of our hands: a mound of ashes. Our book for the ages: a thing of dust. Our dearest child: a passing creature of perpetual change. All our works, borrowed from usurious Time, all are perishable . . . Advancing toward us, inexorably, our last invincible friend and enemy: Time in his dust-gray cowl; Time with his cloud of scavengers; Time with his slow invisible feet, each step of which weighs a trillion tons, since his step will press us into the dust and calm our fevers forever.

This same sentiment I have expressed in my poems, more than once I'm afraid, as in "Nota Bene":

Do not linger long by any man's tomb,
   you who still can travel:
Your time on earth diminishing,
   your own quick days unravel.

Consider a cool truth in your wilderness of fact:
   No matter how ambitious you may be,
      other men are still more ambitious.
   No matter how strong you may be,
      other men are stronger yet.
   And no matter how clever you may be,
      other men are even cleverer.
Yet neither the strongest nor the cleverest
   can lock his door on kingdom come.

So do what you will and will while you can:
   Works complete are all you can leave:
      Ignore the carpers of the day:
         Breath's brief, dust everlasting!
      Unless you do what must
         outlast the pinch of dust,
      who'll waste his living time
      scanning your tombstone rhyme?

One of the classic aims of philosophy is, of course, to prepare us for our exit and coach us in the art of dying well. Death itself is a part of the gift of life: the ultimate change or exchange ought to remind us of the irreversible nature of our minutes in transit, a durable though unpalatable fact which we may prefer to ignore or forget. At eighty-three, Jefferson composed his own epitaph and, celebrating his last Independence Day at Monticello, declared himself ready for the final adventure, "untried by the living and unreported by the dead." Yet the final venture may prove less surprising than we anticipate. We sleep each night and spend about a third of our lives in sleep. This familiar experience furnishes us, I think, with a benevolent preview of our more permanent sleep. To me it seems obvious that each time I fall asleep I am rehearsing the act of death. Hence the state of death itself does not hold any special fear for me; I anticipate no dreams, nightmares, or any kind of awareness after shuffling off the mortal coils.

As for the possible pangs or humiliations that may accompany one's dissolution in case of illness, a hereditary or currently incurable disease such as cancer or AIDS, one would naturally like to avoid those. Modern medical science offers the means to do so. An amendment to the Constitution might assure each future citizen the right to be born to healthy parents; and, as corollary at the exit stage, assure him the right to die well, in dignity, without pain or humiliation, and by his own choice if he prefers voluntary euthanasia.

In view of the above I approach the last scene with some regret but without special fear. I regret parting from loved ones; I regret leaving forever a familiar, strange, mysterious, and often incredibly beautiful earth; I regret having wasted much of my time in pursuit of chimeras. Otherwise, I approach my exit with equanimity.

No one can prescribe another man's course, predict his limits, or proscribe his capacities. Each has his own path to discover, his own row to hoe, his own character to shape.

At intervals in my wayward youth, in an effort to reform myself, I used to deliver brief silent sermons or exhortations to myself: "Avoid mixed motives, divided aims, false values . . . Shun the tame, the trite, the trivial . . . Pay no tribute to mediocrity, however prosperous, powerful, or popular . . . Do not support men or measures or programs that extend the rule of falsehood, greed, hypocrisy, intolerance, however well camouflaged . . ." At seventy-four I retain similar precepts, though I wish I were more rigorous in applying them.

This perhaps sheds light on my belief that all of us have a measure of freedom to choose our direction. Man is not merely a complicated robot of flesh and blood, conditioned by his past and programmed by coded signals from his ancestral genes, his parents, leaders, or televisionary gurus. Though seemingly in bondage to irrational and overwhelming forces, to Mars and Venus, Eros and Thanatos, and though his destination may be problematic, he can choose his direction, up or down a long spiral scale—at any age, at any time. He can choose to change and so, to a degree, control his own evolution. In a poem entitled "The Lost Garden" I have expressed this faith before:

Un-
withering
the old trees stand
in a garden lost
in the world's new wilderness
burdened with the fruit of choice
now as in the beginning.

Unwithering
the tree of life
stands by the tree of death
the tree of bread by the tree of stone
the tree of delight by the tree of thorns.

Unwithering
the tree of evil
stands by the tree of good
the tree of grief by the tree of joy
the tree of lost hope by the tree of promise
the tree of hanged men by the tree of liberty
the tree of old surprises by the tree of new song.

Unwithering
the trees stand
in a lost garden
where no fruit
is forbidden
where each may
pick what he will—
now, as in the beginning . . .

If this is true for me, it may be true for most of my fellows. If I in
my limited way found a measure of freedom to choose my direction,
if only a small step at a time, others can do the same. In this belief,
which may prove illusory, I find a source of courage and hope for man's
future.

Charlotte Zolotow

B. 1915

❧ ❧

Charlotte Zolotow, distinguished writer and editor, has authored more than sixty picture books that portray the everyday experiences of young children and their discovery of the world around them. Her books—including her very first, *The Park Book* (1944)—are written in simple language and with a poet's sensitivity to the sound and color of words.

A native of Norfolk, Virginia, she studied literature at the University of Wisconsin and later joined the children's books department of Harper & Row. She left Harper to raise her two children but returned after a number of years to the junior books department, where she was editorial director, associate publisher of Harper Junior Books, and a Harper & Row vice-president. She is now editorial consultant to Harper Junior Books and editorial director of her own imprint, Charlotte Zolotow Books. For her contribution as editor of books for children and teenagers, she was presented with the Harper Gold Medal Award for Editorial Excellence and the Kerlan Award for distinguished contributions to children's literature. Also a poet, short story writer, and essayist, her work has appeared in several magazines, including *Cosmopolitan, McCall's,* and *Ladies Home Journal.*

A good children's book must be "unpretentious and direct," she says, and it should contain "some universal truth or feeling . . . I love children's books because they are part of the freshness and originality of children, qualities open to infinite variety and theme."

NUDE DESCENDING A STAIRCASE

This is the day before Christmas.

Almost a new year when I will have lived seventy-four years. Another new year!

My commitments as a daughter, wife, mother (the constant daily ones) are behind me. My commitments as an editor, writer, friend are matters of choice now. The rest of the years to come are mine. I get to choose how to spend them, a strange unfamiliar choice! No one's needs but my own to guide my choice. Only my own desire . . . for the first time in my life.

I alternate between continued participation in the rapids of work and friends and theater and contemporary music and books (within the limitations of the lessening physical ability of age) and a yearning to withdraw into a private world, to take back all that has happened to me and relive it by the fire in a way there was never time to do while it all happened.

Time. There was never enough time, and now there is less time ahead than behind me. I am faced with choices and I know I am one of the lucky ones because I do have a choice. I'm grateful. And I'm undecided. And I'm surprised at my own ambivalence. I vacillate, decide and then change course, try compromise and know it is impossible, but with so little time ahead I should choose. Otherwise, like Stephen Leacock's man on the horse, I ride madly off in all directions. It is almost a new year and I must choose.

Choices, lifestyles . . . to continue the old one despite increased difficulties or surrender to memory and to myself. I want to reread books I haven't read in forty years, books I will find rich with experience I didn't understand fully the first time around. I did reread *The Magic Mountain* this last month, straight through during a three-day illness. When I first read it in college, it was a story of love and sickness. But everything it says about time and its passage rose up from the pages this time making the love story only one thread of a much vaster tapestry than I had seen back then. What it says about time and timelessness and the immeasurability of time was important to me now. But when I first read it, it was a different book. (What will I find when I reread Proust and Colette and Hardy and Tolstoy?)

107

Choices, lifestyles! Time! I want to plant and weed and watch my garden grow. I want to sit by the fire and relive, savor things that have happened in my life, people who were with me when they happened. I want the past back in slower motion, an inner reexperiencing of events I didn't finish emotionally (because there wasn't time) when they were taking place. Unresolved emotions, happiness and fears, intensities there wasn't time enough to stop and feel fully. I want to watch the sunlight come in the living room window and light up leaf by leaf the plants I brought in from the garden last fall, the plants I will put out again next spring.

This time of year memories crowd in. Their reality is as strong as the present, this Christmas Eve, and these living guests who will be here tonight.

The smell of pine, the fragrance of traditional foods cooking, ornaments that have survived the friends who gave them to me! I don't say dead friends for they seem as alive to me as the friend across the street who I see in her window.

I go through the living room putting away objects, making place for food and platters and plates and glasses. I take down a Redoute iris print hanging over the mantel of the fireplace. It was given to me by the husband with whom I shared thirty years of marriage, eleven years of divorce, and who shares with me still our son and daughter, leading their own full lives in their own complex households away from us both. I move the print down and put in its place an engraving of Christmas 1963 given to me by a friend and author in my current life. I think of my former husband, I think of this new friend as I remove from the mantelpiece under the print a copper vase that stood on my mother's dining room table when I was a child. I remove the brass humidor full of matches for the fire, which once held my father's cigars. It stood on the table near his favorite chair in every living room of my parents' homes until the day my sister and I had to assort, give away, the objects that survived him when he died.

As I touch the humidor a familiar pain rises up as I remember that my father died alone in a hospital in California three months after my mother's death. I think of them now, not as young parents, but as they were in their seventies, at my present age. I feel them, as I move his humidor and her copper vase to store away until the party tonight is over. I put on the mantelpiece, where the vase and humidor usually stand, a bowl of pine and bright red holly berries from bushes planted years ago when my now grown children were little. I put next to it a brown stone parrot from my son when he was very young, and facing it another stone bird my daughter gave me when she was in her early teens. I see them, daughter and son, existing in my mind as little ones and adults simultaneously.

Memories. Different phases of relationship fill my mind . . . the humidor with its faint scent of my father's cigars in it, the copper vase as it gleamed on my mother's mahogany table. The dead are alive as I touch their things, my children are young and close as I arrange the birds. Someday they may feel this way as they place these same objects in their own homes. Right now my parents, my children, and all the phases of love between us are as much part of today as my friend across the street, getting ready for tonight, hanging ornaments on the tree in her window.

Memory after memory fills the house as real as the smell of Christmas food baking and bubbling in the kitchen.

The transience of life gives it its reality. Death is part of life. Those close to me, both alive and dead, are part of myself. These objects will be here when I'm not, part of the mystic flow that outlasts the giver and the given, the living and the dead. The persons who have composed both the discords and harmonies of my life continue in me, and from me, to the people in whose lives I help compose the discords and harmonies of theirs.

What am I saying? That we are all part of each other? I don't know how to say something I feel. That all time flows together? That the past and the future both are happening now, like Duchamp's *Nude Descending a Staircase*, we are on each step simultaneously. It is all still happening in me as I prepare for the party tonight.

I look across the street to see my friend's tree. It is beginning to snow. Choices, the snow brings me back to choices. I love the snow. I love its whiteness. I love the flakes endlessly falling, covering grass and trees and roofs. I love not only the wind and the wild white, but the shelter of being indoors on such a day, being in a silent house with green plants all around and the comforting hum of the furnace in the basement. I love the freshly brewed breakfast coffee as I stand at the kitchen window and see small protuberances under the snow in the backyard that will be the iris and astilbe and flowers of the summer to come. On ordinary days there is the fireplace, the chair by the fire where I can read and listen to music and spend the day giving in to thoughts, memories, and the intangible, soon-to-vanish physical reality of the ornaments in the room and the friends dead and alive who gave them to me.

It is these ordinary days ahead, when it snows, that symbolize the choice I have to make. I can't go like the man on the horse in every direction at once. I have to choose between contradictory desires, between a peaceful, loving withdrawal into my house and thoughts and my own writing, or going out into that other world I am fortunate enough to still have available to me. It is there waiting outside, through the snow, a world of work and pressure and publishing in which I've worked since 1938. I have scaled down the extent of my activities there, but it is still a frantic, rich, varied, exciting life full of current events and people.

My office is waiting with shelves of books I've worked on editorially over the years. There are appointments with old authors and new authors and artists I've long known and some I never worked with before. There are my colleagues, all younger than myself, energetic, attractive, part of that daily goal of working toward the best books authors and artists can produce. I love many of these younger colleagues, their intelligence, their humor, their talent, their ambition, their excitement. I love the contact with them, the problems and perplexities and feuds and friendships that I would not be part of if I stay at home by the fire. I can enter the real life that is waiting, bundle up and go out into the whirling snow, brave the ice underfoot, the instinctive stiffening of body, the fear of falling, the feeling too old for this.

Or I could cancel the appointments, put apples in the oven, light the fire, watch the snow falling, and be content, surrounded by the records, books and plants and objects, that are more than objects, around me.

Which to choose?

For the young and the old both, there is an indeterminate time ahead. But for those of us who are old the sounds of time's winged chariot are louder in our ears. When the years ahead are fewer than those we've left behind, should we go on working even if it leaves unfinished books and music we have never had the time for? Or should we plunge on as though our bones are not stiffening, and get through to the office, to the comfort of coffee in Styrofoam cups thawing out arthritic fingers before we enter the turmoil and excitement of a day where we know we can give to other people, rather than gathering in life for ourselves only.

I'm greedy. I want both. It is harder and harder to compromise, for then you do neither the one nor the other completely. I know I must choose. I think whichever choice I make will not be right or wrong. But whichever I am doing, I should do completely. No yearning for the alternatives or I'd destroy the essence of the thing at hand. The fuller I round out whatever I am doing, the more prepared I will be for the ceasing or silence ahead, and the more of myself I leave in the people I have touched in my transit on earth.

John Davis

Barrett McGurn

B. 1914

❦ ❦

Providing information to the American public has been the lifework of Barrett McGurn, foreign correspondent, government press spokesman, lecturer, and publisher. He began his career as a cub reporter for his college newspaper, the *Fordham Ram*. Soon after graduating from Fordham in 1935, he took a job at the now defunct *New York Herald Tribune*, where he worked for thirty-two years, sixteen of which as a bureau chief in Rome, Paris, and Moscow. On leave from the *Tribune* during World War II, he became the South and Southwest Pacific war correspondent for *YANK*, the two-million circulation Army weekly.

When the *Tribune* folded in 1966, McGurn joined the government as U.S. press attaché in Rome. He then went on to serve as director of the government press center in Vietnam (1968–1969), as Department of State press officer (1969–1972), as the United States Information Agency World Affairs commentator (1972–1973), and as press director for the U.S. Supreme Court (1973–1982). In 1982 he became the communications director for the Catholic archdiocese of Washington, D.C., and now, at seventy-five, is associate publisher and chief operating officer of the archdiocese's two weekly newspapers, the *Catholic Standard* and *El Pregonero*.

A winner of numerous awards, among them the Military Commendation Medal of the U.S. Army, the Purple Heart, the Polk Award, and the Italian government's Grand Knight award, McGurn has said that "the newsman and the person who speaks for government share the same objective of explaining government policy. The spokesman has an added responsibility—to help government policy succeed. The reporter and the spokesman sometimes are at war with one another, but it is a war on behalf of the same beneficiary: the people."

EXULTING IN WHAT REMAINS

A lthough still in my middle seventies, I find it astonishing that, as a "golden ager," I am entitled to discounts at movie theaters, at the drug store, and on buses and subways. I am even more amazed that pension checks come and that Social Security and Medicare press forward to assist me. The reason, I am sure, is that I am not ready to be old; not in the least bit prepared to surrender the drive, excitement, hopes, and creativity of my younger, less experienced years.

If there is a successful way to age, perhaps this is it: never allow yourself to grow old—at least not psychologically. Certainly this has been my observation over the many years I have studied older people.

From my own early days, back in the twenties, visiting and pondering the thoughts of elders has always been a joy. One of the reasons I valued meeting older people was the opportunity to step back into history's pages, to see the past as if it were present. For those of coming generations who possess nothing but the present, this gift of the past is always available from older people who have observed accurately and understood thoughtfully that part of history's drama which has unfolded before them.

What I found as I talked to the very old was that they were as varied as members of other generations. Some had used each moment of their lives to grow better informed and wiser, approaching their final days still filled with the thrill of life and driving to accomplish something of value for those coming after them. Others without imagination survived emptily for another day, another year, succumbing slowly to melancholy or downright despair.

I think back now to many of those old folks whom I sought out as a young newspaper reporter and later as a United States government official. One of the first was a parish pastor in New York, a man in his tenth decade. I interviewed him as a reporter for my university newspaper, the *Fordham Ram*. At the time, Fordham was a century old, an impossibly long space of time for my young mind to comprehend. I was excited as I went to see the old cleric. Fordham at the time of the American Civil War had been in existence only a score of years, a newly minted institution. What, I wondered, was that young Fordham like? How did it differ? What could our generation see if we were to peer back to those ancient days through the living memory of the old grad?

My interview with the old pastor was one of my first disappointing encounters with the elderly. What was young Fordham like? The aged pastor had little to say: "The curriculum was narrow. It was almost a seminary, rather than a great institution aborning." That was it!

A similar disappointment awaited me a few years later while I served as a cub reporter for the *New York Herald Tribune*, then one of America's foremost newspapers. It was the custom in the late 1930s to have a Memorial Day parade up Riverside Drive, along the banks of the Hudson River, to the tomb of Ulysses Grant. My job each year—a task, it seemed, that would last forever—was to write a story reporting the same old thing: Tomorrow we would have the usual Memorial Day parade with a host of marching war veterans leading the way.

Since novelty is the spice of interesting news copy and repetition the deadliest offense, I always tried to brighten the familiar announcement by interviewing one of the next day's paraders. Each year I sought out the oldest veteran and each year I was saddened with the result. What was it like at the battle of Bull Run, at Manassas, at Barbara Frietchie's Frederick, at the appalling march through Georgia? What was the strategy, what were the tactics? None of my interlocutors could reply. Only later did I realize why. As I hunted up the old warriors I never found a general, a colonel, or even a sergeant. All had been drummer boys, mere children. They had survived to participate in the parade, but their minds were incapable of bringing to me any insights into that horrifying fratricidal conflict. They had never known anything but their own small miseries at the time. They were incapable of sharing anything more than that with the generations that succeeded them. Unable to comprehend in the 1860s, my old vets were equally incapable of passing on insights of value in the 1930s.

As a foreign correspondent for the *Herald Tribune* in post–World War II Europe, I had further occasions to meet the old. These elderly were far more sophisticated than my university's eldest grad or the Civil War drummer boys, but, again, some of them disappointed me by failing to exploit their long and eventful lives in service to the current generation.

I think particularly of a talk with Vittorio Emanuele Orlando on his ninetieth birthday. When the slaughter of World War I came to an end it was Orlando, along with three others—our Wilson, Britain's Lloyd George, and France's Clemenceau—who drafted the Versailles treaty, a document to restore peace and health to the shattered Old Continent. Wilson benignly wanted a new Europe based on the self-determination of peoples, not a new arrangement parceling out the spoils of war among the survivors and thus planting the seeds of bitterness from which a Hitler could grow. Orlando instead wanted a slice of defeated Austria, the South Tyrol, so that his own expanded nation could have a "natural frontier" along the Alpine ridges.

I wondered as I drove the *Tribune* jeep to Orlando's home what the nonagenarian would have to say about the Europe of thirty years after Versailles, the post-Hitler Europe, the Europe still sick from the ravages of yet another world war. For thirty years the ex-Austrians of the South Tyrol had been agitating for a return to their motherland. Orlando's fatal acquisition, an anachronistic possession in an age when rockets soar easily over mountaintop "natural frontiers," had been an enduring thorn of dissension inside Italy's body politic.

Had age brought a mellow wisdom? Not if my observation of the ex-premier was correct. "So you are an American," the old man opened our conversation. "Oh, that President Wilson of yours! He was wrong and I was right!" Far from recognizing lessons from the post-Versailles years, Orlando in his mind was still sitting at that French table of long ago, face to face with the other three treatymakers of a departed generation. It then became clear to me that many older people remain arrested at some point in their past, unable to profit from the opportunities for growth and understanding that each year ought to bring us.

If the encounter with Orlando did nothing to assure me of the special value of seniors, a meeting in the same year with Bernard Berenson had a reverse effect. "B.B." as his friends called him, convinced me that every year of a long life can add polish to a dedicated, brilliant mind.

Berenson was so clearly a man of superior mental gifts that his Harvard classmates in the late 1800s pooled a few dollars to pay his way for a vacation in Europe. One so talented on the Cambridge campus surely would do wonders for society were he to have firsthand contact with the Mother Continent. The Harvard men were right. The "vacation" became a lifetime. Berenson never returned to the States but instead rediscovered the immense patrimony of pre-Renaissance painting in Italy. He became its critic and historian and, as the middle man in collecting many of the paintings for young American art collections, became wealthier than most of the classmates who had invested in him.

Berenson invited me to tea at I Tatti, his villa above Florence, now the property of Harvard. A wispy man of eighty-eight, he was huddled under a knee blanket, a protection against the chill which never left his frail frame. "What is Walter Lippmann saying these days in the *Herald Tribune*?" my host demanded. Before I could think of a way to capsulize the output of the prolific political commentator, B.B. went on: "I don't see Lippmann's column any more. I canceled my subscription to the *Herald Tribune*. Your paper is too interesting. I found that I was getting so deep into it that it would be thirty minutes before I could put it down. A half hour! I don't have half hours to use that way!"

Tea was served to us punctually at 5:45 P.M. and just as precisely, at 6:15, my host pushed back his chair. My allotted thirty minutes were up. "Do see my library before you go," he said. "I must excuse myself. I must get back to the book I am working on."

During those valued thirty minutes Berenson had shared with me a lively, cultivated mind. His conversation was studded with remarks about friends in European leadership and with classical references that were not pedantic. Each year had added to the old man's culture. Each year convinced him ever more deeply of how precious is one more day, one more half hour, of this fascinating existence that each of us can enjoy. Each year, too, had given him a further opportunity to share his vision with society, just as those Harvard men long ago had hoped he would. Writing may become more difficult as the years go by, but that book to which the eighty-eight-year-old returned that evening was finished and made its way to the world's bookshelves before the sage of I Tatti died a half decade later.

Berenson's ability to bring a book to conclusion at the dawn of his tenth decade was marvelous, but by no means a universal experience among the old. I think of Dr. Albert Schweitzer, another man of eighty-eight, whom I visited in the 1950s in his jungle hospital on the African Equator. I crossed the crocodile-infested river beside the hospital at Lambaréné, riding in a dugout canoe. Like Orlando, Schweitzer was interested in me as someone from America. Trying to find common ground, the old physician reached into a past well beyond me: "An American," he mused. "Well, before I came to this jungle clearing there was someone here before me. He was an American. That was in 1910!"

At the turn of the century, Schweitzer had been born on the Franco-German border in an area that shifted back and forth to one country or the other depending on which emerged victorious in the recurring conflicts. Inspired by no desire to kill Germans or Frenchmen and holding four doctorates (in philosophy, music, theology, and medicine), the young Schweitzer at the approach of World War I had come to this spot to minister to some of the earth's most neglected and benighted savages. With the famous doctor was his daughter. She took me aside: "There is one question I beg you not to put to him," she pleaded. "He has followed up his early writings on why we should all revere the mystery of life—life in all its forms, not just human life but even the life of brute animals. He has followed that up by trying to write an even broader book of philosophy. The truth is that it is not coming. So none of us ever ask him what progress he is making."

For me it was another insight into what it is to grow old. While a Berenson could produce yet another book in advanced old age and a Schweitzer could still labor to heal the ills of tribesmen as his own ninetieth birthday approached, all of us face the slow decline of our powers. Senility, writer's block, was overcoming the saint of the jungle.

As the years pass, "golden age" brings differing experiences to different people. For some, the final years are simply wretched. I recall one day high on the Apennine Ridge in Italy when I engaged an old man in conversation. He was seated on a stone wall above a steep valley. I asked for his thoughts. "Everyone with whom I grew up," he answered promptly, "is dead." For him, the summit of the years was merely loneliness—as it is for thousands.

For some, dark old age is the substance of life's third period: first youth, then work, then retirement. To them, "leisure" means the end of productive activity and in turn implies a fading of life's drive. I saw this in different ways on two occasions. The first was in Rome in the 1950s. Jefferson Caffery came to the Eternal City to retire to a suite in the Grand Hotel. We became friends as I tried unsuccessfully to get him to give me his life's story for my newspaper and eventually for a book. I watched with dismay as this former assistant secretary of state and ambassador to France, Egypt, and Brazil faded away, week by week. Retired automatically at sixty-five, the diplomat felt useless. With his purpose for existence stripped from him he was dying.

To live happily, to live at all, each of us needs a purpose. If it is not to be found at the everyday work desk it must at least take the form of a constructive avocation. With other Roman friends we were able to offer the latter to the former envoy. In Egypt he had been a "grave digger," as fans of archaeology are known. He loved the instructive record of the past. All around Rome are monuments of antiquity, few of them known to country-hopping tourists. Caffery had a chauffeured car. We gave him an initial list of little-known wonders to explore. He got to work on them, freshened, and enjoyed another decade of life.

Another insight into the effects of aging with purpose was provided one day at the Supreme Court of the United States in the 1970s. The marshal of the court noticed a man in the lawyer's section, his eyes closed while the contending lawyers debated. The courtroom is not for napping, so the marshal passed a note to Chief Justice Warren Burger: "Shall I eject the man?"

The chief justice held a whispered conference with the senior associate, William Brennan, at his side. Back came a note: "Leave him alone. One day all of us will be where he is now."

Still dissatisfied, the marshal accosted the "sleeper" as the session ended and escorted him to me as the Court's communications director. "Why were you sleeping?" I asked. "I wasn't," he said. "I was resting my eyes. Let me introduce myself. I am past president of the bar association of the state of Pennsylvania. I am a lawyer in Pittsburgh. I go to my office every day. I am ninety-three years old." Apparently, the third-stage blues had never undermined his will to live. He was still in the second stage, the working years. He had never lost a reason to live, and as the century mark approached all he noticed was a need to repose his sight from time to time.

Is work, then, the key to happiness in one's "golden years"? Working for a decade with the justices of the Supreme Court as their press spokesman, it often seemed to me that those wise men of the law did indeed equate life with work. Gray hairs accumulated and then thinned out as the justices ignored the generous retirement arrangements which Congress provided for them. Routinely they passed sixty-five and seventy. Routinely they stayed on as age eighty loomed before them. Justice Potter Stewart, who had become a federal judge in his thirties, was an exception. He retired at sixty-six, remarking that "I was the youngest federal judge in America when I came on the bench; I made up my mind not to stay until I was the oldest." The young Stewart, junior to many of his colleagues, ironically was dead a year or two after retiring. His elders, still on the bench, continued with their demanding labor, each handling five thousand new cases every year.

Were the justices damaging the national interest by clinging to their lifework long after so many contemporaries encounter forced retirement? Was there no danger that people in such an important position of national responsibility would, as one justice's wife expressed it, "lose their marbles"? Justice Blackmun, near eighty, had an answer. He had appointed some trusted acquaintances, he said, to monitor him. Should they detect senility, they would give him binding counsel to step down.

These then, that old pastor of my college days, the Civil War drummer boys, the statesman, the diplomats, and the justices are those whom I have been studying for many years as I have attempted to understand how one can muster the courage to grow old gracefully. I draw on these observations now as I enter my own "senior discount" years.

I know what that old man on the Italian hilltop meant when he told me sadly that every friend of his boyhood was dead. My own mind is peopled now with two or three generations of loved ones who exist only in memory. These are melancholy recollections, but I am blessed with a delightful wife and with great children and grandchildren who bring joy to my days, combating the depression that so many of the old suffer as they live in the past.

I keep working into my eighth decade, mindful both of Jefferson Caffery and of that Pittsburgh attorney whose law office he saw every day of his long life. I am satisfied in my mind, however, that it is wrong to equate work with life and that after present labors cease an avocation—painting, reading, travel, volunteer employment—should be able to fill the void caused by the end of life's second stage.

I enjoy in these "golden years" thinking back over so many fascinating personalities and so many great events with which I have had contact as a foreign correspondent and as an American government officer, but I seek also, while I treasure these memories, not to become their prisoner. Life is too magnificent a gift to be spent, even in the golden years, musing about what is no more. The past and its history are marvelous instructive teachers, but they are no substitute for enjoying the magnificent present and the promising future.

Sure, applying lather for a shave is a surprise when you see that your face has already been lathered. Your physical powers decline. A stroll up a hill brings on heavy breathing. Aches and pains accumulate. This could cloud the joy of the present, but it should not. It did not deter Berenson. And even with writer's block Schweitzer persisted with his healing mission, freeing thousands from their suffering.

Mourn not, then, for what is lost; rather, exult in what remains.

Alfred Painter

B. 1914

After earning his B.A. in business administration in 1938 from Linfield College and working for a year in business, Alfred Painter decided that his true love was philosophy and world religions. He then left business to enroll at the University of Chicago, where he was awarded a Ph.D. in philosophy and the psychology of religion in 1945. While a student at Chicago he served as assistant to the dean of the Rockefeller Memorial Chapel and coordinated student religious activities on campus. In 1956 he was ordained a Methodist minister and for nine years served as the associate minister at Wilshire Avenue Community Methodist Church in Los Angeles. His main career has been as a professor of philosophy and comparative religion. He taught at Bates College, the University of the Pacific, and at Orange Coast College, where he served as chairman of the philosophy department and taught for eighteen years. In 1975 he received the prestigious Salgo Award as the outstanding teacher of the year.

Painter is a past executive director of the Orange County Chapter of the National Council of Christians and Jews and has served on boards for the Red Cross, the YMCA, the University of the Pacific, and the Kiwanis Club. He currently serves on the ethics committee for the medical school at the University of California at Irvine and as a founding member for the Orange County chapter of the Alzheimer's Foundation. He and his wife have led a dozen tours to Europe with college students and have traveled extensively throughout the world.

Although retired from preaching and teaching, Painter is an active public lecturer in Southern California.

REFLECTIONS ON THE ISNESS

There's an ancient Taoist story about a Chinese farmer who had but one home, one horse, and one son to help him cultivate his little plot of ground. One day, his horse ran away and his neighbors quickly gathered to console him. But he said: "I don't know that it is so bad." A few days later the horse came back with two other horses following him. Now the farmer's neighbors came over to congratulate him on his good fortune. But the farmer said: "I don't know that it is so good." A few days later his son broke his leg trying to train the new horses. Again, sympathy from the neighbors followed, with the farmer once more saying: "I don't know that it is so bad." The story could go on and on, but the inference is that most of us spend the majority of our lives passing judgments on what is good and bad and consequently fail to recognize that change is the only constant in life and that good and bad are but relative, endlessly intertwined terms.

Throughout my life I've felt and acted much like that old farmer; and my neighbors, predictably, have always been there with words of congratulation or consolation. I've tried to explain to them that passing judgments with our limited minds and senses is more often dangerous than not, but my message seldom takes. After all, clinging to predictable beliefs and habits is the way in which we ward off the chaos that surrounds us, and none of us are immune to it—the aged being the most susceptible. And yet, accepting change, or having the courage to make a change, is really what growing up—and growing old—is all about.

I developed this outlook long before I'd ever heard of Taoism—or Buddhism or Hinduism for that matter! I was eighteen years old, in fact, and it resulted from something of a "mystical experience." I lived on Queen Anne Hill in Seattle. My favorite pastime was to climb to the park at the top of the hill to sit and watch the city below and the surrounding mountains to the west. One day at dusk, a particularly clear and unusually sunny day, I became entranced by the movement around me and my mind began to tune in to the complex, integrated mass of movement of the humans below me, all interconnected in various ways. I found myself caught up in it as a part of my own being. I became aware of lights turning off and on in the official buildings downtown as well as in the residential areas. I became aware of the red taillights on cars leaving the city as well as of the headlights of cars coming toward the city. Rapidly, I became aware of the many other forms of connectedness. In the distance there were planes coming and going from the international airport. In my mind's eye I saw people from all over the world arriving in Seattle—and leaving it—and I personally felt this massive interconnectedness of life. I saw passenger trains coming and going. I became aware of the towers in the distance sending out radio waves connecting us to others around the globe. It occurred to me that the vast, sprawling city was really like a living organism with the coming and going of the people flowing like blood through the vessels of the planet—and I was an integral part of it.

The overpowering awareness of my inevitable involvement with this mass of constantly changing interconnected life temporarily dissolved my sense of separateness and aloneness. So much so, in fact, that when I "came to my senses" and perceived myself as an isolated human being again I laughed at the thought. The walls that separated me from the world dissolved and a great weight was lifted from my shoulders. Sensing the surge of life in everything around me, I knew, for the first time in my life, that I belonged in the world and that everything was as it should be.

From that day to this, I have never felt alone or left out at any time. And I have never doubted that when things get bleak, the problems I face are those of my own creation, the result of an inability to see or act upon all the possible supporting changes that surround and connect me to what I like to term the "isness" of life. This isness is the meeting place of the past, present, and future, and represents, for me at least, the peace that comes from accepting the universe as it is. Accepting the universe has made it possible for me to accept the changing circumstances of life with a measure of hope and equanimity. Instead of focusing on the disappointments and deprivations that change can bring, I rather look forward to the possibilities for growth that it inevitably brings forth.

Surely the most devastating among the many upsetting changes I've experienced thus far was the tragedy of watching my first wife deteriorate from the meaningless ravages of Alzheimer's disease. For two years I watched her deteriorate into little more than a vegetable. The task of caring for her and teaching full time became an almost unbearable load. The folly of judging the situation to be good or bad became increasingly clear the worse things seemed to get. There could, after all, be no rational justification to account for such a tragedy. It simply was another manifestation of the inscrutable unfolding of the isness. And when she died, what good would it have done me to ask: Why me? Why her? Why, God, did you allow this to happen?

So rather than determine that life for me was over, I took the position that with all the change taking place around me, there must be—simply must be!—some new course to follow. It was then that I decided to develop a series of public lectures on the challenge of change. I was desperately in need of keeping my own mind alive, and I recognized that in the very process of preparing and delivering these lectures I might begin to heal myself.

The lectures were well attended and well received, and in keeping with Taoist wisdom I found that what might have been judged to be a bad experience actually opened the way to a very good experience. Indeed, during the course of these lectures I met my future second wife, who had lost her first husband to multiple sclerosis and had suffered with the tragic implications for years. Through our shared experiences we found a bond and were soon involved in a rich and loving relationship.

Together, my wife and I have learned to live by what I call the wave theory of life. A wave is an interesting phenomenon. It is the result of two forces moving in opposite directions that collide to create a crest. When the crest pitches over and crashes into foam it disperses its energy in many directions and then gathers again to form another wave. It is the energy of the wave that carries a surfer on a short but stimulating journey of carefree excitement until it dissipates, only to repeat itself time after time after time.

Growing older has many parallels to the wave. You find yourself occasionally reaching exciting peaks of experience, only to watch them come crashing down. But after every crash there is eventually a regrouping and a rejuvenation of energy and accomplishment. The loss of my first wife was the crash of a wave, while the finding of my second wife was its reformation.

The wave theory also fits into our financial experience. At one point we thought we were riding the crest of a wave of good investments which would ensure pleasurable retirement years, only to find that our most trusted and respected "friends" had swindled us out of most of our retirement money. And then, of course, the IRS came in and took what was left! So the wave we are riding now is of much different dimensions, to say the least. But we are still involved in the excitement of our ever-changing environment and surviving. Broke but happy.

I have learned that whatever I judge to be good also contains within it—somewhere, if I just look hard enough—some bad, and vice versa. The interrelationships of life are so vast, however, that it makes sense to assume that the force driving it all will continue to regroup into new and different crests of meaning and vitality. Life is an endless adventure moved along by forces beyond our control, but one which we can give ourselves to in trust and confidence. There is always MORE going on than we are equipped to perceive through our limited senses and with our limited experience. This MORE is the root of religious or spiritual life. Change is at the bottom of it, and the more we are a part of it, the more we accept it, the more we rely and trust in it, the more likely we are to uncover the pleasures and mysteries of living.

One of the greater mysteries of life is retirement. It is an experience only a retired person can understand. And I've got to admit that the first months of my retirement left me in an uncomfortable position. I felt I should be doing something that I wasn't doing—but I couldn't figure out what it was supposed to be. Routine had so regulated my life as a teacher that I began to miss it. But I found slowly that rather than being driven by routine and duty, I was now free to do whatever was at hand. I discovered that if you actually take the time to become sensitive to your environment there are always things to do or get interested in that you had not been aware of before. For instance, if a magazine came in the mail, I could actually sit down and read it instead of putting it aside until some future time when I would have time to read it—which, of course, never came. I discovered that a walk in the nearby park could open up conversation with people I had scarcely noticed before, which often led to an enriching experience.

Growing older inevitably introduces you to a body that slowly loses its agility or ability to perform. But when I became sensitive to my physical deterioration (which was accentuated by my freedom to do nothing!) I discovered an exercise class designed to keep older people active. I joined it and am now being told that I look younger and more active than when I retired.

Faced with the lack of intellectual stimulation that results from withdrawal from the daily involvement with others, I found a small group of intellectually active men who agreed to meet every other week for breakfast in order to share their new discoveries or to debate issues of the day. Soon, speaking engagements emerged. They keep me active and stimulated. Then I joined with a group of individuals who were determined to do something about the ravages of Alzheimer's disease.

As I reflect on what is happening to me as I grow older, I not only feel assured that I will be able to face whatever lies ahead, but that my eagerness to discover new and more exciting ways to live and think will never diminish. I recognize that each new day will present me with new challenges, for nothing repeats itself exactly, any more than any two waves at the ocean's edge are just alike. I find this fact stabilizing rather than frightening or disappointing. Realistically, our lives are amazing focal points of change brought about by energy and matter intertwining, endlessly weaving new patterns. Life's meaning isn't found in what we have achieved or accumulated. It is found in our ability to express our uniqueness in the interrelated world in which we find ourselves.

Age does two good things: it equips you with a greater quantity of awareness (which enriches your sensitivity and understanding) and it habituates you to changing fortune. I suppose few of us are truly ready for that "great change" we call death. As for myself, I see no reason to make a judgment about it because I know that I don't know enough to ascertain whether it will be good or bad. Still, I find it comforting to know that whatever may come, it can only serve as an opening to still greater involvement with the eternal isness of life. The only certainty before me is change, and so I face each day with a deep sense of awe, content to let be what will be.

Lohega

Dr. Albert Ellis

B. *1913*

❊❊

Rivaled only by Sigmund Freud and B. F. Skinner, Albert Ellis is one of the most controversial figures in modern psychology. After earning his doctorate from Columbia in 1947, and after practicing psychoanalysis from 1947 to 1953, he rebelled against what he felt was its "dogma and inefficiency." In 1955, after experimenting with several other methods of counseling, he developed his own system of psychology, rational-emotive therapy (RET), a wedding of behaviorism with pragmatic and humanistic philosophy. Although his theories were initially violently opposed by most therapists, he persisted in his talks and writings, succeeding so well that he is now recognized as the grandfather of cognitive behavior therapy (CBT).

Prior to originating RET, Ellis was a pioneer in sex and marital therapy. His prolific writings on the subject, in particular his book, *Sex Without Guilt* (1958), sold millions of copies in the late '50s and early '60s and made him a prime influence in the "sexual revolution" of the coming decades.

The author or editor of more than fifty books and monographs, including several best-sellers, Ellis spends most of his time in New York City seeing many clients and administering the Institute for Rational-Emotive Therapy, a non-profit foundation that trains psychotherapists, operates a psychological clinic, sponsors self-help workshops, and distributes books on RET and CBT. He turns out at least one new book every year, such as his latest one, *How to Stubbornly Refuse to Make Yourself Miserable About Anything—Yes Anything!* (1988).

THE COURAGE TO CHANGE

How do I manage, at the age of seventy-five, to continue to be a confirmed—and, if I may say so, happy—workaholic? With relative ease, I would say. For I still get bored with lying on beaches, with conversational chitchat, with most television viewing, and with other nonactive "pastimes" that so many people, who I do not in the least envy, manage to enjoy. I would much rather work than be bored.

I also have what I called, in *A New Guide to Rational Living*, "a vital absorbing interest" in my work. I have made, for more than forty years, something of a cause of helping people solve their emotional problems. I am devoted to finding better and more efficient ways to do so. I founded rational-emotive therapy (RET) in 1955 because I loathed the inefficiency of Freudian psychoanalysis and of Rogerian client-centered therapy and because I was determined to replace them with a better, more effective system.

I am still determined. So I work seven days a week, from 9:00 A.M. to 11:00 P.M., seeing scores of clients, leading five therapy groups, supervising a dozen therapists, giving many talks and workshops, directing a large institute, and writing, writing, writing scads of articles and books.

Has older age slowed me down? Yes, a little. I sleep a bit more. I procrastinate slightly on important things while barging ahead with less important ones. I take a few daytime naps on weekends, which I never took in my early life. I spend less time, because of my aching back, sitting up at the typewriter and more time using speedwriting or dictating in my comfortable lounge chair.

I also live with, and adjust myself to, my diabetes and some of its hazards. For over thirty years I have rigorously coped with the diabetes, but now I have to use more insulin than ever and stick to a rigid schedule of blood testing and eleven carefully timed meals each day. What a pain in the ass! How time-consuming! But, highly motivated to live and work, and still determined to improve on the theory and practice of RET, I uncomplainingly forge ahead.

What have I learned, by reading, writing, talking, therapizing, and supervising, about the courage to grow old? Several important things, I think. Let me mention some of them.

Let me first say that the courage to grow old has several salient aspects, most of which include healthy life philosophies. The first two of these philosophies are incorporated in the oft-quoted statements of St. Francis and Reinhold Niebuhr, which have been adapted into the serenity prayer of Alcoholics Anonymous. The RET version of these statements, which I have used with my clients for several decades, omits any reference to prayer and to help from any assumed deity and therefore goes as follows:

> I am strongly determined to acquire the courage to change what I can change, to accept unfortunate events that in spite of my efforts I cannot change, and to acquire the wisdom to know the difference between the two.

At any age, this is a wise and workable philosophy, but it is particularly relevant to the courage to grow old.

Let me expand on the first part of this homily—which often gets sadly neglected. Not all older people are rigidly set in their ways. But all too many are! It is easy, at least in the short run, to repeat what you have been doing, thinking, and feeling for many prior years. Change is wrenching—often "risky" and "dangerous." But older people can change, often do. In fact, they have several advantages that abet innovation. For example, economic security, retirement from career responsibilities, and little need to care for and guide others. But change still has its risks, such as the rupture of old pathways, scandalization of others, possible economic sacrifices.

Courage means risking these dangers and accepting the consequences of change. It means reassessing what you have commonly been doing, refusing to follow long-imposed conventions, untoadying to people you don't really like, doing a number of criticizable things. Yes, change means change. And in spite of—and sometimes, wisely, because of—decreased energies you can have the courage to force yourself to modify some of your lifelong habits. Because you no longer really want to trod the old, well-worn paths. Because you truly enjoy doing what you've rarely (if ever) done before. Because in your relatively few remaining years you desire to try new and different things.

The wisdom to accept unfortunate situations and things that you can't change is, again, an attitude hardly confined to old age. Any age group could well benefit from it. But growing older almost inevitably means more unavoidable restrictions on your powers. Like it or not, you can't—or damned well had better not—push yourself to do some things, such as prolonged exercise, that you could fairly easily do when younger.

Too bad—but not awful, horrible, or the end of the world. According to the principles of rational-emotive therapy, under such conditions you can accept—yes, gracefully lump—the restrictions you dislike and happily enjoy what you still can feasibly do. No, you don't fool yourself and Pollyannaishly tell yourself that you like surrendering some of your former interests and occupations. You can even legitimately hate their loss or curtailment. But you can still tolerate what you don't like. Yes, sensibly tolerate.

Even more, you can enjoy the challenge of living with restrictions. You can make a fascinating project out of an antiwhining attitude toward unavoidable deprivations. You can take pride in stubbornly refusing to kvetch and complain when conditions force you to settle for less than you want. Let other frustrated senior citizens rant and rave, as they often will. Need you? Not if you accept the challenge of standing some necessary gaff.

The other challenge you can pleasurably accept is that of finding new involvements. Instead of jogging, you can walk. Instead of certain active sports, you can read, write, paint, listen to music. Are you complaining that there is practically nothing you can now enjoy? Hogwash! Give alternative hobbies and interests some real thought. Do a little research. Talk to your friends and relatives about what they find interesting. There are so many possible diversions that you can find that your turning up with nothing absorbing to do is almost beyond comprehension.

Especially look for, as I noted above, "a vital absorbing interest." This means something big, ongoing, and personally important to you. A cause, for example, worth fighting for—or against—a political, economic, or social position. Or collecting something—stamps, antiques, art, or what have you—that will provide you with a project that is endless and that you will never completely finish. Anything big and anything that you, personally, find engrossing. Have you never had sufficient time for such an avocation in the past? Now you probably do. Why wait?

Finally, you can accept, especially as you grow older, the prime principle of RET and other cognitive-behavioral therapies: that you don't get upset by old age, but choose—yes, consciously or unconsciously choose—to needlessly disturb yourself with it. The ABC theory of rational-emotive therapy says that when unpleasant Activating events occur at point A (such as the restrictions of old age) and when you then experience disturbed emotional consequences, at point C (i.e., anxiety, depression, rage, or self-pity), the main causes or creators of your disturbed C's are not your A's but your B's about these Activating events. B stands for your beliefs about your A's. At point B, you can choose to have only rational beliefs or preferences, such as, "I don't like what's happening to me at point A, but I don't always have to get what I want to stay happy. I can still lead a reasonably happy life despite my advancing age." On the other hand, you can choose to subscribe to irrational beliefs or absolutistic shoulds and musts, such as, "Because I dislike what's happening to me at point A, it absolutely should not, must not happen! I can't stand it! I don't want to grow old! I will not grow old! I'm no good for letting it happen! What a horrible place the world is and will always be!" You thereby make yourself feel panicked, depressed, enraged, and/or self-pitying.

Your greatest challenge in life is to accept the ABC's of RET; to admit that you needlessly choose to upset yourself and therefore had better work hard to dispute (and consequently limit) your irrational shoulds, oughts, musts, and other dogmatic commands on yourself, on others, and on the world. In this way you rigorously stay with your preferences, values, and desires and really surrender your absolutistic demands. If you have the courage to accept this challenge, your old age can be remarkable and enjoyable. The choice—at any age—is yours.

Do I, at seventy-five, accept this choice and challenge for myself? Do I use RET to live successfully with the disadvantages of my aging body? Not perfectly, I am sure. I inwardly complain somewhat more than I need to do about the limitations of advancing age, and I am a little less energetic than I actually could be in pushing myself to my realistic maximum involvements. But I try to retain most of the high frustration tolerance that was typical of youth, and I stubbornly refuse to put myself down when I fall back to lower frustration tolerance. I thereby continue to accept myself even with my limitations and thus follow one of the most important goals of RET. And although unconditional self-acceptance hardly stops my aging process, it definitely makes bearing it a hell of a lot lighter!

Bachrach

Lee Loevinger

B. *1913*

❧❧

Lee Loevinger is the granddaddy of "jurimetrics," a word he coined in 1949 and which is now accepted as the term to describe the field of law that studies the relationship between law, science, and technology. Over a long and productive career as a legal theorist, judge, and attorney, he has found time to serve not only his profession, but also his state and country. He is a past supreme court justice of Minnesota and served as the assistant U.S. attorney general under the Kennedy administration, in charge of the Antitrust Division of the Department of Justice.

Currently of counsel in the Washington, D.C., law firm Hogan & Hartson, Loevinger is actively adding to the more than one hundred and fifty books, monographs, and articles he has published in the fields of jurimetrics, jurisprudence, and antitrust, administrative, mass media, and nursing law.

He is quoted as having said that "the dominating passion of my life has probably been curiosity—the desire to know and understand. This involves a peculiar paradox: Ignorance increases faster than knowledge, as each new fact or principle opens new frontiers for intellectual exploration. Thus, with greater learning comes intellectual humility and skepticism. So, after reaching seventy I am less certain of anything than at thirty I was of everything."

LIFE BEFORE DEATH

Reflecting on the question of whether it takes courage to "grow old," I have come to the realization that aging is a process that all living persons, from the newborn babe to the centenarian, experience. Everyone grows older by the minute, hour, day, month, and year. As we grow older many things change, and one of the most important is our attitude toward aging.

I still have a vivid recollection of agonizing at an early age over the dilemma created by my emerging self-consciousness, as an awareness of mortality began to intrude on me. Extinction seemed an awful fate, almost unbearable. On the other hand, immortality—existence literally forever—seemed equally intolerable and inconceivable. I never did resolve this dilemma but rather outgrew it as it became obvious that it was insoluble, at least in the terms that I then perceived it. Many years later I learned that nothing in the universe is ever really created or destroyed. Matter and energy are always conserved; only the patterns, the states of matter and energy, change. Perhaps this is the ultimate answer to my youthful dilemma, if indeed there is one.

Each person has his or her own method of accommodating the inevitability of death. For many it is embracing or renewing a faith in life after death, usually in the framework of a religion. For some it is simply a supine surrender, a passive waiting for death. For others, including myself, it is more important to be concerned with life before death than with life after death, whatever form that may take.

There have been numerous calumnies against those who are older, uttered, naturally, by those who are younger. A few years ago the young were proclaiming that a mere thirty years was the great divide between the young and the hopelessly aged; and the youth brigades were marching with the battle cry: "Don't trust anyone over thirty!" It is undeniable that as we grow older our bodies become more frail and we become subject to physical limitations not experienced when we were younger. Fortunately, modern medicine is able to repair, replace, or maintain many of the bodily organs that degenerate or fail with the passing years.

More significantly, scientific investigation has now shown that in normal adults there is no deterioration of mental abilities associated with aging. Indeed, cerebral exercise can benefit the brain, and the brain continues to grow in ability when stimulated by an enriched environment. Many of the elderly have employed their time to become more learned and to develop better judgment than their juniors. For me, this is the essence of growing older. I believe that physical prowess is not the essence of living. The essence of existence as a human being is intellectual activity, the content and use of the mind, or of what some would call the "soul."

Others have thought and felt this and expressed it more eloquently. In the sixteenth century Sir Edward Dyer rhapsodized:

> My mind to me a kingdom is,
> > Such present joys therein I find
> That it excels all other bliss
> > That earth affords or grows by kind . . .

Two centuries later, a youthful John Keats confronted his intimations of mortality by writing

> When I have fears that I may cease to be
> > Before my pen has glean'd my teeming brain,
> Before high-piled books, in charactery,
> > Hold like rich garners the full ripen'd grain;
> > then on the shore
> Of the wide world I stand alone, and think
> Till love and fame to nothingness do sink.

I believe that the very meaning of "growth" for the human being is the cultivation and development of the mind. Growing and learning are substantially the same thing. The important thing for me is to pursue an interest in learning more about as many things as possible. Of course, this is an endless task. The more you learn, the more there is to learn. This is true not only for an individual, but also for groups comprising any discipline, and, indeed, for any society with pretensions to being civilized.

As science has learned more about the nature of matter and energy that are the elements of the universe, it has found itself confronted by questions that were unsuspected, and would have been unintelligible, to earlier generations. Human beings know a few things about the surface of the small globe on which they live. But our globe is surrounded by a vast darkness. The darkness is ignorance. It can be driven back as we create light in one place and then another. As more lights of learning are lit, the area of illumination around us grows, but always beyond it there is an even greater circumference of the darkness of ignorance. Our knowledge will never be final or complete. The pursuit of knowledge is never-ending; thus there is always the opportunity for growth.

Since I have enjoyed learning, it hasn't taken much courage for me to grow older; indeed, I've really enjoyed the process—which is simply another way of saying I've enjoyed living. But this does require the confession that I've mainly been lucky. I have survived at least an average number of physical disabilities, through the skill of surgeons and the miracles of modern medicine. These have included removal of a birthmark and excision of tonsils and adenoids in childhood, later repairs to both lower ends of the gastrointestinal plumbing system, removal of an inflamed gall bladder, exchange of a deteriorating (stenotic) heart valve for a new one made of animal tissue, and removal of a cataract and implantation of a synthetic optical lens. These, together with an average quota of mild maladies, such as flu and common colds, have not prevented me from generally feeling the sensation of vigorous good health.

The most dramatic crisis I remember is World War II. Having believed myself a conscientious objector to all war and military service during earlier years, I suffered torments of doubt debating my conscience immediately after Pearl Harbor, and the declaration of war against Japan and Germany. However, within two weeks it became clear to me that there was only one course my conscience would permit: I had to do more than deplore the evil represented by the German Nazis—I had to fight it actively. So I volunteered for the Navy and requested overseas duty. Assigned to the amphibious force, and then to the small American group that accompanied the British Navy in the invasion of North Africa in November 1942 ("Operation Torch"), I confronted the imminence of mortality while still in my twenties. I had then, deep in my gut, an irrepressible terror of death. Yet even then the fear was that of losing the opportunity to live a life I had just begun, the frustration of ceasing to be before my pen had "glean'd my teeming brain." Despite the terror, I did what I was supposed to do. If that was courage, and I make no claim to it, it was probably the major episode in my life that comes closest to such a virtue. My only feeling is that I did then what I thought was the right thing to do, and I have tried to do so since. I cannot do more and will not do less.

The principal difference in attitude that I perceive between myself as a young man and the man I am today is that I have become more tranquil. Perhaps this is because most of the crucial decisions that will affect my life have been made and the range of choices is now less. Perhaps it is because, as the body becomes somewhat more frail, the spirit becomes more sturdy. Although I can still become indignant about much that goes on in the world (who can't?), I am more tolerant of the opinions and foibles of others that are contrary to my own or even those that denigrate my own ideas. I have developed and clung to a principle which I call the "Doctrine of Insignificance." This states that if a matter is not genuinely significant as far as you are concerned, then you should be indifferent to it, or at least avoid becoming angered. Almost daily, anyone can observe myriads of people who have not yet learned this simple lesson. A prime example is those who complain when an elevator they have just entered stops at several floors before reaching the desired destination. Another common example is the driver who cannot tolerate it when a traffic light turns red just as he arrives at a controlled intersection, not to mention the motorists who vent their traffic-generated frustration with gunfire, or those who complain because their newspapers are not delivered to precisely the right spot before their doors each morning.

Young and older, we all become impatient or annoyed when we are inconvenienced. But age and experience bring a degree of tolerance and patience. This may seem anomalous, since it suggests that we are willing to endure more time waiting even as the time allotted to us grows shorter. But ire and impatience expended on insignificant matters gain nothing and cost something in personal comfort and health. It is not merely philosophy but quality of life that counsels: If it's really insignificant, relax and be indifferent.

To this point I have written of growing "older" but not of becoming "old." I think there is a great difference. In my view, those who are still growing are not old; the old are those who have stopped growing. You are old when you lose interest in learning. So long as you are seeking to learn, you are growing and continuing to grow older, developing and improving your mind and spirit, possibly even becoming learned—but you are not old.

In my own case, I have spent most of my adult life as a lawyer, working with words and their proper arrangements, and occasionally penetrating to the underlying concepts they represent. But this is not enough to understand the modern world. The language of science, for example, is numbers, and the concepts they represent are usually different from the concepts of verbal symbols. Thus, to say that a person is large or small conveys very little by way of precise information. To specify an approximate height and weight in numbers is much more informative. This is an extremely simple illustration. An understanding of the significant aspects of modern society, the world, and the universe we live in, requires a much more complex mathematical approach. It requires not only literacy, in the sense of skill in understanding and using words, but also numeracy, which is some knowledge and understanding of the quantitative and numerical data of science.

I have been fascinated by science ever since my undergraduate days in college, but have been too busy most of my life to indulge more than a dilettante interest in it. Yet, I have remained a scientist manqué at heart. Now, after more than fifty years as a lawyer, I am beginning to find time to study and learn more about science. I have no illusions that this will lead to a second career. But it will surely provide me with a vast new area for thinking and learning—that is, for growth. So I shall continue to grow older, I hope for a very long time to come; but the emphasis here is on "grow" and not on "older." I am encouraged in this by the counsel of scientists that optimists are healthier, happier, and longer-lived than pessimists.

Age is a matter of insignificance, and thus of indifference, so long as I continue to grow. To be blunt about it, "old" is a condition that afflicts you, like rheumatism or atherosclerosis, when you have lost your sense of curiosity and have stopped learning. It is a rheumatism or atherosclerosis of the mind and spirit. While I sometimes may fancy myself unusual (or, in exuberant moments, possibly distinguished) in some respects, I think that these views reflect fairly common attitudes toward aging among those who have attained true maturity.

So, having surmounted the successive crises of confronting my own inescapable mortality, I have ceased to worry, or even think much, about what comes after death, if anything. Surely if there is such a thing as "life after death" it must be something quite different than anything known as "life" on this planet. Consequently, I am concerned only with life before death, a thing which I do know something about, and which will surely engage all of my efforts and occupy all of my time so long as I remain alive. I intend to walk upright, interested, curious, and learning about the world and the universe, until my end comes, whenever that may be. At the age of seventy-five I am not yet old, and I hope to grow much, much older. But I am determined that—come what may—I shall die before I become old.

Chapleau-Osborne

Anne Marx

B. *1913*

✕ ✕

The quality of Anne Marx's verse—her range of subjects, depth of feeling, and mastery of poetic form—have earned her the reputation of being one of America's outstanding contemporary poets. Her achievement is all the more remarkable because she did not begin writing in English until she had reached adulthood.

Born in Germany, she was a medical student at Heidelberg when her first small book of poems appeared. With the rise of the Nazis, she fled Germany and came to the United States in 1936, where she settled in New York. Her first book in English was published in 1960 and won for her the American Weave Chapbook Award and immediate recognition as a poet. Since then she has published thirteen books of poetry and has won numerous awards, among them several annual awards from the Poetry Society of America and the Poetry Society of England.

Mrs. Marx has traveled widely to teach, lecture, and give workshops and readings throughout America and abroad. Her enthusiastic contributions on behalf of poetry include eight years as an officer and vice-president of the Poetry

Society of America, and as national poetry editor and later as editor of *The Pen Woman*, a journal of the National League of American Pen Women. Her most recent book is *Hurts to Healings*, published in the United States, England, and her native Germany. She believes that "to be undeterred is the key to any achievement that is important to our lives. Undeterred by detractors asserting that one's goal is impossible to reach. Undeterred by blame or praise. Undeterred by demands of custom and fashion. Undeterred by all but the most essential bonds of family and friends. Undeterred even by the knowledge that there will be no greatness at the end of the long climb—only satisfaction that we have tried to bring out the best that is in us, that we have added to our years that special ingredient we needed most to add zest to existence."

IN LIFE ENGROSSED

Around the age of twelve I made a secret pact with God. My life to that point had been filled with an inordinate amount of tragedy, so I asked God (whom I visualized at the time as a benign father figure) to spare me any further troubles or pain in the years to come. Confident that he had heard and responded to my prayer I felt safe in the knowledge that any and all misfortune was now behind me; I could look forward to a trouble-free life. I had to learn, both gradually and painfully, that life does not balance out its gifts or its blows in equal proportions. God cannot be bargained with and maturing means dealing with problems as they arise.

One of the most significant problems I've had to deal with in my life occurred four years ago, when I was confronted with the stark fact that I had a well-advanced cancer. It wasn't beyond repair, but lengthy treatments were required. First I had to take radium inserts within an isolated room where my radioactive body could harm no one else. Nurses came but intermittently, and my husband was allowed just a five-minute visit every half hour. Sleep was impossible, because I was asked to remain motionless for forty-nine and a half hours. (I am still pondering the significance of that extra half hour!) It seemed as if I were in an isolation tank, cut off from the present but reliving the past. Reviewing my life in the utter calmness of that tank, it seemed inevitable that I had contracted cancer. During my twelfth year my father had died from cancer, and the very thought of it had always made me shudder. When the doctors inquired into my family medical history they looked meaningfully at each other. And they wondered what my mother had died from at the age of twenty-six? She was a victim of the worldwide flu epidemic that hit just after the First World War. If penicillin had been available then she might have lived to a ripe old age. And if they had had chemotherapy treatments when I was a youngster my father too might have lived. These strange accidents of timing occupied my thoughts. Here I was with cancer and yet, to a certain extent, feeling fortunate! Wasn't it fortunate to have been born in this century, with all its advances in medicine helping me get well, rather than to have been born in the nineteenth century of my parents? And I couldn't help but think of my grandmother who was firmly anchored

in the Victorian age. "A woman is born for suffering," she used to say—
a notion that I thoroughly rejected, even as a child.

I emerged from that room temporarily weakened physically, but per-
manently strengthened spiritually. In one way, I felt in charge of myself.
I knew now that I could cope with a grim situation. In another way,
I had learned to surrender to a power outside myself without rebellion.
The force beyond, who had long ago refused to bargain with me, was
now in charge of my fate. I had become a submitter.

After a second, briefer visit to the isolation room, I resumed my
mental field trips, while keeping my body still—oh so still—to get the
full benefit of the treatment once more. This time, I was able to engage
the creative right side of my brain. I composed poem after poem in my
head. Alas, there were no handy notepads around for jotting down a
few key words for subsequent recall. Where did they disappear to, those
poems? I believe they still exist in my subconscious. Others may have
materialized already without my even recognizing them. But any loss
is only my own; the world will not be greatly deprived. Yet I believe
that nothing is truly lost that is so deeply felt.

When this second phase was over, I had earned a "vacation," which
I spent in a tranquil part of Maine. Every day was a new and amazing
birthday gift. Creative ideas were flowing. A new collection of poems,
already in the hands of my publisher for some time, needed rethinking
and revising. In particular, the title required much deliberation and
correspondence. This book had to reflect my recent experience, to imply
an extension of life, yet without sounding maudlin. Eventually, the title
came: A Further Semester. It still pleases me, because that is what my
life really is right now. I gazed into the distance of death, found no fear,
and came back for another sojourn. The title also seemed significant
because this book contained so many poems dealing with old age and
death. In one long sonnet sequence I contemplated the recent lives of
my contemporaries and the various ways in which they coped with
illness and loss. Many managed magnificently, while others were sadly
lacking in both fortitude and faith.

Strangely, all those poems were originally written and first published
long before there existed the slightest suspicion of my cancer. Who can
say what caused my preoccupation with sickness, loss, and death? It
was more than the sum of past experiences. I am inclined to believe
that my body was sending messages to my mind, providing an uncanny
awareness and preparation. Doesn't it take a well-advanced growth a

long time to "advance" to the danger point? Who can say whether our antennas are not equipped to sense such physical upheavals and thus prepare us for the trials ahead?

The following poem is a sample from *A Further Semester* and the sequence entitled "Coping With Losses":

A MUTUAL GIFT

Rising as we arrived, the gracious host
as ever through the long decades we shared
from heights to valley, he put us at our ease
though lately in appearance like a ghost
of his young mountain self. Relieved, we dared
to chat and laugh without restraint, to please
our friend ignoring the malignancies
of fate. He poured the wine, aware we cared
and felt like grieving, yet honoring his cue
performing naturally. Nobody stared
at limbs like ropes as he stood up to toast
friendship; and as he locked the door, we knew
that we had brought one needed gift in lieu
of flowers—one hour of lives in life engrossed.

"In life engrossed"—this became a kind of leitmotif. When the planned operation was at last performed in September of that year it was almost anticlimactic. Presumably, this was now merely a shriveled "defused" organ that had to be removed. After the usual initial discomforts of a major operation, I bounced back joyfully. It was all over! I was still alive. I wrote a new poem on hospital stationery called "Checking the Vital Signs." Some resident doctors and fellow patients were interested in my books. Nothing makes a poet feel more alive and rejuvenated than people's interest in his or her work, no matter how modest! I felt exhilarated and almost normal, although the body lagged behind for a while. "We got it all"—that testimony was glorious music to accompany our journey home.

Stray malignant cells, however, might be lurking somewhere. Now it was necessary to tackle the final stretch in good spirits, by undergoing outside radiation for several months. This too became a new learning and growing experience. In the hospital, I had trained my thoughts to be positive. In Maine and at home, I had tried to be considerate and loving toward family members and friends, suppressing all negative impulses. I read many books on positive thinking, mind over matter, healing by laughter, and similar themes located in our library. May Sarton's books, written after her own various setbacks, left me with a deep impression of her stubborn strength. But up to then I lacked the total, all-encompassing compassion I first experienced in the radiologist's waiting room several times a week. Here I began to care about the other patients, men and women of every age, race, and circumstance. We talked to each other like sisters and brothers. Later, I wrote a poem which received a prize, called "Radiant Hope." The award itself is no world-shaking event; I mention it merely because it launched the poem along an extensive route to fellow sufferers. They responded with letters and equally hope-inspiring messages. A network of mutual sustenance was created.

By the end of the year, my treatments were finished. I was declared well. Medication, however, continues indefinitely. Regular checkups since then have been satisfactory. Life goes on as before, but with a fundamental difference. I am older and wiser, rather fearless, and much more concerned with all of suffering mankind. I feel an overwhelming identity with a mighty force of commiseration and kindness, never experienced to such a degree before. My own troubles have shrunk to insignificance compared to some of the others.

Aging might well have occurred, less consciously, at a slower rate, had it not been accelerated during my cancer episode. In either case, it simply does not take any particular courage to face the inevitable. Applying that realization to my illness, it will serve me equally well during the continuing aging process. I hope to react in the same spirit to dying. Legions of living creatures have left this earth before me. Willingly or not, they met their end in innumerably different ways. So why not I?

I believe that the final state of death may be a mercifully oblivious one. Before the end, I hope to be spared prolonged pain and to spare my loved ones the helpless agony of seeing me suffer. Increased disorder and inertness would be the hardest conditions to accept. However, since I have no choice about that either, I can only try to slow up the process of deterioration by remaining active and alert as long as possible. One might say that "the courage to grow old" is synonymous with the will to keep going. Keeping busy and stimulated seems to be one of the key factors in leading a satisfactory life at any age. Fate may force us eventually to give in to limitations, but nothing should make us give up altogether.

One point, though, is especially important, namely, not to cram too much into one's day so that it passes without one's real awareness. It is increasingly necessary to stop and look along the way, to take a leisurely walk, pick a violet, read a poem aloud, listen to favorite music—in short, to be attuned to a somewhat slower rhythm of salvaged time.

AS MY FACE LIFTS TO FALL

Straddling summer's high wall,
Leaping lightly past fences,
Once I gathered tall spires
Of hollyhock.

As my face lifts to fall,
As the season advances,
I get high on small flowers
Right on my block.

Ira Wallach

B. 1913

❧ ❧

Ira Wallach, whom Martin Levin of the *New York Times* calls "one of the defest satirists at large and a master of the fragile art of parody," is the author of several books, plays, and theatrical sketches. His better known works include sketches for the revue *Phoenix 55*, starring Nancy Walker (1955); the play *Drink to Me Only* (with A. S. Ginnes, 1955); his book, *The Absence of a Cello* (1960); and the book for the off-Broadway musical *Smiling the Boy Fell Dead* (1961). His screenplays include *Hot Millions* (1968), which won an Academy Award nomination for best original screenplay and the Writers Guild of Great Britain Award for the Best British Comedy Screenplay. His books include *Hopalong-Freud* (1951) and *Muscle Beach* (1959).

Mr. Wallach used to fly a light plane because, as he said, "there is no more perfect solitude than to fly alone over the countryside." As for his work, he remarks, "I enjoy writing and never give much thought to my motivations."

STROLLING TOWARD
THE FINISH LINE

As a child I caught frogs and butterflies, incarcerated fireflies in empty milk bottles, held grasshoppers over the back of my hand and waited for them to "spit tobacco." (The grasshoppers, when captured, expelled a brownish fluid that I suspect is some sort of defense mechanism.) I also trained for hours every day in Miller's lot to reify my dream of becoming a professional baseball player.

In 1913, when I was born, IBM could have paid the national debt out of its petty cash drawer, radio was a futuristic fantasy, television and space exploration the bread and butter of science fiction, and a bulky office adding machine was deemed technological sophistication. I believe that my generation has experienced more explosive societal changes than any generation in history, including the generation that grew up during the Industrial Revolution. I know that I am an extension of the boy who caught frogs and made grasshoppers spit, and yet he is almost a stranger to me. The connection between what I was and what I have become grows increasingly tenuous. Today I look in vain in the mirror for a reflection of the swashbuckling image that once smiled back at me. The baseball player became a tennis player, the tennis player has become a golfer, and the runner a walker, but my physical ills are insignificant and I am reasonably certain that my head functions as well as ever.

I have little patience for people who refer to the elderly as having reached the "golden age." Age brings with it deterioration, and deterioration is not golden. The advertisements aimed at "mature" (read "old") people usually show a handsome white-haired woman holding hands with a similarly white-haired man while both look off, misty-eyed, to distant and alluring horizons. This is the Mary Poppins approach to age, and while Mary Poppins may entertain me, she does not provide me with wisdom.

Mary Poppins, however, will be delighted to learn that I do not find aging to be painful or distressing. Age brings with it certain advantages. One advantage is that we have in reserve more experience to draw upon and this helps us deal with life more wisely. Except for muggers and other oafs, white hair inspires courtesy in others, and people call

me "sir" more often than "meat head." Aging even brings certain physical advantages. If in my earlier days I had been a champion golfer, a
professional with many tournament wins, my game would now be
going downhill, but because I came to the links rather late in life, my
game can and does improve.

People often observe that as one grows older, the days trudge slowly
on, but the years fly by. I find that not to be true, at least for myself.
Yes, the years do fly by, but so do the days. Possibly that is because I
am a writer, I work every day, and I find the work exhilarating. I know
that I am fortunate in this. For others, I believe that enforced retirement
of the physically and mentally able is gratuitous cruelty.

I also enjoy studying. Now I am trying to fill a cultural gap by learning
French. I look forward to the hours I spend with my French books and
cassettes, even though I sometimes grow impatient with myself because
I cannot achieve a Gallic fluency by injection.

I never ask myself what I consider the rather absurd question, "Why
am I here?" To me, the only conceivable answer is that I am here to
play my infinitesmal role in evolution, an act inseparable from living
but quite separable from volition. I don't trouble myself by asking the
meaning of life because no one has yet come up with an answer that
hasn't made me giggle. I also note that those who claim to know the
meaning of life are not one whit more content than I.

In my writings, now as always, I try to do the best I can, but dreams
of immortality have never spurred me on. I seriously doubt that Shakespeare ever aspired to immortality. He had his work to do, he did it as
best he could, and his best was quite good enough. The only time one
can enjoy one's immortality is when one is alive. Furthermore, it is
essentially quite bizarre to think that we can ever assess who will and
who will not be immortal. We do not know of any immortals who
existed before the absurdly brief time-span of oral and written history.
Recorded history can be reckoned only in thousands of years, but we
reckon the existence of the human brain in millions. How immortal
will be those immortals who have been among us in the last three or
four thousand years? Will they persist in the memory of man when we
have added twenty or thirty thousand years to human history? Will
Shakespeare then be still among the immortals? Or Moses, Christ, Bud-
dha? Only the rash would dare an emphatic answer.

In his book, *War*, Gwynne Dyer wrote of the battle of Megiddo:

It is impossible to care much about who won the battle, because both sides lived long ago and far away, and most of what they cared for—their family and friends, their language, their religion, their personal and political hopes and fears—has vanished utterly. That is not at all the way we feel about the Normandy invasion of 1944, but if history goes on long enough, the day will come when Megiddo and Normandy will seem on a par: equally futile and equally meaningless . . . The man in the ranks of Tuthmose III's army of Armageddon was deluded about the importance of his death, but the man in a Chieftain tank (or a T-62) in Germany today is not. And I am the Queen of Sheba.

Ambition does not burn my belly. I think an overpowering ambition is a certain recipe for discontent. The feelings that George Jean Nathan expressed about ambition in his book, *The Anatomy of an Attitude*, coincide with mine:

Ambition is a commendable thing, but too much pious nonsense has been preached about it. The ambitions of all of us should properly be bounded by a critical appreciation of our own limitations. I, for example, should like nothing better than to be able to afford the ambition to write criticism as profound and fine as John Dryden's, but I have enough critical instinct to know that such an achievement is beyond my capabilities.

Now to the standard question: Would I like to live my life over so that I could avoid some of the more egregious errors I have committed? My answer is no. For one thing, had I my life to live over I am quite certain I would not make the same mistakes, but I am just as certain that I would make new and possibly more unfortunate ones. Errors are teachers. They help us learn. Besides, although I relish living, the process of aging is one that convinces me (and others) that once around is quite enough.

Long ago I spent many years as a communist. The depression of the early '30s and the painful problems associated with it impelled me toward Marxism. I could say that those were mistaken years, but I think my mistake was to confuse the criminal distortion of Marxism with Marxism itself. Yes, those were misguided years, but they were also fruitful years. It was not my ambition to establish gulags or sanctify firing squads. My ambition was to contribute whatever little efforts I was capable of to trying to make society more equitable, and I still think that a worthwhile goal. Those years made me think. They broadened my world-view. They impelled me to try to make sense out of much of what I perceived as senseless in society. My allegiance to the Communist party was an allegiance to what I thought it was and not to what it actually was.

Time is the element that is most important to me as I continue to age. With each passing day, the time left me is one day shorter. I am therefore jealous of time and determined to use it in the best possible manner. I believe that the best possible use of time is the avoidance of boredom. Now I avoid fools, but when I am in their presence, I suffer them (but not gladly). I am tolerant of their foolery. Once I could never get myself to stop reading a boring book in the middle. I felt morally obliged, as though I had a commitment to the author, to wade through the damn thing right to the last page. Now I toss away any book that has neither engaged nor edified me by the time I reach page forty or thereabouts. If what I see in the theater is clumsy and inept, I walk out after the first act. Since I am intolerant of the play but not of the players, I wait for that first act curtain so as not to tread on their feelings. Public opinion no longer sways me in such matters. When all New York was acclaiming the Kabuki dancers, I walked out on them before I yawned myself to death. (But I am willing to concede that my failure to enjoy them may be my weakness and not theirs.) I avoid those of my contemporaries whose idea of a scintillating conversation is a recital of their physical woes, a comparison of medications, and a blow-by-blow description of the latest surgical encounter. And I hereby declare to all within listening distance that I definitely do not want to see pictures of your grandchildren.

Philosophically, I believe that what has influenced me deeply is Spinoza's humbling injunction that we view everything under the aspect of eternity. That injunction has encouraged me to accept death and to believe in it. Aha! I hear someone saying, "Gad, he'd better," paraphrasing Emerson's alleged rejoinder to Margaret Fuller's fatuous remark, "I accept the universe." I am not much possessed by death, but when I say that I accept it, I am also saying that I avoid the pitiful ploys so many use to deny it. Whoever worries that a biological line may come to an end is avoiding an acceptance of death. The preservation of a biological line provides only a bogus immortality. Had I a grandchild, I am certain I would welcome it with interest and love, yet the lack of a grandchild disturbs me not at all. The human line will continue, with or without my descendants, unless we collectively manage to blow ourselves off the face of the earth.

The aging person who selects a burial plot with a good northwest view of the Hudson River in an elevated spot on a grassy knoll is also avoiding acceptance of death. Right now he or she can enjoy the view from the graveyard, but the body that will be interred there couldn't care less. Bury it under the outhouse and it will be just as content with oblivion.

Whoever leaves instructions for ash-scattering is also using another death-avoidance ploy. Alive, a man may be deeply moved by contemplating the spectacle of his ashes being strewn over Lake Tahoe at sunset. When he is actually reduced to ashes, those ashes will be very good-natured. You can flush them down a toilet (as in a Dorothy Parker story) and they won't complain.

The notion of future oblivion does not obsess me. Oblivion, after all, has no emotional content. I am enjoying life, although I live it at a different level and a different pace than was formerly my habit. The sight of lovely young girls continues to delight me, and although I may stare avidly (but with discretion), I do not fall into the dirty-old-man category because I preserve my dignity by not taking rash and inappropriate action. I now have no intention of giving up any bad habits that afford me pleasure. I believe in keeping minor ailments a secret from my doctor lest he make of me a pill and nostrum repository. My wife, daughter, brother, and stepson give me the considerable pleasure of their company, and I have good friends who do likewise.

When oblivion comes, I will have left unsaid many kind words and a few trenchant ripostes, and I regret that. But then, of course, unless we have become vegetables, we will all leave some things undone.

My only legacy will be my books and plays, and the memory of me for those who choose to remember.

Look me up in the encyclopedia twenty thousand years from now, but please don't be disappointed if I'm not there. Shakespeare may not be there either.

John Tebbel

B. *1912*

❧ ⬩ ❧

When asked what advice he could offer aspiring writers, the veteran journalist, historian, and teacher replied, "Epictetus said it all in his *Discourses*, and I've repeated it for more than twenty years in my fiction workshops at New York University: 'If you would be a writer, write.' " Heeding his own advice, John Tebbel has authored or ghostwritten (about half and half) more than eighty books, among them *George Washington's America* (1954), *The Inheritors* (1962), *From Rags to Riches* (1964), the highly acclaimed, award-winning *A History of Book Publishing in the United States* (1971–81), and *Between Covers* (1987).

Tebbel began his writing career at the age of fourteen as a stringer for state dailies in Michigan. By 1935 he was city editor of the Mount Pleasant, Michigan, *Times-News*. Later he worked for *Newsweek*, was managing editor of the old *American Mercury*, and held editorial positions for such papers as the *Detroit Free Press*, the *Providence Journal*, and the *New York Times*. In 1943 he became associate editor of E.P. Dutton & Company, simultaneously launching his career as freelance writer and editor. Leaving Dutton in 1946 to pursue writing full time, it wasn't long before "the constant anxiety of the freelancer's life" turned him toward teaching. In 1949 he became an assistant professor in the Department of Journalism at New York University, and by 1954 was a full professor and its chairman. Pleased with this move, Tebbel later remarked that "I found teaching and writing an ideal combination as a way of life, particularly since teaching gave me nearly as much satisfaction."

After retiring from NYU in 1976 after twenty-six years, eleven as chairman, Tebbel occupied himself much as usual, writing books and adding to the list of more than five hundred articles he has written for both popular and scholarly publications. He also listens a great deal to music and follows sports. "I write to the constant accompaniment of a good New York music station, and I hear a lot of music, both classic and jazz, at other times, often from my large library of records and tapes. I'm also interested in sports, some of which I follow on television. I see as much theater as possible. In fact, I have never met an art I didn't like."

LIFE ON
A SHRINKING ISLAND

In a special issue of the Johns Hopkins University alumni magazine, years ago, a panel of contributors from many disciplines considered the phenomenon of growing old, feeling their way around the subject like the blind men with the elephant. One metaphor from that examination persists in my memory. "Growing old," said one writer, "is like living on an island which gradually grows smaller and smaller."

As an inhabitant of that island, watching the sea relentlessly creeping in around the edges, I'm increasingly aware of the shrinkage, particularly the contraction of foreseeable time in which I may, if lucky, continue to inhabit my island.

There is, for example, the matter of books. My considerable library has been a useful research tool all these years. It contains a good many books I've done no more than sample, and some I've never read. I estimate there are at least half of them I want to read. Simple arithmetic tells me that will be impossible, so the question arises: How is triage to be applied? What should be given priority, and which ones must I reconcile myself to never having opened?

All of them, sadly, must compete with new books, a category I find myself curtailing more and more. Do I really want to spend the time reading this new and promising novel, when it means the time will be taken from something well tested from the past? As a historian, I want to read the best new books from that area of knowledge, but I find myself mentally trying to estimate whether a particular book is anything more than merely interesting. There are thousands of "interesting" books I would like to read, but my standards are considerably higher now.

In a way, the choices of what to read are beginning to sound like that durable cliché, "What books would you take with you if you were going to be marooned on a desert island?" Thinking of whatever hereafter there may be, should I give consideration to the philosophical equivalent of "How to Build a Raft"? That is, should I reexamine religion, and if so, how to choose among the vast number of religious books available? Better, maybe, to stick with the Bible; it seems to be having a revival of its own, although of course it remains a perennial bestseller, and surely is the greatest body of literature ever produced.

Daily the choices become more difficult as I look upon my bulging library shelves and read the book reviews. Obviously, the time will come when these choices are certain to be impossible. What solid rock will I retreat to then, if death is only delayed and not sudden? To that question, deponent cannot return an answer.

But there is also the matter of my own books. Since I have already written more than eighty, of mine and other people's, shouldn't that be sufficient unto the day? I don't know any writer who would accept such finality. Currently, I have three books in various stages of preparation, and that will account for at least two more years of writing time, so the question is, What next, if anything, can be deferred?

I keep thinking of the apocryphal story about Horatio Alger, Jr., of how in his last hours he struggled to get out of bed, seized the paper and pen he kept ready, and made one last attempt to write the great novel he had always believed he was capable of. His sister, so the dubious story goes, put him back into bed, pulled up the covers, and said firmly, "You've written enough, Horatio." The lesson here is that only forcible restraint will prevent a writer from writing until he is no longer physically able to do it. I know that I'll never write all I want to write, or be able to resist making one more attempt to produce what reason tells me is not within the range of my talents.

Relatively speaking, these are happy dilemmas I've been rehearsing here. Every day I realize how extremely fortunate I am to be able to do what I've always loved doing since I was very young, and to know that I can keep on doing it until illness or sheer physical disability precludes it. In that respect, my lot is different from most of the 4,300 people who live with me in a retirement community, where only I and a few others are actually not retired, but are still able to pursue a career. The less fortunate ones are not idle, by any means, but most have had to exchange one way of life for another, and to face growing old with whatever resources they can muster.

Except for a few, these are not people with financial problems. Some are comparatively rich, others are what was once described as "comfortable"; still others have enough for present needs but live with the knowledge that they could be wiped out, or near it, by health events of a catastrophic kind. Otherwise, they face the common problem of how to fill their remaining days. Most of them do it with considerable grace, bolstered by a kind of gallows humor embodied in what is now a too common expression, that they are living in "God's little waiting room."

For some, the waiting room represents an opportunity to do things they've always wanted to do. Executives who were once too busy making money to have any other interests find themselves pursuing full time what were once part-time hobbies. Women who had been either preoccupied with careers, raising children, or both, now have completely different interests, and the village attempts to provide the means to satisfy their needs. Add to this the universal, ongoing interest in the lives of grown children and grandchildren. Consequently, growing old here doesn't appear to require any particular courage, but simply the creative ability to fill up the days with what were once hobbies, or sports, or cultural pursuits, or simply socializing with friends who have similar interests. There are new friends, new interests—a kind of life-enhancing process.

If I thought of my own lot and that of those around me as typical, I would have reason to ask, "What do you mean, the courage to grow old?" But there are no such illusions here. We have learned enough of the world by this time to know that for a great many people, growing old does take courage, and if we hadn't learned it before, we would learn it quickly enough from what goes on around us. Beneath the apparently tranquil surface of this retirement oasis, the dramas and tragedies of growing old are played out every day, and they spawn the kind of courage the human condition has always produced under stress.

To be aging and ill requires the greatest courage, it seems to me. To see someone taking care of a wife or husband with Alzheimer's disease, for example, opens the door to a particular kind of hell that must take extraordinary courage to confront every day. Growing old in such circumstances means giving up one's own life for another, and doing it over what is usually a long period of time. The same could be said for cancer and other diseases whose outcome is known and inevitable, soon or late. For the aging patient (except for the Alzheimer's victim, who loses the ability to understand what is happening) it means growing old with a minimum of dignity and hope. For those who must take care of the afflicted it is a life haunted by financial fears as well as the agony of a loved one's life ending. To face this kind of aging, day after day without faltering, demands courage of the highest order.

There are, inevitably, those who do falter. Our village has its quota of people who have succumbed in one way or another, whether from illness or other causes. Those living on fixed incomes as costs go up relentlessly lead lives of advancing desperation. Simple loneliness is another serious problem. We have more than a thousand single women living in the village, nearly all of them widows. There are less than a hundred single men.

Most stave off loneliness by filling their lives with activities of conventional kinds, from bridge to golf, and they have their own friendship circles. For others, because of temperament or unavoidable circumstances, it isn't possible to construct a satisfactory life alone. Alcohol becomes the anesthetic to endure growing old, and we have an alarming number of those whose days are measured by the bottle. No one knows how many mental health problems there are among the aging population of the village because attempts to identify and help them have failed, for the most part. Courage fails here. These people are in full retreat.

Sometimes, confronting the shortening years, it may seem that, whatever advantages old age may bring, the unavoidable disadvantages are far greater. Yet, given reasonably good health, aging has its own peculiar rewards. Friends, for example. By now, we have not only those friends we've known before in other places, whom we write to, speak with on the telephone, and see now and then, but the new ones we've made.

In my own case, I have the added satisfaction of memories or continuing friendship with thousands of students I've taught in two universities. Some of them have become lifelong friends, whom I see fairly often; others keep in touch by telephone or letters. I observe the accomplishments of these men and women in newspapers and magazines, and on television, believing, as they often assure me, that I contributed something to the making of their lives. Teachers know what it is to have such an extended family, and if they are old teachers, they know that former students provide a rich legacy to enjoy in the last years.

In later life, whatever it was that one most enjoyed in the past becomes doubly meaningful. The enjoyment of music, next to books, has been one of the greatest joys of my life. Memory tells me that I have heard the best of what the music world has had to offer in the past half-century, and against that backdrop, what I hear today on radio and television, as well as on less frequent visits to the concert hall, gives me a depth of appreciation I could never have known when young. Like books, music gives me a special kind of courage to endure whatever may happen in old age. It is always there, always rewarding. Friends and family may drop off one by one, but music remains and endures to the end.

Even illness, the inevitable accompaniment of aging, can on occasion impel us to view the process with a peculiar kind of satisfaction. Unless the outcome is adverse, even an operation can be rejuvenating. Most of us who have had one know what it's like to emerge from the hospital and view the world again. The sun, the clouds, every blade of grass, or even an expanse of snow, take on a new meaning because we're part of the world again, and we no longer take it for granted.

There is something perverse about old age, too, in giving us the courage to face with some measure of equanimity the possibility of calamitous events. Even something so mundane as flying from one part of the country to another carries these days a worrisome element of risk—crowded skies, lunatics or terrorists among the passengers, failures of overworked aircraft and crew. If the flight is to another country, the possibilities multiply.

Nagging fear is natural. Not many would want to leave the scene in exactly this way (although it's better than a lingering, terminal illness), but on the other hand, the aging passenger may face these possibilities in a more relaxed frame of mind than other people. The race has been run, or nearly run, the rewards have been achieved, the failures belong to the past, and there is nothing to be done about the regrets. An appointment-in-Samarra feeling may envelop the aging passenger, who believes he (or she) has had a good run for the money. The hope is for an encore or two, but if not, let the curtain come down.

As for apocalyptic visions that haunt the dreams of those who are informed about what is happening in the world, they may be somewhat mitigated in the minds of those headed toward the exit. Again, as in the case of air accidents, no one would look forward to being incinerated, or overcome by some form of pollution, or sharing the last gasps of a dying planet. But if greed and stupidity, the curses of the human race, bring about one of these catastrophes, there is a satisfaction among the old in reflecting that, once more, we've had the best of it in this century, and it isn't as though our promising careers are in jeopardy, or that we won't live to see our children grow up, or that we won't have an opportunity to do all the things we wanted to do. No encores needed. Let the doomsday curtain fall if it must. If this seems selfish of the old, so be it.

Fear may be the one element calculated to destroy courage and everything else among the aging. Nothing can be enjoyed or contemplated if fear dominates the mind, regardless of whether or not it's justified. It would be irrational, of course, simply to deny fear. We are right in sometimes having dread anticipations of what might happen to us in any given situation. When the body, for example, begins to send us signals that something may be terribly wrong, fear and anxiety are logical results. Yet we know that fear is also the enemy, and that we need to muster up whatever courage we can summon to deal with all the enemies within us, if we hope to survive.

And most of us do hope to survive, I think, unless ill health or some other calamity has made life an intolerable burden, and release from it is our only hope. If the mind remains alert, we survive because we want to see "how it all comes out." Those of us who are children of the twentieth century have surely seen the greatest show since recorded time began. A few of us have spanned two centuries. Oliver Wendell Holmes, living into his nineties, knew both John Quincy Adams and Alger Hiss, while his mother could recall looking out a Boston window as a young girl and seeing the British troops leave town.

Born in the seminal year of 1912, I have seen with my own eyes an era that encompassed the rise of motion pictures, radio, and television; the triumph of the automobile; the miracle of flight and exploration of space, and the presence of man on the moon. I am living on in a new technological era that, even with the unlocked atom threatening the world's existence, promises further wonders.

When I was six years old, we moved to my grandfather's farm, and he met us at the station with a horse and buggy, taking us to a farmhouse without electricity or running water. (The paradox is that even in this high-tech age there are so many places in the world today where the same conditions prevail.) But the world I live in now would have been beyond the comprehension of my grandfather, much less my great-grandmother, who lived to be 108, yet in whose lengthy lifetime there was nothing to compare with what I've seen.

Having witnessed so much, my appetite has not been dulled. Those of my contemporaries who tell me they've become detached from the world, who don't read the newspapers anymore and have lost interest in anything except their immediate concerns, seem already as good as dead. To paraphrase Samuel Johnson, who declared that a man who had lost interest in London had lost interest in life, it must surely be true that those who no longer care what's happening in the world have also lost interest in life itself. For life is not simply what happens to ourselves, but what happens in our relationship to an infinitely complex and endlessly fascinating world. To face the troubled present and uncertain future in old age doesn't require courage so much as curiosity, and a feeling of attachment to all living things—and dead things, too, for that matter.

This curiosity extends to the contemplation of life beyond death. People may say they never think about dying, but it's safe to assert that this is a thought always lurking in the conscious and subconscious of everyone. Philip Wylie once remarked about the conversations between patients and their physicians which begin, "Doctor, lately I've been noticing . . ." To which Wylie adds sardonically, "What they've been noticing is old George T. Death peering over their shoulders."

We all think about George from time to time, if only fleetingly. Death is the certainty in everyone's life. Facing it may require the greatest courage of all, because death is a fact so fearful, when it comes down to the individual, that many refuse even to talk about it, partly because of superstition, partly out of an inability to cope with the fear it generates.

Without meaning to denigrate religion in any way, I believe it is the great anesthetic that enables so much of the human race to deal with the fact of death. If we believe, we are assured of another life in which those we have lost will be restored and we ourselves will not again be burdened with the cares and sorrows of this world. Rewards and punishments will be meted out according to the doctrines of a particular faith.

But even for those who reject the specific dogmas of organized belief, the idea of religion is still a comfort. Those who have studied comparative religions see unifying factors in all the beliefs to which humanity adheres, no matter how much they differ on specifics according to cultures. The central belief is that another life does exist beyond death; people disagree only on details. It could be said that those naysayers who tell us, "When you're dead, you're dead," are like those tired of London—they, too, are tired of life itself. They may also be deluding themselves, since the human mind cannot absorb the concept of nothingness.

Those of us who are nearer to the Great Uncertainty than others find this very inability a consolation in itself. We who have loved life cannot imagine nonexistence. Instinctively, we turn to the idea of a life beyond the grave, and we only disagree about what it may be like. Curiosity again—perhaps courage in another form.

A few days before he died, my father told me he was not afraid, just immensely curious to see what was going to happen. It would be a new experience, he said, and extremely interesting to find out. I found myself agreeing with him, and it made the contemplation of his imminent death and my own ultimate departure much easier.

Of course, the naysayers may prove to be correct, and death indeed is final. But in that case, we'll never know it, and consequently there's nothing to worry about. Scientists, however, tell us that matter is indestructible, and if so, surely it isn't beyond the capability of whatever kind of god there may be, who was able to set this incredible universe in motion, to reassemble the finite particles of our lives into the same or a new form of life through all eternity—proving, as Einstein suspected, that time doesn't begin or end but constitutes a continuum in infinite space.

If we have the courage to believe that much, growing old becomes only another stage in a journey so long we can't even visualize it, and there will be no necessity, as Dylan Thomas urged, to rage "against the dying of the light." That light may be turned up again in another room, where who knows what may happen.

George Woodcock

B. *1912*

An incredibly prolific writer, scholar, adventurer, "ex-anarchist, and now free-wheeling radical," George Woodcock has journeyed in Mexico, Peru, Egypt, India, Ceylon, Southeast Asia, Japan, China, Pakistan, Lebanon, Iran, the United States, most of western Europe, and throughout his native Canada. These travels have resulted in the scores of highly acclaimed travel books he has authored over the past fifty years. In addition, he has become noted as a poet, essayist, historian, and biographer.

In his twenties and thirties, while working as a farmer and railway administrator, Woodcock became an anarchist and an advocate of communal living. He voiced these views forcefully in many of his early books, among them *Anarchy or Chaos* (1944) and *The Basis of Communal Living* (1947). Although his desire to see "society emerge out of natural impulses as opposed to imposed ones" has never entirely abated, as the years went on he focused most of his time on travel, writing about his travels, and on his poetry and biography. *The Crystal Spirit* (1966), a biography of his friend George Orwell, was praised by

Malcolm Muggeridge as "far and away the best of the numerous books, essays, and other writings about Orwell since his death."

In addition to the over fifty books he has authored or edited, he has written hundreds of articles for British, Canadian, and American publications, including *Horizon*, *The New Yorker*, *Saturday Review*, *New Republic*, and *London Magazine*. He has also authored several scripts for the British Broadcasting Corporation and the Canadian Broadcasting Corporation and for many years served as professor of English at the University of British Columbia.

Woodcock believes that the uniting feature in his work has been an "immense and zestful and lasting curiosity about the world and the beings who inhabit it; I was aware of this already as a small boy reading great books of the nineteenth-century travellers and naturalists. Related to that curiosity is a desire to understand and empathize, which has led me into the study of Asian philosophies and if not into fiction, certainly into drama as a means of understanding human motives by personifying them."

ON PRUFROCK'S LAMENT

I grow old . . . I grow old. . . .
I shall wear the bottoms of my trousers rolled.
Shall I part my hair behind? Do I dare to eat a peach?
I shall wear white flannel trousers and walk upon the beach.
I have heard the mermaids singing, each to each.
I do not think that they will sing to me.

T. S. Eliot was still a young man when he wrote those inimitable lines, though many who knew him felt that his sense of age came not from growing old but from being born old. The point I want to make at the beginning is that the sense of oldness, the feeling that powers are failing, that one is being by some dreadful magic transformed into a less complete being, can come at any age. Or not at all. Oscar Wilde once quipped of Max Beerbohm that when he was born the gods had granted him the boon of perpetual old age. There are many who carry that boon like a burden, having never really lived their youth, just as there are people who hardly see themselves as old until the moment of death is near.

For there is surely no other area in human existence where the physical and mental aspects of our lives move in more erratic relationships than in this matter of aging. There are those who begin—as so many of the Victorians did—to fold their tents at fifty. There are others to whom the sixties, the seventies, sometimes even the eighties, are the times of peak achievement. And I suspect, from what I have observed, that we have reached a time when for many people—more people than in the past—the mental life transcends the physical one in the sense that there is no longer an automatic shutting off of capacity as a man or a woman grows older. I have seen so many writers and artists who are my friends and who have had brilliant careers in youth, who have seemed to decline or at least to withdraw in middle age, and then, on the edge of what was once thought of as old age, have had an apparently miraculous second flowering, often producing work that is richer creatively, and deeper in understanding, than anything they have done before.

Of course, there were individuals in the past who performed marvelously in old age; Goethe comes to mind, and Titian, and a nineteenth-century fellow countryman of mine, Philippe Aubert De Gaspe, who wrote his only novel—a masterpiece about old Québec—in his seventies. But in the past these were the exceptions. Artistic geniuses tended to die early of the killer diseases that were so much more prevalent then in young adulthood, collapsing of tuberculosis like Keats and Chopin, of syphilis like Baudelaire and Maupassant, and if they did not pass away young, the likelihood was that their work would taper off into routine dullness as if, in a favorite phrase of the period, "they had outlived their time."

Was that a physical process or a mental one? An individual one or a social one? Probably all these elements entered into the situation. We live on the whole more healthily today, in spite of the manifold pollutants in our food and air of which we are all aware, partly because of better medical care, but even for those who never see a doctor, from the steady conquest of infections and contagious debilitating sicknesses. Even when we are old by the calendar, we are usually in far better shape than our forebears. I have lived long enough to remember when a man on the Shropshire countryside of my childhood was thought elderly in his early fifties, old by the time he was sixty, and ancient by seventy; if you read Jane Austen, who wrote a century before that, you will find people in their forties described as old.

But even there I think the question of attitude comes in, and attitude is both individual and social. We are often told that modern North Americans are youth-obsessed. If youth obsession means consciously imitating the young and trying to rejuvenate oneself physically, then it is clearly an aberration. But if it means rejecting the stereotypes of aging, then that's another matter.

Again, I can remember in my rural childhood enclave, where Victorian attitudes lasted long, older men and women actually dressed the parts (there were fashions of garment and even cloth for different age groups), and assumed the manner of grave dignity appropriate to their age. "Be your age!" in fact was one of their favorite sayings, and I can remember its being levelled pointedly at my grandfather, who in his sixties had a taste for cuddling young women at church socials.

Yet in those days families and societies still held together, and the old, if they survived in good physical shape, had their roles as elders in the family and community, dispensing wisdom which increasingly fewer people chose to hear, but at least respected and cared for as if their lives had a meaning for those around them.

Nowadays there is a situation among the old that favors the knowing few and insidiously militates against the unknowing many. It is much easier nowadays for the person who has mental vigor and remains in physically good shape to continue a productive life, particularly if he has prepared himself by cultivating some kind of self-employing occupation that does not have the built-in penalty of a mandatory retirement. As long as his mind continues to work well, and he can move about with reasonable facility, he will be accepted for his own worth. I know this from experience; at the age of seventy-six I still find myself at the peak of my literary productivity and at the same time accepted as an equal member in the Canadian literary world to which I have so long belonged.

But for an alarming number of old people age means a collective loneliness, an expulsion from the rest of the population in a much sharper way than ever in the past. Having lost the protection of families and small well-knit communities, they have become the responsibility of society as a whole—yet another social problem, like alcoholics and single mothers, but on a larger scale.

The appalling effect of this situation is a steady ghettoization of the old. It is more convenient to deal with them if they are detached from the rest of society and herded together. So they are encouraged to move into old people's homes or into apartment complexes or even housing estates specifically designed for them. There are whole communities, in Florida and British Columbia and elsewhere, that become known as old people's retirement places. In southern California there is a large one called "Leisure World," jokingly referred to by the surrounding populace as "Seizure World." The pseudo-science of geriatrics provides the ideology of old-age ghettoization, tacitly assuming that aging itself is a disease rather than a variable combination of the physical wearing out of the body with certain socially imposed attitudes about being old.

Of course, there are mental changes as the body ages, just as there are in other phases of life, though these are often in the direction of enhancement and maturity of vision rather than deterioration. I don't think my general view of life has changed much since it was formed during my twenties, but I have found in myself in recent decades a steadily more intent attention to the details of nature, a growing aesthetic appreciation of the savor of life and even of the elements of my own craft—thoughts and words. I am aware that my ear for language is sharper than it ever was, and I still feel even now, as all writers and artists must do if they are not dying on the vine, that my best work is yet to come. I hope it does.

But I also realize that the way to sustain my flow of creativity is not to mingle with old people just because they are old. I do indeed mingle with old people, but for good reasons other than age, either because they are my friends or because they are on the same kind of artistic and intellectual quests as I am. Otherwise, I still count my friends and associates among the whole field of people who share my interests; I still find in every new acquaintance the opening to a promising new world, which I am eager to explore if it shows interesting prospects. I steadily take up new projects. I have learned that while to some it may seem absurd to be old and in love, the essence of a good life is constantly to engage the absurd in existence, which then becomes the wonderful. If all this leads to anything, it is to the relationship between human life and freedom. If we are truly free, not bound by conventional ideas about the aging of the mind and the roles of old people, then we can still live to the fullest even though we are subject to the necessity of decay and, as Yeats would have it, are "tethered to a dying animal." For it is further true, as Yeats also said, that

> *An aged man is but a paltry thing,*
> *A tattered coat upon a stick unless*
> *Soul clap its hands and sing, and louder sing*
> *For every tatter in its mortal dress,*
> *Nor is there any singing school but studying*
> *Monuments of its own magnificence.*

I have talked only obliquely, and at the end, of death. And that is doubtless because I have walked through the valley of the shadow and to my surprise have feared no evil. Indeed, on a night when I hovered on the very verge of death I was given a dream that has guided my life ever since, teaching me the necessity of incessant and conscious choice, of incessant creation as long as one can continue to create.

I remember from childhood the hymn we used to sing in the little evangelical churches of the Welsh borderland, and which ended with the refrain:

> *Work for the night is coming*
> *When man shall work no more.*

I used to see "work" as "toil" and hate the hymn, but work for me is now creation, and I care not much what I do. I now like to believe that the writer of the hymn really meant that by the human activity of work the night was held at bay and that the night consists of nonworking, noncreating, hence nonbeing. In the same way I sense that creation defines and limits its own night, which is death, and that there is a sense in which, creating, we move out of time and therefore out of death. And of that earnest of eternity age cannot rob us until we ourselves surrender to the night.

Rosemary DeCamp

B. 1910

She was James Cagney's mother in *Yankee Doodle Dandy*, Robert Alda's mother in *Rhapsody in Blue*, Sabu's mother in *Jungle Book*, and Ronald Reagan's mother in *This Is the Army*. It therefore came as no surprise when Rosemary DeCamp, well-known character actress, suburban housewife, and mother of four, was named, in 1948, the "Mother of Distinction" by the Institute of Family Relations for doing "more to glorify American motherhood through her film portrayals than any other woman in the past decade."

In addition to the more than fifty films she has appeared in, DeCamp has starred in numerous television series, including "That Girl," "The Partridge Family," and the "Bob Cummings Show." Most recently, she has made guest appearances on "Love Boat," "Fantasy Island," "Hotel," and "St. Elsewhere." On radio, she was a member of the cast of the long-running serial, "Dr. Christian." She is also a nationally recognized enamelist whose works have been shown at several museums, has written newspaper columns and a book, and has been active in Democratic politics in California, where she makes her home in Torrance.

FROM THE DRAGONFLY
TO THE OLD LADY

When I think about the courage to grow old, which isn't very often, the only kind of courage that strikes me as necessary is the courage to grow old graciously—to forgo complaints, to stifle symptom-sharing.

Our youth and most of our middle years are spent like the life of a dragonfly skimming the water; we seek the sun, flowers, and food, unaware of the depths below or the sky above. We are glittering and beautiful, absorbed in self-needs and all the lovely surfaces. As the years pass, the dragonfly disappears, hopefully replaced by a being with enough curiosity to search the past, to ask the perennial questions: Who am I? How did I become what I seem to be? Way below, down deep under the surface in a pool rich with memory, answers and questions float and intertwine: love and discipline, sibling jealousies, mother, father, friends made and lost, circumstances, accidents wiping out security, cruelty, despair, love and luck, joy and death, roads not taken, places not visited, the beauty of faces . . .

And there too in this pool of reflection are the guilts—ugly, poisonous kelp, clouding the beauty of waters much deeper. Perhaps there is nothing more important than learning to excise these guilts. And yet to do so takes the same kind of courage we need to remember our virtues and kindnesses, the gifts we've given with love and generosity. If this isn't true for you, it certainly is for me. My Puritan-Episcopalian background finds it as difficult to praise myself immodestly for good deeds as to wipe out blame.

It was Socrates who first said, "The unexamined life is not worth living." If we've examined our lives and found some perspective, what lies ahead? How about our surviving children or grandchildren? Here, unless we were very lucky, we may need more courage than we can possibly hope to muster. And if we can't generate that, we surely need to generate some compassion and understanding. For our disappointments concerning the behavior of our children stem mainly from exaggerated expectations. "Oh, Johnny's such a student, he's going to be a lawyer." "Annabelle has a lovely voice. We're giving her all the lessons she can take." "Ronnie will get a football scholarship. Look at those shoulders." Who'd be prepared to admit that their children are nothing more than "average"?

But our children are not extensions of ourselves. They are people, separate and distinct. They are not alive to provide the successes we've missed. I told myself this over and over with each of our four daughters, but too often failed to follow my own instructions.

My husband and I share a figurative scrapbook library of frenetic and frustrating years in the rearing of our offspring. There is a lot of humor too. Some of the memories get funnier with distance: the fishing and camping trips, untangling trout tackle for ages four to fourteen, the thousands of miles journey into central Mexico with six in a station wagon during the big petticoat era. Then there was the Elvis period, the waterbed fixation, the Beatles sounds, and heavy rock. These memories may fade with time, but they did leave tidal marks and laugh lines.

We have friends driven to despair by their young with drug addiction, dropping out, running away, even suicides. One couple we know took a "survival course for parents"; another couple "sent their children packing." To quote the old plaint, "We brought 'em up and they brought us down." And we haven't entirely escaped our share of divorces, car accidents, citations, bail, and, of course, fortunes happily expended on schools, colleges, and universities.

Emotionally, in me, love and commitment to my children run deep. I wonder if men feel the same way. There is a thrill of belonging to a child that runs like a cord through my body, heart, and mind. It's frazzled and worn in some places, but stays elastic enough to survive through all kinds of crises. I confess that the thrill of cradling and baby-nuzzling diminishes when they begin to throw food and other objects, but the love lasts and, if we are lucky, is tinged with respect.

Grandchildren—how cute, smart, strong, sweet, etc.—seem to be an inexhaustible subject among my peers. But I must confess that I find other people's grandchildren boring. I do not want to see pictures of them or hear about their teeth or clever sayings. I suppose this highlights something of my own character. I have one grandson, an eighth grader. We enjoy watching TV and movies together. We both like Benny Hill and "You Can't Do That on Television." At this point that is about all we share—but laughter is the best bond.

Ogden Nash once wrote that "senescence begins and middle age ends when your relations outnumber your friends." I suppose that's where I am now; I can expect some surprises—not all of them chuckles. I held up my arm one day in the sunlight and was startled to see all the little crinkles in my skin. Who has been pasting crepe paper on my arm? No one. It's fun to try all kinds of creams and lotions, but they make little difference. The crinkles and wrinkles multiply, and we realize that all our tissues inside and out are changing. It is really quite wonderful that everything works as well as it does—swallowing, breathing, perspiring, weeping, laughing. How remarkable it is I sometimes think that despite the visible differences I've not been brought to a halt . . . yet.

At the risk of aping Pollyanna, I think my hearing loss has made me a more agreeable person. I really pay attention now to anyone speaking, look them right in the lips in search of their meaning and intentions. This is not only flattering but makes for a warmer and more accurate exchange. As a child I recall my numerous relatives shouting and yelling at each other, so my loss must be an inherited defect. Of course, in those days our marvelous little microphones hadn't been perfected. Grandpa could just tune me out with his little dial-on-a-box if I became too demanding.

I'm asked on occasion if actresses have more ego problems dealing with aging than do housewives or secretaries. I think they do. If an actress has been a great beauty, in this youth-oriented society of ours, she will suffer time's tricks less calmly. Also, female stars live in and out of mirrored lives. Few of them ever get accustomed to reality. And what could be more real than facing the transitory quality of life?

I think I was lucky because I didn't begin to work in pictures until I was thirty years old, which is long in the tooth for film. I had already received a B.A. and an M.A. from Mills College and had taught there my fifth year. As a character actress, I was "aged" in makeup until I could finally grow my own wrinkles and bags. However, I worked for so long and made so many appearences in TV shows and feature films that these bits and pieces keep circling the globe to appear in other countries. The fans, bless them, have grown familiar with my name or face. There is a flourishing business in the sale of old stills and addresses. Consequently, I still get glamorized photos of myself from faraway places with bits of money, stamps, or international postage. Vanity prompts me to reply: "We both know I never looked like this, but thank you sincerely . . ." They usually want a "now" photo, but that would hardly grace their wall, so I send along a fuzzed up picture of me as an improbably benign "Mom." The euphoric effect on me has worn off, though my ego is manifest in continuing this rather costly correspondence.

To deal with the advancing years I do a couple of things. One is to give myself little pep talks from time to time in which I affirm to myself that I've still got a purpose. "Don't complain," I say to myself. "You have a function here. Unload the dishwasher. Do the shopping. Make the salads. You are a part of an enclave. Fulfill your function, and don't grouse!" The other thing I do is to play games with myself and family to avoid some unpleasant task. "Darling," I say to my husband, "would you mind getting this and such for me? I'm a little tired." Or, "My hip is bothering me. Please take the dog for a walk. Poor thing really needs the exercise." This is game stuff. But as long as I'm not fooling myself, it doesn't matter to my family. They will play along or just say, "No, Mom, you need the exercise. YOU go."

My friend Shirley Gordon, author of many delightful children's books, keeps a notebook of useful quotes. The other day, I found one there from the psychologist, David Byrne, that startled me: "Action precedes motivation." Oh, no! This can't be true. Shirley said, "Oh, yes. I'll prove it to you. Go upstairs and find your motivation." So I went upstairs and found a number of things I had intended to do and proceeded to do them. When I came downstairs, Shirley laughed and said, "See. You had to act and then found your will to do." She was pretty smug, but I got the point. It brought to mind an old saying in a college psychology course: "See the bear. Run. And be afraid." So, emotions very often do follow actions. Clap, and you feel enthusiasm. Nod your head, and you begin to experience agreement. In short, when in doubt, act—and keep a positive frame of mind while you're doing so!

I often wonder, is fear essential to courage? Can courage trudge along by itself without the prod of fear? There was a year in my life which required a totally rash commitment of courage. It was in 1963, when the Cultural Affairs Division of the State Department, through some friends of ours, asked my husband and me to go to Pakistan. I was asked to teach theater and drama. My husband was to lecture on law at various universities. We accepted happily without sufficient cultural briefing. For months I memorized plays and planned courses in dramatic reading, poetry, speech, and pantomime. But as I read more of the Koran, I realized that we were about to enter a deeply religious society in which the representation of the human form was forbidden. This meant no sculpture, photography, or theater. In addition, most women could not appear in public unveiled. "Not to worry," I was assured. "English is the second language. Many women are liberated and modern theater productions are being performed with great enthusiasm." But my doubts grew when I read Pakistan's literacy figures—four to eight percent! Literacy in English closer to three percent. Plays with a large number of women in the cast (over two!) would be impossible to perform. Those clamoring for theater wanted Eugene O'Neill, Arthur Miller, and Tennessee Williams. Ah-ha! Modern are we? And male oriented.

Courage reared its head and came to a fine flowering when we arrived in Karachi, where I was informed I would have to perform a play and recruit students. This to take place three nights hence at an outdoor Cultural Affairs garden party. My husband helped me cut selections from three O'Neill plays in which I would play all the parts. I will never forget that hot night in the subtropical garden surrounded by turbaned and bejeweled nabobs eating sweetmeats or chewing betel nut. They remained impassive as I screamed and shouted my way through O'Neill's *The Emperor Jones*. At least they didn't laugh—probably not understanding why this middle-aged blond lady was so disturbed.

The next morning there were thirty-four students waiting for me in an old marble mosque in downtown Karachi. They must have enjoyed the racket in the garden. This teaching assignment repeated itself for months in eight different cities and was successful enough to leave behind a school in Lahore bearing my name.

I detail all of this because during that year courage was basic for me in each daily appearance. I had to psych myself up for every class and every piece of critical praise for those dear, often ill, ignorant, aspiring students. So I think the courage I exhibited in Pakistan was mainly based on fear of failure, fear of inadequacy, fear of hurting my country's image. Courage doesn't grow by itself, then, but has to be fertilized by fear.

In my own life, I have little to fear just now. But how about the man who rises daily to face debt and frustration and marches off to long hours of work he despises? At night he returns exhausted to repeat the whole process day after day, year after year. Now that is courage. Is he afraid? Or is he just conditioned?

The long journey from the dragonfly to a seventy-nine-year-old lady has been fascinating. But then, too, I think it is the only life I have lived. Courage for the crises was essential, but my overriding emotion is one of profound gratitude; gratitude for what I have been allowed to see, hear, and feel.

The most I can hope for is that this state of gratitude will remain until I am ready to depart. Until then, I will continue to remind myself of the importance of meaningful activity by reciting to myself an old, anonymous, and, probably, Oriental saying:

The young man said to the very old man, "What is your greatest burden as you grow old?" The ancient one replied, "That I have nothing to carry."

Sarah McClendon

B. *1910*

The Texas-born reporter, news service executive, and television and radio analyst is best known for her sharp, direct questioning of presidents, cabinet members, and other public officials. Since 1944 the questions she has put to nine different presidents have had broad impact throughout the nation. She forced Kennedy to clamp down on security risks in the State Department; brought pressure on Eisenhower for sending troops to Lebanon without first asking Congress; encouraged Nixon to clean out the entire Veteran's Administration for failing to send out Vietnam veterans' checks, and embarrassed Reagan for his failure to combat laws that discriminate against women.

Sarah McClendon currently operates her own news bureau, McClendon News Service, in Washington, D.C. She is the author of "Sarah McClendon's Washington," a syndicated column, and "Sarah McClendon's Report," a newsletter on people and events from Washington. She is featured weekly on ABC Radio's "The Michael Jackson Show" and has appeared on every major television talk show in the nation, among them "Meet the Press," "The Today Show," "Donahue," and "Crossfire."

Ms. McClendon is a member of the Hall of Fame of the Washington, D.C., Society of Professional Journalists, and has won numerous awards, among them the Media Award from the Veterans of Foreign Wars, the Public Relations Award from the American Legion National Commanders, and the Woman of Conscience Award from the National Council of Women.

NO TIME FOR A ROCKER

I never think of myself as an old lady, although I am seventy-eight years old. I keep looking at older people and thinking that they are "old," not I. I suppose I have developed some sort of mental approach to being a part of the present and therefore somehow feel ageless.

But I would not be young again for anything. I do not want to relive those experiences, any of them, with their uncertainty about the future. I would not want to relive the pain of the Great Depression. I would not want to relive President Roosevelt's death march, which I experienced on crowded Washington main streets. I would not want to relive President John F. Kennedy's death when we in the press marched behind the casket from the White House to the Capitol where he lay in state. And I hate to even think of the riots in Washington following Martin Luther King's death. Nor do I wish to relive the turmoil over the marches during the Vietnam War, or the sadness I felt when Richard Nixon departed from the White House.

I now work seven days a week, twenty hours a day, and I like it. I am fortunate in having a profession that permits me to work as an independent, to be my own boss and to be creative, which makes me happy. I can keep writing as long as my mind works and my fingers move. I realize that other people are not in such a happy profession, but I do feel strongly that they should keep working at something and keep up with current events. When elderly people cannot remain in a job, they can find all sorts of interesting public service organizations that really need their help. A good example are the elderly men and women who tutor school children in math and reading, and the many excellent foster parents or foster friends who serve the young as role models.

How does one face the realization that he or she is growing old? It does not require courage as much as it requires adjustments. Since I thrive on work, my greatest problem is coming to terms with the fact that I cannot work as much or as hard as I formerly did. I often say I wish there were two of me and that there were more hours in the day and two extra days each week so that I could turn out more work. What I do is get facts, check out information to avoid inaccuracy and contradiction, and then piece it all together into a story, much like a housewife puts a meal on the table, ready and hot.

There are certain things I must avoid in old age. If I raise my voice too loud or criticize too much or fuss too often about not getting all the information I want from the White House or the various federal agencies I cover, I would readily be declared a shrew. That would partly be due to my age. A younger person would simply be described as overly ambitious. Another thing I must be careful about is the way I dress and carry myself. I must look neat at all times, even though I'd rather let my hair down. I must hold my shoulders high, even though I feel the hump of old age.

I hate to exercise because I find it boring, but my brain works better if I keep the blood flowing. And exercise cuts down on my arthritis. (I remember my father at ninety-five saying that he had to walk every day or he would get stiff.) I also take daily vitamin pills and calcium tablets, and eat plenty of fruits and vegetables. I eat less red meat, more fish, and more chicken (minus the delicious, seasoned fatty skin). I must be careful not to fall when I walk since I have a highly successful artificial hip which I must protect. I still take lovely soaking foamy baths, but I am extremely careful when getting in and out of the tub. I always turn over on my stomach before getting out of the bath because this makes it easier for me to rise to my knees, grab the support bar, and pull myself up and out.

I won't sit in a rocking chair, since that is a symbol of wasted old age. I hope I will never find time to sit in a rocker. There are too many other interesting things to do.

I wish the government would help us more in developing long-range planning for the second life of the elderly: life after retirement, etc. I personally think that our government could help us much more. But so many people in this country are afraid of government because they have worked for it and seen its many faults. Others simply do not wish to be controlled in their individual tastes and consequently perceive government as a threat. Still, I have always thought that some inspired leadership could devise and then carry out a program that would enable the elderly to keep on being active and useful; that would cut down on loneliness, which is probably the worst problem the elderly face. The idiosyncrasies of the elderly arise from lonely living to a great extent, and this in turn makes them distasteful to younger people. So I think we need to invent jobs for the elderly or suggest ways for them to work for either fun or profit—or both. The great need is to have society using their talents so that nothing of value goes to waste.

I would start such a program by registering all the elderly in the United States under the guidance of the government. In this way we would know where they lived, how to get in touch with them, what they could contribute, what their physical limitations were, and what they would like to do. Along with this we could have a register of needs for talented elderly volunteers. They could check with this register to seek jobs and opportunities for productive living in late life.

Given what I've said, I believe that it is tremendously important for the elderly to organize for political power and clout. We need to sign petitions to pass new laws, to improve existing legislation, and to check on current regulations in the health field. We need to keep watch on congressmen and other public officials and must make our desires known.

The elderly could and should serve as mentors and guides to on-coming generations. We should guide young people to think always about how to improve life in this country, both political and private. We must ask them to reflect upon the heartbreaking scene of the home-less elderly sleeping on grates near government buildings; we must alert them to the discrimination against women which is prevalent in our society and which hits so hard on elderly women; and we must make them aware of the fact that increasing homelessness results largely from the inflation of home mortgages, caused by governmental policy.

During my life I saw poverty on the farm near my home, the biggest oil boom in history with its attendant rags-to-riches stories, much progress in health care, and considerable improvements in communi-cations. I have seen the nation go in cycles only to return, it seems, to the place where we started. What I perceive is the need for improve-ment, and this is what us talented oldsters must help bring about.

Robert Finkel

Frederick Franck

B. *1909*

Frederick Franck, whose drawings and paintings are part of the permanent collections of a score of museums in America and abroad, including the Museum of Modern Art, the Whitney Museum, the Fogg Museum, and the Tokyo National Museum, is an uncommonly versatile man. He holds degrees in medicine, dentistry, and fine arts. For three years he served in Africa, where he founded a dental clinic on behalf of MEDICO-CARE at the Albert Schweitzer Hospital in Lambaréné, Gabon. He was the only artist to record all four sessions of the Second Vatican Council (1962–1965).

His twenty-six published books deal with Africa and Albert Schweitzer, with the Vatican, with religious experience, and with his concept of drawing, among them *Days with Albert Schweitzer* (1959), *Outsider in the Vatican* (1965), *The Zen of Seeing* (1973), *The Awakened Eye* (1979), *Art as a Way* (1981), and *Echoes from the Bottomless Well* (1983), and *Life Drawing Life* (1989).

In memory of Pope John XXIII, for whom he has unbounded admiration, he converted the ruins of an eighteenth-century watermill near his house in Warwick, New York, into "Pacem in Terris," a "trans-religious oasis for reflection and reorientation." It offers a yearly series of chamber music concerts and stagings of Franck's contemporary variations on the medieval themes of the Play of Everyman, the Passion Play, and others.

"Pacem in Terris is not tied to any particular religion," says Franck, "but to all and to none, for I hope that it may also appeal to all who shun religious labels, but who just as intensely share in the specifically human search for meaning and for values to live by. It is meant for the inwardness, the quiet, and the freedom that is at our very center."

GOD DOES
NOT READ RESUMÉS

I was born in 1909 at that southernmost tip of Holland, which, like a narrow appendix, lies squeezed between the German and Belgian borders. It seems a providential spot to select for one's birth, for precisely here four cultures and four languages have met and mingled for centuries. Here, one becomes a polyglot by age four: we spoke Dutch at home, French about a mile to the south, a Flemish dialect to the west, and German half an hour's drive to the east. I began to suspect very early in life that borders are arbitrary lines and that similar humans live on either side.

The spot would have been even more providential if both world wars had not exploded here. I was five years old when at my grandfather's hand I stood, on that August day of 1914, staring at the proclamation I could not yet read, but which, Grandfather said, announced the mobilization of the Dutch army. Holland was to remain neutral in World War I, but the next bloodletting would not spare it.

As if it happened yesterday I remember watching from my attic window the town of Visé across the arbitrary line go up in flames, the constant booming of the Big Bertha guns, a zeppelin cruising like a huge cigar through the murky red sky. Then came the endless streams of refugees pouring across our border. For four years improvised ambulances, trucks, and pushcarts passed below our windows with bloody heaps of living flesh in the tatters of Belgian, French, and German uniforms. In churches and schools camped the wretched refugees, for whom our mothers cooked pea soup and porridge.

It was a strange childhood: safe, yet overwhelmed by horror. I was an inveterate hiker, a loner, who roamed through the hills on our peaceful side of the border, responding ecstatically to the glory of white clouds over meadows full of buttercups, daisies, and poppies, but bewildered by the constant alternation of this bliss with utter terror and powerless compassion. It made me allergic for life against all physical violence, all the avoidable cruelty to whatever is alive. I had read about some Japanese fishermen who begged forgiveness from the fish they caught, and of Red Indians and Bushmen who seemed to have a similar understanding of the sacredness of all life. Had we lost this completely, were we no longer human? "What is it to be human?" I began to ask myself. I am still in the process of answering this question, for we live to solve it—not in words, but in the process of living itself.

I shall add very little to this story of my childhood, for autobiography is a self-indulgent form of fiction, and my adventures are not so important. Suffice it to say that I studied medicine and dentistry, earned degrees from the universities of Brussels, Edinburgh, and Pittsburgh, and served in Australia as a consultant to the moribund colonial Dutch East Indies Government. After World War II I started private practice in an office off Madison Avenue. I did my utmost for my patients, but my interest in oral surgery was far from overwhelming. I had been tricked into the health professions by family tradition and manipulation, for art and "religion," in the widest sense, were my passions, as they still are. For some years I led a schizophrenic life: two or three days a week I was the respectable professional in a white coat, while the rest of the time I painted and wrote in a dilapidated Greenwich Village loft. I had my first one-man exhibition on 57th Street in 1942, had more shows, won some prizes, got somewhat of a name. But I saw my private practice as a pushcart operation and as far as art is concerned, the reviews, the prizes, the occasional museum purchases were very nice, quite wonderful for one's resumé, but man does not live on resumés alone . . . and God does not read them. I had to answer the question of my own human truth quite personally or else I would have lived in vain. It is as simple as that.

I was serving on the medical staff of Albert Schweitzer at his legendary jungle hospital in Lambaréné when the Grand Docteur was well into his eighties. Only while at Schweitzer's did my professional skills give me real satisfaction. I treated people in dire need who came paddling down the Ogowe in dug-out canoes, and the unfortunates from the leprosarium which Schweitzer built with his Nobel Prize money. But I did more. I drew and drew, and so I came to terms with African earth, with African faces. I penetrated and was penetrated by African ways of being human, for to draw is to become what you draw. Once, returning from New York, I carried thirty letters for Schweitzer in my briefcase. They had been written at the behest of a sixth-grade teacher at a public school in the South Bronx. I had gone there to speak about Schweitzer on an invitation I hesitated to accept until my wife, Claske, said: "If it had been the Sierra Club, you would have jumped at it." And so I talked to these thirty slum kids of whom not two seemed to be of the same genetic mixture and very few who grew up with both their parents. "You don't have to read all these," I said to the old doctor, "but may I drop them a line of thanks on your behalf?" "No," he said, "read them to me! These are the things in life that are really important." Then, bent over his table, I saw his arthritic hand start to write a long, warm letter to Bella, the teacher in the Bronx: "I know how hard a job yours is. I come from a family of teachers . . ." Puttering in his drawer, he found a photo of himself with his pet pelican and another with Peter, his baby gorilla, resting on his arm. "Send these," he said.

I thought that by this time I knew a thing or two about Schweitzer, but as I saw the old Nobel laureate laboring over that letter to the Bronx I realized as never before that this man, who had pushed each of his extraordinary potentials as a doctor, a philosopher, a theologian, a musician, to their utter limits, was a human being of awesome authenticity. Since 1913 he had been a pioneer: of foreign aid—without any political strings attached; of missionary action without the obsession of converting people; of a practical ecumenism that excluded no one; and, at eighty-seven, he once more pioneered: he was the first man of such prominence to protest loudly against atom bomb testing. He had solved the primal question: he had lived his own human truth.

I had returned to America when on October 11, 1962, I happened to read Pope John XXIII's opening speech to the Second Vatican Council, which he had convocated in order "to open the windows" of his Church. Angelo Roncalli, the son of poor peasants, was seventy-seven when he became Pope John XXIII. I was so inspired by the youthful vigor, the unconventionality of what he said, by his trust in humanity's future in the midst of the Cuban missile crisis, that I felt his Council might be a watershed in the dismal inhumanity of this century. I followed an overwhelming impulse, a blind urge, and flew to Rome. I would respond as the artist I happen to be. I would draw the drama and its main actors. It was not easy to gatecrash St. Peter's, for the Council was a tightly closed shop. But this outsider in the Vatican succeeded, and drew all four sessions from 1962 to 1965. Some eighty of these drawings now belong to the St. Louis Priory; another hundred are in the collection of the University of Nijmegen in my native Holland.

In 1963 Pope John died at the age of eighty-one, but only after having proven himself as a pope for all seasons, a friend to all people, within or outside his fold. All that happened since has failed to undo what this genius of the heart achieved, as he ripened into his ageless old age.

My third teacher in growing old instead of waning into senescence was Daisetz T. Suzuki, the Japanese Buddhist sage who almost single-handedly initiated the West into Buddhism, especially Zen Buddhism (according to Arnold Toynbee a historical event comparable in importance to the invention of nuclear fission). To Professor Suzuki I am indebted for confirming and deepening my profoundest intuitions about the ego and the True Self. When I met him in 1953 he was teaching at Columbia, a venerable octogenarian. In 1966, at the age of ninety-six, death interrupted him in the midst of writing another book. His essay, "The Unattainable Self," written at ninety, was the most profound and brilliant of his long career. Shall I have another ten years to follow his example? I'll act as if it were guaranteed . . .

A Protestant doctor, a Catholic pope, a Buddhist sage had shown me beyond all doubt that the art of "growing" old could be mastered, just as it had been mastered by Martin Buber, Einstein, Hokusai, and a great number of incognito fellow travelers on the Way.

What did they master, these human beings who seemed to have solved the problem of living and indeed "grew" old to bestow blessings on their fellow mortals? I think that perhaps I know: "A viable universal ethic," said Albert Schweitzer, "can only be based on Reverence for Life." It is indeed the opposite of this reverence, the blatant contempt for life, that is still adding daily to the hundred million corpses which sheer barbarity has caused in this century, and that is still inflicting unspeakable suffering on those countless living beings, calves, pigs, chickens, furry animals, who are bred, tortured, killed, desecrated by the antihuman technology of our factories of living flesh.

But then I reflect that Schweitzer's "Reverence for Life" is quite unthinkable unless seen in the context of what I call "the Specifically Human." There are namely a number of behavior patterns and brain functions, like self-awareness, foresight, imagination, and compassion that distinguish humans from all other species. My cat's genetic coding lets her be born as a cat to die as a cat. Our human genetic coding, apparently, lets us be born as not yet fully human, as "pre-human." It includes the potential, however; hence the life-task is to awaken fully to the Specifically Human at our core, notwithstanding the power of the reptilian and mammalian components of our brain that survive in us.

It is the overcoming of this reptilian component with its blind, murderous impulses that constitutes the fulfillment of our specifically human destiny. Significantly, the most recent evolutionary development of the human brain is that prefrontal cortex which empowers us to identify with, to feel empathy and compassion for other beings.

The three old men who keep inspiring me did not slide into their dotage, but kept on ripening into their own truth, transcending the barbarian, the reptile within, until their specifically human genetic coding was wholly actualized. Each one did it in the context of functioning as a doctor, a pope, and a philosopher. Each one proved that one may be too young to love, but never too old, as I am beginning to experience now: love for those who are close to me, for the trees around the house, for life itself becomes ever more intense and conscious. I feel no age. I may not run as fast as I once did, but I am not tired. Or rather, when tired of writing, I start to draw. When tired of drawing, I play my piano. Bach always refreshes me and I just discovered that playing Telemann equals a double espresso. My hand is still steady. It is not that I am "still" drawing, I draw more intensely than ever! My eyes still work and see more keenly, more deeply. I do admit to wearing a hearing aid. I don't really need it for Bach and Telemann, but I can switch it off to shut out pretentious chatter and exasperating musical junk.

I have just finished another book on seeing/drawing and still give my workshops on the Zen of Seeing. I bless the day I changed careers in middle age, for I still have dozens of these workshops scheduled in this country, Sweden, Holland, England. Each time it is a new delight to help people recover the lost art of seeing, to open their eyes again, so that instead of "looking at" the world around them passively, they see it again afresh, and discover their capacity to draw what they see, regardless of any previous art training. I shall continue to give these workshop retreats as long as I can, and shall go on writing and drawing, trusting it may be given to me to do my best work at ninety, and to have solved the primal question: "What is it to be human?"

John Rice

Dan Q. Posin

B. *1909*

❧ ❧

After earning his doctorate in physics from the University of California at Berkeley in 1935, Dan Q. Posin continued his work as an experimental physicist, concentrating his efforts on radar, microwaves, and the use of artificially radioactive substances in biology, agriculture, and research. By the close of World War II, however, he was deeply disturbed by the atrocities committed by the Nazis and by the power of the atom bomb, "harnessed to crematoria." From that time onward he dedicated his life to peace. Convinced that his friend, Albert Einstein, was right when he said that the fate of the earth would ultimately depend on the "decisions made in the village square," he began to deliver talks about the atom bomb and the conditions for world peace at every opportunity. He visited farmers, business leaders, PTAs, women's groups, Kiwanis Clubs—any group that cared to listen, Posin cared to address. As of this date, he has delivered over 3,000 such talks to groups around the world. In recognition of these many "village visits" he has been nominated six times for the Nobel Peace Prize.

In addition to his peace work, Posin has spent much of his life trying to

199

educate laypeople about the wonders of science. To this end he has written hundreds of articles for popular magazines and, for many years, was science columnist for the *Chicago Tribune*. He has also authored twenty-six textbooks and popular books on physics, astronomy, and chemistry, and has produced some of the most highly regarded educational television shows on science. He has won six Emmy Awards from the National Academy of Television Arts and Sciences for his broadcasts in Chicago, including awards as best educator in television and conductor of best educational programs. He has served as a science consultant for the *World Book Encyclopedia*, the *Encyclopaedia Britannica*, and the Columbia Broadcasting System.

Although he has lectured and taught at several universities both in the United States and abroad, Posin has spent the majority of his time at De Paul University, where he was professor of physics between 1956 and 1967, and at San Francisco State University, where he has served as professor of physics and astronomy since 1967.

Posin visits the "village" whenever possible and continues to teach at San Francisco State. "And I intend to stay," he says, "until they carry me out."

VISITING THE VILLAGE

When World War II ended, and my work on radar at MIT's Radiation Laboratory slowed down a little, I tried to organize a National Congress of Scientists to explore what could be done to prevent future holocausts such as those that had been perpetrated by the Nazis and atomic bombs. So I wrote to Nobelist Ernest Lawrence and to Robert Oppenheimer, both of whom had been my professors at Berkeley, asking them to come and be speakers and leaders at the gathering. I also wrote to Einstein.

Ernest replied that he preferred to return to his prewar work, cyclotrons and other such machinery used in unraveling nature's secrets, while Oppie did not reply—perhaps he was still beset with postbomb concerns if not badgered about going on with the H-bomb, the "Super." Einstein wrote that he would like to come to the Congress, but that the state of his health was not good. He offered, however, to do all he could to contribute to the work of the gathering and wrote a two-page letter for me to read at the opening meeting. But with all the principals unable to attend, the Congress died aborning.

I stayed on at the MIT Radiation Laboratory one more year—investigating the basic nature of radar waves—and then left for North Dakota to become chairman of the fledgling physics department there. While setting to work at Fargo I thought about Einstein's work on the unification of the forces of nature and wondered why not unification for humanity, for all the forces of the human species? I felt a deep need to explore and pursue the possibility of world peace through the assistance of the scientific method and a humanizing scientific spirit. And then, something specific happened, something which led me, perhaps subconsciously, to try to live a long time—I received an invitation to speak on war research to an engineering club in Fargo.

After the luncheon with the members of the club I gave my talk. I went into a thirty-minute performance of what nuclear energy is, acting it out, spontaneously, and as vigorously as I could. I tried to show how the Bombs work, and what they do to living things, particularly human beings. I talked about the only defense possible: the defense of the human spirit through the establishment of just world law for all humanity in a great unification.

One day I received a pamphlet from Einstein, who had formed a committee to spread information about the Bombs. The name of the pamphlet was "Only Then Shall We Find Courage to Surmount the Fear That Haunts the World." In this pamphlet, he wrote ". . . Our representatives in New York, in Paris or in Moscow depend ultimately on decisions made in the village square . . . To the village square we must carry the facts of atomic energy. From there must come America's voice . . ."

Now I would redouble my efforts, and gird up for the long run. There was much to do. There were many villages in the world. I had to live a long time. And so the years passed by, in a dream of villages, in a dream of faces, gatherings, a dream of questions, appearances, travel, teaching, travel, teaching, travel . . . villages . . . in the spring, summer, fall, in the snows of winter . . .

Slowly, in the early '70s, little by little, I found it desirable to take naps between classes. Sitting in a chair in my office was not good enough. So I brought some blankets and a pillow from home and laid them out on the crowded floor of my office between the sink and the desk. After setting the alarm clock I found rest, often oblivion, until the clock trilled the signal for the next class.

Now, in my eighties, I still teach full time, have not retired. And I intend to stay—until they carry me out. I teach four different courses, to a total of some six hundred students every year. In the astronomy course, my students and I set out on journeys to the villages governed by that nearby star, our sun—to the villages of the orbiting planets. In the class on the theory of relativity I journey with my students through the villages of Einstein's world, where, en route, we discuss the nature of the four-dimensional universe through which we pass while light and other electromagnetic waves come and go as the curved space-time undulates, signaling a happening . . .

We also make our imaginative journeys to the villages of Russia and America, where great scientific advances have been made in the construction of ingenious death-dealing devices: Uranium Bombs, Plutonium Bombs, Hydrogen Bombs, Neutron Bombs, Fission-Fusion-Fission Bombs. All this we study thoroughly together and then wonder about Earth and its destiny. We also study Star Wars Weapons: the laser beams, the X-ray lasers, the charged particle beams, the neutral particle beams, the kinetic energy missiles. In sadness, we ask together if science and technology are enough. Something seems to be missing. "All that is necessary for evil to triumph," wrote the British statesman Edmund

Burke, "is for enough good people to do nothing." So we think about that, too.

There is another group of scholars whom I instruct, and with whom I travel on my village journeys to the sparkling domains of honest science, honestly used. These are men and women between the ages of about fifty and ninety—the students of the Fromm Institute for Life-long Learning. To these scholars I present sometimes eight, sometimes sixteen lectures each year. Strikingly, the concept "old" is nowhere in the air at the institute. Though some of these students may walk more slowly than they did forty or fifty or sixty years ago, I get the impression that they are neither old nor growing old, but rather staying young. Perhaps I take on some courage from witnessing "elderly" scholars striving, and successfully, to stay in touch with the world.

I recall a case in point. Not long ago, the president of a fine university, a splendidly tall and rugged-looking man, a very busy man, retired after years of heavy service. And shortly after that he dropped dead. An eminent scientist at the university, terribly saddened, remarked in private conversation that "he stopped—and everything stopped."

But death eventually comes to all things that live, whether they "stop" or not. First, life, then death. As a physicist, I believe that life is a mechanism that defies the second law of thermodynamics, while death is the ultimate triumph of this law. What is this second law? It states, in effect, that all natural processes tend to degrade, to lower the levels of energy in every potent system, in an irreversible manner, unless the system is refurbished. A forest, for example, burns and spreads heat and gases far and wide. No energy is lost, but the fire-heat is diluted over the entire planet, rendering this energy less available for any powerful use. Physicists say that this unavailable energy increases as time passes, and they call the measure of the accumulation of this unavailable energy "entropy."

But living things do not allow their energies to be degraded completely. They eat and drink and replenish their energies. Thus, they defy the second law of thermodynamics. That apple which you eat does have its energy depleted, degraded—it is no longer potent—you have taken its power unto yourself. The apple has been made to abide by the second law, but the eater has defied it.

Life is a mechanism that defies the second law of thermodynamics as long as possible, and so I teach my students to defy this law in any way they can—to fight, in other words, for life. Better still, to fight for the lives of all peoples, for there is no shortage of edible or growable life-sustaining resources. There is only mismanagement of those resources.

Nevertheless, all living organisms experience deterioration of some sort as time passes; and the dynamics of defiance, the power and capability of defying the second law, gradually or suddenly diminish and eventually it is normal to come to terms with the second law, the law of aging. Living things do not lose the last fight against the law; they merely play out the game according to the rules of the universe. But it is good to play out the game with verve and strength and audacity and dignity and compassion toward our fellow beings. And, who knows, in the long run of the universe, out of the diluted energies, the faster atoms may regroup, and a new you might somehow return through a cosmic recycling. "It's a question of probabilities," I tell my students, "a question of how the atoms play out their game." Perhaps, too, as Norman Cousins—from another point of view—seems to suggest, it also has to do with how well *you* have played out *your* game. Thus, in some remote recycling, you or your friend may reappear in one form or another, as a blade of grass, or an oak, or a butterfly, or . . .

Stars, too, like everything else, have a life and death. All stars do two things while they live: they make energy, such as starlight, radio-type waves, and X rays; and, starting with hydrogen, they create all the elements, the atoms, that we know: helium, carbon, oxygen, phosphorus, copper, gold, tin . . .

The most massive of the stars, the supernovae, do all this creating relatively quickly, overheat, and explode, showering the space around them with vast clouds of their created atoms. The clouds of atoms swirl and twirl while the atoms of this stardust choose partners to create amino acids, the forerunners or building blocks of proteins, the molecules of life for biological beings. The twisting and turning and combining continues, eventually producing a modest-sized star with planets and moons. "Physicists and astronomers believe that our solar system was created in this manner," I tell my students. "From the stardust of one or more supernovae, everything in the solar system, including every living thing, is created. Indeed, all living things are bits of stardust, including you." One evening, I wrote a poem entitled "Child of the Universe":

You are a bit of stardust
Endowed with dreams.
The world, it seems,
Clamors for "reality"—
Draining your vitality
To live the dream.
Recall—"We are such stuff
As dreams are made on"—
Come, walk, with eyes
Fixed on the heavens
Whence you came—
Not progeny of Mars,
But offspring of the stars.

"How sad it is," I say to my students, "that very few people know this and do not sense the awesome grandeur of the creative act—the stars are for life—the heavens are for life." Immanuel Kant came very close to divining this fact long before the secret work of the supernovae was known when he wrote: "There are two things which fill me with eternal wonder—the starry sky above us and the moral law within us."

So a great fact remains largely unknown: the intimate connection between the labors of the stars and the dawning of living rational beings, who, at their best, look to the heavens, to their original mother. The starry sky and the moral law within us are as one. If only the movers and the shakers on Planet Earth knew and truly realized their wondrous celestial heritage, they might, just might, go to the village.

Alex Gotfryd

Margaret Cousins

B. 1905

❧❧

Margaret Cousins was born in Munday, Texas, to pioneer parents, and grew up in Dallas. For many years she pursued an editorial career in New York City, where she was managing editor of *Good Housekeeping* and *McCall's* magazines and fiction editor of *Ladies Home Journal*. At the same time she contributed short stories, essays, and poetry to other popular magazines. She is also a distinguished author of children's biographies. Her most popular book, *Ben Franklin of Old Philadelphia*, has been in print for more than thirty-six years. Others include *The Story of Thomas Alva Edison, Uncle Edgar and the Reluctant Saint*, and *Boy in the Alamo*. For her many contributions to American literature she was awarded the George Washington Medal by the Freedom Foundation at Valley Forge.

Margaret Cousins was graduated from the University of Texas at Austin, which recently named her Distinguished Alumna. In 1980 she was awarded the degree of doctor of literature by William Woods College of Fulton, Missouri. She makes her home in San Antonio, Texas.

ONE MORE ADVENTURE

In my childhood, the subject of growing old rarely came up. We were too concerned with our immediate survival to spend time thinking about the future.

I grew up in a small town on the great Knox Prairie in western Texas, the child of latter-day pioneers. Both my grandfathers were homesteaders whose families had gone west after Sherman marched to the sea and Lee surrendered at Appomattox. My mother had been brought to Texas from Kentucky in a covered wagon at the age of five months, a journey from which her own mother never recovered. My father had left home at the age of fifteen to become a cowpuncher and join the cattle drives headed north. Life was more difficult back then. It is hard for people today, who enjoy lengthened life expectancy, to realize the primitive state of medicine, surgery, immunology, and the paucity of resources for treating illness, which was commonplace in my youth. If my people considered the possibility of living to ripe old age I think they would have been more likely to approach it with joy than courage. Courage was mentioned those days only when concerned with the ominous—a funnel-shaped cloud or a rattlesnake.

I was fortunate enough to be born into a family whose members consistently stressed the basic values of a good life—morals, manners, respect for work and achievement, consideration for others, honor, truth, affection and love, discipline and self-reliance. I was consistently exposed to these and other philosophical principles, and my father had a profound determination about discipline and self-reliance in which I was thoroughly grounded with the aid of a peach limb. While I took a dim view of these matters at the time, I am eternally grateful for this grounding, for discipline may be more important at eighty than it was at eight.

Perhaps these beginnings account for the fact that I have never thought much about longevity. I have always had friends of all ages, and one of my best friends as a child was an elderly gentleman who had been a captain in Hood's brigade. He was a great storyteller and provided me with a bird's-eye view of the Civil War.

When it was finally brought forcibly to my attention that I was growing old I had neither the background, education, nor experience to cope with it. The corporation for which I had been working for several years retired me on the morning of my sixty-fifth birthday—the "automatic age," as specified in their pension plan. I reacted with outrage. My record reflected profitability. I was working actively with a large number of accounts, several of which showed lively promise. I was scheduled to leave on a speaking tour. I could not believe that this great company, almost a hundred years old, could manage without me! If I had ever read the pension plan, I had forgotten what it said. But I reread it and it was plain—automatic age! After a few screams, cries, and hot tears, I accepted the pension and flounced out to get another job. Needless to say, the corporation survived.

My new job provided me with a few years of fascinating experience in the workplace, but one day, when I was going along minding my own business, I was reminded of the unlikelihood of my becoming the first female Methuselah. Hastening across Madison Avenue on 55th Street in New York City, at high noon, my left knee buckled involuntarily, without warning, and I fell sprawling in the middle of the street, just as the lights changed to green for onrushing traffic. I believe my life was saved by a bearded street person who rushed into the street, held up his hands to stop traffic, and literally dragged me to the curb, whereupon he disappeared. While this gallant if undignified rescue was in progress, I remember thinking woozily, "Time to retire!" This instinct deepened when my doctor diagnosed the perfidious knee ailment as rheumatoid arthritis, which can only get worse.

The desire to maintain self-reliance encouraged me to carry out this decision to retire, made under stress severe enough to constitute an omen. To maintain my independence I felt that I must seek a simpler existence. For the first time, I experienced the necessity of courage as the fountainhead for old age. Courage persuaded me to examine the possibilities, make choices, devise new plans, and render accomplishment of them possible. Courage fueled optimism.

First I examined as many of the aspects of aging as I could ferret out. One of the most consistent and depressing attitudes seemed to be resistance to change. This mind-set on the part of the elderly cropped up in all my studies. Old people simply fear the unfamiliar. They do not want anything to be different. They want everything to be the way it was.

Change, of course, is intrinsic. There is no way to prevent it and no profit in fretting about it. It occurred to me that the only way to cope with change was to join it. When I retired, then, at the behest of my arthritis, I determined to change everything about my life. I decided to move to a place where I had never lived, where I had no contacts. I chose an old city with diverse cultures that had always attracted me, but which I visited only on holidays. I opted for an apartment in an old building, downtown, on the bank of a river, where there were few full-time residents. I decided to get rid of my car. Everything about my life underwent change. This took all my reserves of discipline and self-reliance, not to mention physical strength. But it accustomed me to change, sufficient to last a lifetime, and it challenged me to invent and build some sort of future for what must be euphemistically known as my "declining years."

I can truthfully say that the last decade since my retirement has been one of the most exciting periods in my whole life, and I am profoundly grateful for the experience. Sudden access to unlimited time and declining demands of activities and energies provided me with a long-lost opportunity to review certain aspects of myself and my modus operandi. A good many of these turned out to be mired in the concrete of habit. I had grown so accustomed to my ways of thinking and acting and talking that I was looking backward instead of forward. I had become conservative, conventional, and stuffy.

The necessity for acquiring new occupations and making new friends drove me to discovering new possibilities. I became a volunteer, exploring church work, docentship, public service, fund-raising for worthy causes, educational projects, literacy campaigns, animal rights, preservation and conservation, local politics, storytelling, and even babysitting. An energetic, effective, enthusiastic world existed, which for sheer lack of time I had never experienced. I never said no to any feasible suggestion.

Along with these things, which I found generally fascinating, I began to discover interests, about which most of my new friends were already aware—computers, word processors, audio, video, stereo, microwaves, cordless telephones, electronic marvels, modern music, postmodern art, minimal literature, aerobic dancing and exercise, fitness, running shoes, nouvelle cuisine! I won't say I liked all these earmarks of emerging culture, but at least I learned they existed and had mass followings. Inevitable change is always more a beginning than an ending. Late in life I was gifted with one more adventure.

Of course, there is no gainsaying the disturbances of old age—the stiffening joints, the declining faculties, the fading memories, the inescapable slowing down of every movement, the little flutters of panic, the unaccustomed fears. One's pride suffers at one's inability to stay the course. Hope wavers when it comes to exploration—the declining possibility of going and doing. Most devastating of all are the departures of the beloved ones, the boon companions, the long-term friends, the people who remember the same things we remember. Nothing recompenses us for these deprivations—nothing—and only courage can hold us together . . .

But then—consider the morning light, streaked with gold; the sickle moon dogged by Venus, the night sky, full of stars. Think of wildflowers swarming down a rocky hillside, the taste of ripe peaches, the sound of music. Remember the wild surf, breaking six times to the horizon, the faces of children, the undeviating loyalty of old dogs!

How could I get closer to this world? What could be more important? "World, World," wrote Edna St. Vincent Millay, "I cannot get thee close enough." My sentiments exactly.

Sam Nocella

J. A. Livingston

B. *1905*

Understanding the whys and wherefores of the American dollar—why it goes up, down, and what smart investors ought to do with the ones they have—has been the lifework of J. A. Livingston, nationally circulated Pulitzer Prize–winning economics columnist for the *Philadelphia Inquirer*.

Livingston began his writing career in 1925, working for a variety of newspapers in Brooklyn and New York. In 1930 he became investment columnist and editor for the *New York Daily Investment News* and by 1936 was economist for *Business Week*. Since then he has served as an economics columnist for a number of papers, among them the *Washington Post*, the *Philadelphia Bulletin*, the *Philadelphia Inquirer* and other papers. As far back as 1978, with his series, "The Decline of the Dollar: An American Tragedy," he has said that "the world wants to be shown that deficit spending is not the permanent American way." The continuing tragedy, as he has written repeatedly since, is that the world still has to be shown.

His writings have appeared in the *Saturday Evening Post*, *Nation's Business*, and *The Reporter*, among others. His numerous awards include three Loeb

Newspaper Awards for special achievement, the E. E. Fairchild Award from the Overseas Press Club for outstanding business reporting from abroad, honorary doctorates from Temple University and the Philadelphia College of Textiles and Science, and the 1965 Pulitzer Prize for international reporting.

AGING IN LUCK-SHURY

I t doesn't take courage to grow old, it takes luck—the luck of having parents and grandparents who handed down the physical strength to resist illness and the mental agility to profit from error.

That's personal luck. It's a stepping-stone to economic and social longevity. Impersonal luck also is required—the luck of not being in an accident in an accident-prone world.

What takes courage is fending off the lacks of aging. As of now, I'm lucky to have eyesight, physical mobility, and some hearing, though I need hearing aids. My lack—and it's a lack I need courage to overcome—is people, special people on whom I depend.

I write a twice-weekly column for newspapers on economics and finance. I've been doing it since 1945. To do it well, I have to accumulate persons with whom I can talk and think things over. They are government officials, university professors, lawyers, accountants, financial analysts, colleagues in journalism, and fellow economists. Alas, as I age, they decumulate. So I lose contacts. Hence, alas and alack!

I still feel the loss of my close friend, Karl R. Bopp, who was president of the Federal Reserve Bank of Philadelphia. He died in 1973. He was an economics philosopher. He was always willing to talk to me, but he also was always discreet. He would never reveal what Federal Reserve policy would be, but how he said what he said—his emphasis and deemphasis—helped me avoid judgments that would mislead readers. It's hard for me to believe that for fifteen years since his death I have managed to continue my column bereft of his grasp of economic trends and developments around the world.

I also miss Oliver Pilat, author of *Drew Pearson—An Unauthorized Biography* and *Westbrook Pegler—Angry Man of the Press*. He was a rival reporter on the *Brooklyn Eagle* when I was a reporter on the *Brooklyn Times* about fifty years ago. In later years, as a friend, he'd criticize my column at times, but more frequently he'd praise it. Praise from him was a stimulant, an incentive to continue, for his judgment was hardened by experience. I felt honored when chosen to reminisce about our experiences together at his memorial service in 1987.

I can think of several others whose wisdom, observations, and affability I miss: George W. Taylor, the great labor mediator, who died in 1972; Lawrence M. Stevens (1970), investment broker, with whom

I would exchange views on the stock market in between games of backgammon; and Leonard A. Drake (1961), who was for many years the economist of the Philadelphia Chamber of Commerce. After Drake died, the chamber ceased to have an economist. But why should I continue with my list of missing persons? It is better incomplete.

"A little society is needful to show a man his failings," wrote Robert Louis Stevenson. I'd alter "a little" to "a lot," and add that a lot gets harder and harder for me. Aging is a handicap. Persons in their thirties and forties, who would make ideal friends or contacts, don't cotton to octogenarians who are out of the bustle of hiring, firing, promoting, and recommending people. So it's increasingly difficult to acquire the society I need to show me my failings. And often, out of respect for old age, younger persons are too polite to be forcefully and honestly critical.

Finley Peter Dunne, creator of the Irish sage and philosopher Martin Dooley, said, "Old age is a disease like other infirmities and people are afraid they'll catch it from you. Besides, my notion of hell is having to outlive my friends, and mine are going fast."

In *The Theory of Moral Sentiments*, Adam Smith wrote that each man has within himself an "impartial observer" who approves or condemns his own conduct. In my work I require critics and judges to let me know if my ideas and thoughts need to be reshaped, revised, or accented. And, as Smith wrote: "The only looking glass by which we can measure ourselves is the eyes of other people." To measure my ideas I need the yeses and noes of others. Discussion, like great novels, poetry, and plays, is an intellectual grindstone that sharpens, smoothes, and widens understanding. And in this era of globalized change, I can't get along without it.

Will I become a worn-out columnist, like a prize fighter who knows little else than fighting and continues punch-drunk toward defeat and obscurity? Will I become word-drunk and idea-empty?

The treadmill keeps me occupied. It's what I'm habituated to and what I enjoy. I struggle for an idea, get one, do research, talk to people, put words on paper, rewrite, and rewrite, then edit and reedit before I finally type "30," the number journalists use to signify the end or finish of an article.

Prize fighters learn that they are through when boxing promoters don't find matches for them because people won't pay to see them perform. That could be my fate, and I hope that before the *Philadelphia Inquirer* and other newspapers signal that I'm ready for retirement by not using my column, I'll be perceptive enough to beat them to it. I hope self-criticism would dictate: "Joe, you're writing has deteriorated. You're no longer up to columning. Quit."

I'm growing old pleasurably because I'm doing what I wanted to do when I first learned to read a newspaper. I grew up in New York and was brought up on Walter Lippman, Heywood Broun, David Lawrence, F.P.A. (Franklin P. Adams), Westbrook Pegler, Grantland Rice, Don Marquis, Damon Runyon, and other great columnists. I'd say to myself, "If only some day I could be a columnist." And that I have been, and, at this writing, still am.

Forty years ago, it could be said: "As the U.S. goes, so will go the Western world." Then what the U.S. president said, other nations heeded. Today, when an American president talks, the heads of other nations listen, but it may not be in their interest to follow what he says. The U.S. is no longer the dominant frog in the world muddle. It's a big frog—yes, the biggest frog—but other frogs have gotten bigger and competitive. That has changed economics. America no longer is *über alles*.

I have to reorient to such a change. Treading on the treadmill—turning out nine hundred words twice a week—requires more effort when aging dequickens one's hands and mind. Words, names, and dates now escape me. Synonyms are not at the tip of my fingers on the typewriter. Names of persons I know well don't always come to mind. Even spelling becomes elusive. Alas, alas! Far away and long ago are the school days when I won spelling matches. Now I have to look up things I used to remember: the dates of presidents, the capitals of states, the unemployment statistics which came out only yesterday. I think of Frank Sullivan, who wrote me that he can distinctly remember what happened fifty years ago but not five minutes ago. Amid such debility, I sometimes think, "Why not t' hell with it, why not quit the grind and enjoy life?"

But would I enjoy?

When I was fifty-five and sixty I wondered: Would retirement leisure be a pleasure? Could I thrive both mentally and physically on an un-deadlined existence—gardening, going to museums, traveling, and so on? The more I thought, the less I thought of leisure. I still get pleasure out of my yesterdays and therefore want future yesterdays to be my tomorrows. But are the tomorrows deadlined?

In this era of radio and television, when people are apt to look and listen rather than read and think, I still obtain the multiple joys of columning—the joy of completing a piece, the joy of seeing it in print, and the occasional joy of having someone say, "Gee, Joe, that was a fine column." So there's past joy, present joy, and what I trust will be future joy—the joy of deciding what had been written was exceptionally good.

To be successful, a columnist has to "attach"—habituate—readers to his or her column. Changes in style and subject matter are necessary. Readers must occasionally be surprised, so that they pick up a column expectantly yet can't be sure of what they'll read. Frequently, I will have Dr. Rashonall, an economics professor I've created, testify to a Senate committee on why certain policies are desirable or undesirable. Sometimes I will let Alice-in-Wonderland characters deal with the nonsense of economics. And every month I do a column in which Bull, Bear, and Quandary debate: Is business good or bad? Is the stock market going to rise or fall? It always ends with Quandary in perplexity. It's universally popular, perhaps because when it comes to the stock market, people almost always are perplexed.

I'll resort to verse occasionally to enliven a column. In 1984, I began a column on computers as follows:

FEARFUL BALLAD

If I could overcome my dread
  I'd see if I could work it,
But dancing round and round my head
  Is "Relax, why not shirk it?"

Yes, I am scared, I really am
  And this is my enigma,
I'd like to take it on the lam,
  But that would be a stigma.

Though I can type and calculate,
  This box requires tutors,
I wish I could annihilate
  The makers of computers.

To live and not to be able to produce columns, that will take courage. Some afflictions of age I find tolerable—not being able to play handball, being less effective at badminton, and no longer desiring to swim regularly. But I enjoy dancing with Rosalie just as much, maybe even more, than when we were at the University of Michigan. Again luck! We're companions in aging. That gives me courage. We were married in 1927.

I received a letter dated December 25, 1987, from Vincent A. Ciaccia, of Philadelphia. It was a keep-it-up Christmas present. It said: "Your articles are of immense intellectual interest to me. They are a continuing education and I am enjoying a 'post' college course for free. My grandson, Paul, and granddaughter, Adrienne, are encouraged to read your articles whenever they can. Paul is on his way to age 18 and showing an interest in becoming a lawyer. Adrienne is just past 16 and has a natural talent for being an artist."

That has been my objective as a columnist—to educate and interest people in economics and to enlarge their understanding. That doesn't take courage, it takes desire, and I'm lucky that I still have the desire and that my column is still being printed. I've been living a life of luckshury. So it hasn't taken courage for me to grow older. I've had the good luck of being hale and being read. And on May 15, 1988, I was awarded an honorary degree of doctor of humane letters from the Philadelphia College of Textiles and Science. So I've also had the good luck of being noticed!

Bill Rettberg

Dr. Gairdner Moment

B. *1905*

꧁ ꧂

After receiving a B.A. from Princeton in 1928 and a Ph.D. in zoology from Yale in 1932, Gairdner Moment accepted a teaching and research position in Baltimore's Goucher College, where he became a professor of biology and later chair of the department. He served on numerous national biological committees, was a member of the Governor of Maryland's Task Force on the Siting of Nuclear Power Plants, an associate program director in the National Science Foundation, and secretary-general of the XVI International Zoological Congress in 1963. From 1960 to 1963 he was coordinator of the Voice of America's biology programs. He is now a guest scientist in the National Institutes of Health and on the Johns Hopkins Recombinant DNA Safety Committee.

Author of numerous research papers and several books, among them *General Biology* (1950), *The Biology of Aging* (1978), (with O. F. Kraushaar) *Utopias: The American Experience* (1980), and *Nutritional Approaches to Aging Research* (1981), Professor Moment is editor of *Growth*, a quarterly journal publishing original research on problems of normal and abnormal growth.

Primarily a laboratory scientist with a lifelong love of the out-of-doors, he has camped and hiked since childhood. He is a fervent believer in human unity and says that "a peaceful and prosperous world divided up on racial and national lines is an impossible dream."

ACCEPTING THE UNIVERSE

What is the secret of attaining the truly good life, the dolce vita vera, in old age? The same things, I am convinced, that generate a productive and thoroughly enjoyable career in the prime of life. By career I am not referring to any particular profession or occupation, for the career to which we are all born is life itself in its totality. The career of being a child or an adolescent is as significant as the career of being old, a well-tempered, that is, a strengthened and resilient, octogenarian. Each age should be ordered so that it can be lived and enjoyed to the full, whether one is enmeshed in action or, as Thomas Gray would have it, "far from the maddening crowd's ignoble strife."

Of the many factors involved in making that truly good life, none is as central as the confession made by Margaret Fuller, American transcendentalist, friend and associate of Emerson and Thoreau, literary editor of the *New York Tribune*, and ardent feminist. Margaret Fuller finally announced that she had decided to "accept the universe." Emerson reflected the view of many of his friends when he exclaimed, "By Gad! She'd better."

There are, of course, many ways of accepting the universe, just as there is more than one path that can lead to that well-tempered octogenarian. However, regardless of the path chosen, a key part of accepting our universe is to recognize that no one can fulfill his or her total range of potential. When Auguste Renoir was a youth in Paris painting porcelain and window shades and singing in the cathedral choir on the side, no less a musician than Gounod saw great musical talent in him and tried to persuade him to study music. Whether or not Renoir had a struggle in making his choice, he chose one profession and one profession only as the vast majority of us must.

Like many young Americans of the 1960s, I have longed to own and operate a small generalized farm. My desire was further fed by the fact that I knew of exactly the place where an old farmhouse stood close against the foot of a hill and facing a valley with productive fields crossed by a sparkling stream; beyond it, a range of mountains. Such an idyllic career might have been possible for me, a happy and chronic workaholic, but what of my desire to become a professional biologist, or a carpenter, or owner of a small summer hotel? These are high among the kinds of problems that make college, especially the freshman year, so stressful. Consequently it is essential to recognize that the wonderful thing about life is that it does offer a large variety of choices. So when you attain your eightieth birthday it doesn't make sense to chastise yourself because the road not taken might have been better. It also might have been worse for you and in entirely unexpected ways. Accepting the universe includes accepting the past.

In my own boyhood I saw at close hand two men who accepted the universe, my grandfathers. One was a Methodist preacher whose parents were born overseas, while the other was a Connecticut Yankee, one of whose ancestors took up arms against his king and who believed religion was a lot of nonsense. What I noticed about these two men was that they were very much alike despite different backgrounds and religious opinions. Neither smoked, drank, or swore. Both were caring husbands and fathers. Both had five affectionate and admiring children. Neither was interested in organized sports, but both were enthusiastic fishermen. They were realists, and perhaps that is why there was never any confrontation between them. I remember my grandfather Bostwick pointing out, as only a realist could, that if people had to pay money to get dandelion plants for their lawns as they did for crocuses, they would appreciate how truly beautiful dandelions are. Each enjoyed the line of work he had chosen and each worked until within hours of his death, both from heart attacks in old age.

I think they were both right in part and both wrong in part. Neither had the whole "truth." Who does? Put together, the message that I inherited from these two men is simple: The world is a magnificent place where it is possible to live a triumphant life in love and honesty, gaining strength from Christian values as seen after two thousand years of accumulated experience. I also learned that the truly good life is possible without the heavy overload of myths and superstition that many religions carry.

Like a host of people, I do not think of ultimate reality in terms symbolized by an old man with a beard walking in a garden with a talking snake. Rather, I expect to return to the clay to which poets have long said we shall all return. Even "Imperial Caesar, dead and turned to clay," as Shakespeare says, has no exclusive rights over that deep universal embrace which will receive us all. From time immemorial, clay has been a symbol of the creative power of the potter. In our own day we have discovered what a truly remarkable substance it is. Clay is found in many varieties, yet all clays are silicates; silicon chips, the heart of modern computers, are a product of clay. It now appears from new and pertinent evidence that latent among the incomparably wonderful properties of clay lie the origins of life itself.

Happily for me, I am one of those, as William Cullen Bryant wrote in his American classic "Thanatopsis," "who in the love of nature holds communion with her visible forms" and has heard some of her "various language." If I have not caught a falling star as John Donne urged, I have at least held out my hand to catch a snow starlet and held an emblem of eternity in my palm. Snowflakes do not evolve. They are the same today as billions of years ago and there is every reason to believe that they will remain the same as long as the world shall last. If water ice forms on some planet of the farthest star we can be sure that the snowflakes there will have six points and not any other number.

Not everyone can see with William Blake, "a heaven in a wild flower or a world in a grain of sand," but all of us can understand that every grain of sand is a full participant in the vast system of planets, asteroids, and comets that circle the sun. Thus I am assured that all those I love and I myself, indeed the whole splendid phenomenon of life, are an expression of something as deep set in the fabric of the universe as the lightning flash or the silent colors of a rainbow. Arising from those deepest levels of reality, we are the thinking dust that dreams, and in that dust our conscious selves flow back into that immanent God in whom, as St. Paul explained to the Athenians, "We live and move and have our being" (Acts 17:28).

Acceptance of this perception of the world does not mean anyone should think, like the fool in Psalm 14, that there is no God and therefore anything goes. Far from it! Whatever your conception of the nature of Diety, everyone can agree that the human race is social and like any social creature is provided with inborn attitudes and behaviors that make social life possible. Social life requires some mutually accepted framework of behavior. From the evolutionary standpoint, social chaos doesn't work. Go to the ants! Go to the baboons! Go to the wolves! All live in structured societies, different, but with structure nevertheless.

One of the commonest of the destructive results of failure to accept the universe is the "Why me?" syndrome. It afflicts especially the middle-aged and older and robs us of the contentment we should rightfully have. I have heard the Reverend Dr. C. R. Shallenberger, chairman of chaplains at the Johns Hopkins Hospital, say that "Why me?" was by far the most frequent question he was asked by patients and their relatives. It is asked as insistently by Jews, as Rabbi Harold Kushner relates with great poignancy in his book, *When Bad Things Happen to Good People*. Such questions arise endlessly, as when a daughter is the only one of five teenagers killed in an auto accident; or when, in the prime of life, it is found that the head of a family has inoperable pancreatic cancer; or when a child, happy, loving, talented, is the one in a thousand to develop a devastating brain fever from a common childhood disease; or when a long-wished-for child is born with hopelessly defective eyes. Such tragedies lay hold on the heart and refuse to let go. Yet they do not justify survivors torturing themselves with vain regrets or an overwhelming sense of sin that can poison the rest of life.

Of course life can never be the same after a tragedy, any more than it can be the same after a great joy. Those who do permit tragedy to poison the rest of their lives should read how one of the greatest of religious teachers expressed his acceptance of the universe. A group of followers of Jesus, on seeing a man blind from birth, asked, "Rabbi, who sinned, this man or his parents, that he was born blind?" Jesus answered, "It was not that this man sinned, or his parents" (John 9:2–3). Jesus then turned to the task of healing. There is a similar statement in the middle of the Sermon on the Mount shortly before the Lord's Prayer is presented: "Your father who is in heaven . . . makes the sun to rise on the evil and on the good, and sends rain on the just and on the unjust."

The people who blame God when bad things happen to them never seem to turn the situation around. Who are they to say that they or their friends are so virtuous that no evil should befall them? Have they never heard the voice of the Almighty asking them, as he asked Job when he complained about the world's design, "Where wast thou when I laid the foundations of the earth? Who determined its measurements? On what were its bases sunk?" Such people, whether Jewish, Christian, or Islamic, seem to have forgotten the many prayers in which they profess to be miserable sinners unworthy of so much as the crumbs of divine favor, the complete servants of God.

Endless regret for the road not taken or a sense of guilt for ancient wrongs can have a multiplier effect on events that will shake anyone with normal human feelings and produce a damaging depression. In the loss of a cherished ability, perhaps athletic or musical, or the loss of a good friend or a child, accepting the universe means accepting the time you were gifted with whatever talent was yours, or accepting the time you knew that dear friend or held your child in your arms and rejoicing in it anew.

Unfortunately, even the best of octogenarians can become unable to care for themselves, and be left cold, neglected, and lonely, utterly wretched with aching bones and aching hearts. Here is where tempering throughout life, in its joys and fires, even vicariously, can confer that high perspective which enables mortals to see life steadily and to see it whole, a vision that can ease the aching heart if not always the aching bones.

A crushing sense of depression can occur without tragedy and despite achievements and honors of undeniable authenticity, as I have found not just in my case but also in the experience of several others I know well. At such times I remind myself that I have had a successful career and have been honored for my contributions numerous times. I even had a building named for me, an honor usually reserved for the deceased! I joke with myself that it is an impertinence for me to be alive. Still, I wake at night desperately worried, although sometimes I can't remember what I'm worried about! And this all occurs surrounded by the support of a warm and loving wife and our affectionate children. Just to write it down shows me how absurd such feelings really are.

Many individuals have a variety of home remedies for depression. These include a warm shower or tub, a sound sleep and the avoidance of fatigue, a list of jobs to be accomplished, supportive music, a lump of sugar with a drop of peppermint oil. For me, none is more effective than continuing the work of Adam, cultivating our garden.

Accepting the universe also means having the courage and the good sense to accept the human time frame. The myth that indefinite duration, either here or in another world, is the determinant of value and that without it life has no value is understandable but simpleminded. Is a lily for a day worthless? Should sunsets be canceled because even the most glorious don't last forever? Does not the delicate red and gold columbine, growing among the rocks, hold its own with the giant two-thousand-year-old redwoods? Each snowflake is unique in its loveliness, its life spans but an instant of a circling year, yet it bears the imprint of eternity. I remember that in a similar way each of us is unique, in our case by virtue of the many millions of possible genetic combinations made possible by our genes, and that, however brief is the life span of a snowflake or a man, both of us are expressions of the deep-set properties of our universe.

The world we live in is a place of continuous change, of process. The continents are in constant motion, separating and colliding, sending earthquakes across the land. Mountains arise and are eroded into plains. New animal species appear and become extinct. Perhaps Margaret Fuller accepted more than she realized when she accepted the universe.

We have no choice but to accept the turbulence of the world of nature. Only in its human realm can emerging love make a significant difference. Over two millennia ago Sophocles correctly realized that "of all the wonders known to man, none is more wonderful than man himself." Therefore let us rejoice that in our own brief lives there is time to be both spectator and participant in the processes of a universe that expresses itself in a bewilderment of wonders. More than that, there occur in many lives experiences, revelations, or epiphanies that are so soul fulfilling that they leave the conviction that life is now complete although not necessarily over.

I see no good reason to echo the cry of Dylan Thomas, "Do not go gentle into that good night, Old age should burn and rave at close of day; Rage, rage . . ." Much less will I follow the destructive course of Captain Ahab, shouting defiance at the skies and fruitlessly driving the *Pequod* and her crew, save one, to their deaths at sea.

Rather, I have looked out upon the far horizons of the world, and at the vast realm of life arising from the clay beneath my feet, and recognized my home. Then, Bryant's "Thanatopsis" comes to mind, declaring that anyone "who in the love of nature" has heard her "various voices" has no need to go, driven "like the quarry-slave at night," but can "approach the grave like one who wraps the drapery of his couch about him and lies down to pleasant dreams." That great mother of us all, the earth, will receive each one of us in her transforming and creating embrace.

William I. Nichols

B. *1905*

❧ ❧

The veteran editor and publisher says that "as the years go by I often think back to a line from an old insurance company ad: 'Never complain about old age—it is a privilege which is denied to many.' "

Of old New England background, Nichols graduated from the Milton Academy in 1922, and from Harvard magna cum laude and Phi Beta Kappa in 1926. He attended Balliol College, Oxford (1926–1927), where he was a Rhodes scholar. He then served as dean of freshmen at Harvard (1927–1929), as publicity manager for the National Electric Power Company (1929–1932), as director for electrical development for the Tennessee Valley Authority (1934–1937), and as the editor of *Sunset* magazine (1937–1939). In 1939 he became the managing editor of *This Week* magazine, a Sunday weekly that appeared for several decades in as many as forty metropolitan newspapers and reached, at its peak, more than fifteen million American families. Upon retirement from *This Week* in 1970, he had served as either editor or publisher for over thirty years. Since 1970 his time has been divided between Paris and New York.

A close friend of the late Herbert Hoover, Nichols edited two of the president's books: *On Growing Up* (1962) and *Fishing for Fun* (1963). He was also the editor of *Words to Live By* (1948) and *New Treasury of Words to Live By* (1962).

Mariethé, his "beautiful and brilliant wife," was born in Czechoslovakia, lived in France, and then after a year under Nazi occupation, escaped to the U.S., where she met Nichols and married in 1942. There followed what Nichols describes as "forty years of a joyful marriage and then four years dimmed by the slow, relentless twilight of Alzheimer's disease." Mariethé died in 1986.

Although he is willing to concede that "growing old has many compensations," Nichols believes that "the saddest and hardest part of aging is the loss of those one loves."

LETTER TO A FRIEND

Coincidences work out in surprising ways. On the same day, and in the same mail, I received two letters. One was from the editor of this anthology, asking me to write something on some aspect of growing old. The other was from a longtime friend, neighbor, and college classmate—now over eighty as I am—telling me of his wife's long, painful death.

I have decided that I can do no better than to answer both letters with the same reply. To understand what follows, you should know that my wife, Mariethé, died a year ago, after forty years of joyful marriage and then four years dimmed by the slow, relentless twilight of Alzheimer's disease. My friend's wife, also long an invalid, died some months later. His letter showed that he was still in a state of shock and, perhaps unconsciously, seeking comfort and help. Here, slightly edited, is my reply:

Dear Frank,

It gave me a warm feeling to think that you would write me as you did, especially since back in our college days we hardly knew one another. It is only, now, some sixty years later, that we are united by a force much greater than a dozen class reunions.

For me, October 21st will be the first anniversary of Mariethé's death. According to the people round about, I have made a "fine adjustment." I am glad they think so, for that is what Mariethé would have wanted. She had no patience with glum and mournful people. "Des rats morts," she used to call them. But, inside, the fact is that I still think of her and miss her more and more. She is always with me. Sometimes, alone, I find myself talking to her as if she were still here.

Increasingly—and more vividly—memories of the "good years" come tumbling back. In one way this makes me glad. It is a reminder that, compared to many others, I am fortunate (as are you) in having so much happiness to look back on. But then, with memories come moments of sharp reaction and pain: "Where is she?" "Why isn't she here, and with me NOW?"

Here is one way I have found to help cut the pain. It is very simple. Almost a trick. Everything in the apartment is exactly as it always was. Mariethé planned it and loved it. Often toward the end, but when she could still walk, she would say: "Let's look at OUR house!" Then, arm in arm, we would walk through each room, remembering the objects, one by one. I say "everything as it was," but there is one exception: in a corner of the bedroom I have kept the hospital-style reclining chair where the nurses placed her for several hours each day. Now, whenever the sadness hits, I look at the "relax"—as French nurses call it—and thank God that she isn't here and that her suffering is finally over.

Which brings up something else. In your letter, you spoke of going to "ten different churches." I know all too well why, as I have done the same. But this much I have learned from my visits: there is not much that any priest can say, and even less any pastor, which can give us what we want, which is to break through to what Mariethé always called "The Other Side" and to feel that we are still "in contact."

Again, I have found a solution, though it may sound strange to you, especially if you still think of me as a Waspy descendant of three generations of Unitarian ministers. Much later, at the time of our marriage in 1942, I became a Catholic. Not a very good one, for the new Mass has, for me, taken most of the holiness out of the regular observances. But in the meanwhile, the good part is that I have discovered, and made friends with, Saint Anthony of Padua, who is the best, kindest, gentlest, most understanding, most practical, and most believable of all the saints. I doubt if there is a Catholic church or chapel anywhere that does not have a statue of him with a little child in his arms, surrounded by lighted candles.

Even during the good years, we both had the habit of dropping in at Saint Patrick's Cathedral in New York to "talk with Saint Anthony." Mostly, then, it was about immediate problems—lost objects, job problems, selling our place in Vermont, etc. The same thing during our trips to Europe. Once we even made a stopover in Padua. His tomb was there. Mariethé called it his "headquarters."

It was all in fun then. But later on, it was different. During the final illness, I found myself going almost daily to light a candle, and always with the same prayer: "Please, Saint Anthony, cure her. But if that is not possible, then please take her." And he did—just at the moment when the very worst was about to begin.

And now, with Mariethé gone, it is as if I were impelled by some outer force. Almost automatically, I still go and light my candle and, along with my prayer, actually feel as if I were talking to her—through him. With that comes a wonderful sense of calmness and strength.

By now these visits have become a sort of necessity. Wherever there is a church, I drop in. Last Monday, it was the glorious cathedral in Cologne. Now, back in Paris, it is the next-door church of Saint Germain-des-Près. But it can be anywhere. There is even a church across the street from my dentist! One is never out of touch.

There is something else which has sustained me. In our bedroom is a bookshelf wall. One long shelf there contains only small, framed photographs. Some are of Mariethé, of course, some of us together. But dominating the shelf are many pictures of our dearest friends. Pictures through the years, very informal, taken in all sorts of places and with an infinite variety of costumes and postures. It faces our bed—and so it is the first thing I see in the morning, the last thing at night.

Most of the friends in those snapshots are gone now—to Mariethé's Other Side. Soon the rest of us will be going, too. But it really isn't necessary for us to take time out to debate the exact nature of that Other Side. Let the theologians worry about the specifics of heaven and hell and the sex of the angels. All we need to know is that the people we love—those deep in our memories and our hearts—are waiting for us there. Yet at the same time, they are also with us here. This is the miracle. The miracle of love.

The French sum it up in the saying: "One who loves, lives forever." Even better, I think, are these words which the sculptor Ivan Mestrovic had engraved on a cathedral bell:

> Learn the secret of Love, and you will discover
> the secret of Death—and belief in Life Eternal.

So, dear Frank, so much for me. Perhaps too much, and too personal. I suppose all I really wanted to tell you is that you are not alone.

With all my best,

Bill

Fred Schulze

Harry Lee Shaw

B. *1905*

❧ ❧

The well-known editor, writer, and teacher has contributed widely to national magazines and is the author or co-author of twenty-three books, most of which are in the fields of English composition and literature. His best-known books include the *Dictionary of Literary Terms* (1972) and the *Dictionary of Problem Words and Expressions* (1975). For a number of years he was director of the Workshops in Composition at New York University and taught classes in advanced writing at Columbia. He has worked with a large group of writers in the Washington Square Writing Center at New York University and has been a lecturer in writers' conferences at Indiana University and the University of Utah and a lecturer in, and director of, the Writer's Conference in the Rocky Mountains sponsored by the University of Colorado. In 1969, he was awarded the honorary degree of doctor of letters by Davidson College, his alma mater.

In addition to his work as a teacher and lecturer, Shaw has had a distinguished career as an editor. He has been managing editor and editorial director of *Look*, editor at Harper and Brothers, senior editor and vice-president of E.P. Dutton & Co., editor-in-chief of Henry Holt & Co., director of publications for Barnes & Noble, and editor at W.W. Norton & Co.

A TOTAL COMMITMENT

At the age of five I received my first intimation of mortality. I was playing in my front yard with an older companion when a funeral cortege passed by. We interrupted our play to watch the solemn procession. I was puzzled by the sight and asked my friend for an explanation. He told me that an old man whom we both knew had died and was being taken to a cemetery for burial.

That confrontation with death and its association with old age would trouble me, even torment me, for half a century. Time out of mind I would shudder to think of advancing age and its connection with death and burial. Again and again I said to myself these lines from the poet Andrew Marvell:

> But at my back I always hear
> Time's wingèd chariot hurrying near;
> And yonder all before us lie
> Deserts of vast eternity.

Decade after decade I struggled to keep youthful, to cheat advancing years. I watched my diet and weight, I exercised regularly and strenuously. I played tennis summer and winter. I walked, I jogged, I rode a bicycle, I swam. I persisted in deluding myself that I was younger than my years. Whenever possible, I sought the company of persons younger than I. When I remarried I was fortunate to win the hand of a woman years younger than I. I fathered a girl and boy when I was approaching the age of fifty.

Instead of facing oncoming years with courage I met their steady and inexorable approach with disdain and ever-present fear. I tried to conceal my age, refused to acknowledge it, and deplored any mention of it by family or friends.

As the years mounted, I became increasingly dissatisfied with my life. Materially and physically, all was well, but in mind and spirit I grew more and more despondent and even hopeless. Slowly and hesitantly I began to seek solace for my growing depression in the use of alcohol. My work as an editor and publisher provided many opportunities for drinking, and I gradually proceeded from a nondrinker to an occasional drinker, a social drinker, a heavy drinker, a problem drinker, and finally into outright alcoholism. With the cunning and deception of an addict I successfully managed to compensate for my illness and to perform my duties well enough to avoid the dismissal that my conduct really merited.

Descent into the bottle provided no panacea, and I grew ever more dispirited. I sought help from two general practitioners of medicine, a psychiatrist, and from the minister of my church, which I doggedly continued to attend. As I grew increasingly miserable I slowly became reconciled to sinking into old age and inevitable death.

But then, some twenty-five years ago, a miracle occurred. A friend who was well aware of my predicament and who had conquered his own addiction, took me to a meeting of a program designed to help alcoholics achieve sobriety.

I was immediately impressed with the friendliness, the fellowship, of the assembled group of men and women. My friend, who later became my sponsor, took me to meeting after meeting. I stopped drinking and began to hope that I could stay stopped. I found warm and caring friends at the meetings I attended, loyal and close friends who encouraged me, supported me, and kept me dry and sober, day after day.

The recommended steps of this program became an integral part of my life. I came to believe that a power greater than myself could restore me to sanity. I decided to turn my life and my will over to the care of God as I understood the concept of God, although my belief in a divine power had withered and my understanding of God bordered on agnosticism if not atheism. I attempted to take stock of myself by making a moral inventory of my assets and liabilities as a human being. I admitted to myself and to others in the program the nature of my wrongs and shortcomings. I decided that I was ready to have a power greater than myself remove my character defects and asked that they be taken away. I made lists of people whom I had harmed and tried to make amends to them, except when doing so would harm them or others. I learned when I was wrong to admit my error. I tried through meditation to improve my attitude toward God as I understood Him and asked for guidance. Having had a spiritual awakening as a result of trying to take and live these steps, I attempted to carry a message to other similarly addicted persons and to practice these principles in all my affairs.

This awakening revolutionized my life. I began to take a genuine interest in others, both alcoholics and those who were unhappy or depressed for other reasons. I made it a practice to see and talk with other alcoholics every day of my life. I welcomed the opportunity to carry the message of sobriety to persons who were still addicted. I took individuals who expressed a desire to stop drinking to meetings of the program. And, whenever asked, I spoke at meetings of my own experiences with alcoholism and sobriety. By focusing on others I gradually became less and less concerned with myself and with what advancing years were doing to my body and mind.

Instead of viewing life as a grim, gray monotony, as "merely one day after another," I began to live each day as if it were special. I tried to embrace the thought expressed in a prose poem by the 4th century A.D. Indian poet and playwright Kalidasa entitled "The Salutation of the Dawn":

> Look to this day
> For it is life,
> The very life of life.
> In its brief course lie
> All the realities and verities of existence:
> The bliss of growth,
> The splendor of action,
> The glory of power.
> For yesterday is but a dream,
> And tomorrow is only a vision,
> But today, well lived,
> Makes every yesterday a dream of happiness
> And every tomorrow a vision of hope.
> Look well therefore to this day.

But as I grew in sobriety and found my temporal life taking on new and vivified meaning, I began to feel that I was missing spiritual growth and dedication. I missed, and missed poignantly, the faith, the firm belief in God which I had had as a child and as a young man. The concept of "God as I understand Him," frequently mentioned by fellow recovering alcoholics, was virtually meaningless to me. I deplored my lack of belief but could not bring myself intellectually to accept and subscribe to a divine power.

And then, after more than twenty years of sobriety, I experienced another miracle. A lovely woman, a close friend of my wife and of me, suggested that I attend a religious retreat. I demurred, but because I was so eager for renewed faith I finally agreed. This friend took me on a Thursday night to a session of Tres Dias and left me there. And for three days and nights I lived a remarkable life.

The Tres Dias movement began in Spain after that country's civil war. Its originators were devout Roman Catholics who were devastated by the destruction of their churches and the loss of spiritual guidance as a result of war. The movement, known as "Cursillo," was brought to the United States by a group of Spanish Air Force officers training during World War II. The movement became ecumenical, was opened to Protestants, and became known as Tres Dias.

At the retreat I attended, a group of thirty men, called "candidates," was immersed hour after hour in inspirational talks, prayer, meditation, and spiritual fellowship. We were led, instructed, and encouraged by an equal number of men who had been on previous retreats and who had renewed their faith in God and Jesus Christ.

For three days and nights we were totally isolated from the outside world. No newspapers, television sets, or radios were available. We were asked to put away our watches and were advised to make and receive no telephone calls. Our focus was entirely on God and Christ.

As a result of this three-day experience I found myself once again possessed of a firm faith and with renewed belief that life could be worthwhile and rewarding. My activities in and out of the program for alcoholics took on a new meaning as I came to realize that my sobriety was really a gift from God. Each day since that retreat I have been encouraged to face advancing years with a heightened degree of calmness and fortitude.

As the shadows lengthen, I receive inspiration and courage from several selections that I have memorized. I find myself daily murmuring the words of the prayer attributed to St. Francis of Assisi:

> *Lord, make me an instrument of your peace.*
> *Where there is hatred, let me sow love,*
> *Where there is injury, pardon,*
> *Where there is doubt, faith,*
> *Where there is despair, hope,*
> *Where there is darkness, light,*
> *Where there is sadness, joy.*
>
> *Oh, Divine Master, grant that I may*
> *not so much seek*
> *To be consoled as to console,*

To be understood as to understand,
To be loved as to love.

For it is in giving that we receive,
It is in pardoning that we are pardoned,
It is in dying that we are born to eternal life.

My fears of old age and its inevitable culmination have been largely obliterated by my acceptance of the thought expressed in a sonnet by John Donne, a poem that is also a part of my daily recital:

Death, be not proud, though some have called thee
Mighty and dreadful, for thou art not so;
For those whom thou think'st thou dost overthrow
Die not, poor Death, nor yet canst thou kill me.
From rest and sleep, which but thy pictures be,
Much pleasure; then from thee much more must flow,
And soonest our best men with thee do go,
Rest of their bones and soul's delivery.
Thou art slave to fate, chance, kings, and desperate men,
And dost with poison, war, and sickness dwell,
And poppy or charms can make us sleep as well
And better than thy stroke; why swell'st thou then?
One short sleep past, we wake eternally
And death shall be no more. Death, thou shalt die.

My efforts to interact with others and my renewed religious faith are enabling me to face old age with the attitude of the pig in the following story: A hen and a pig were walking along the street one day when they passed a billboard that carried an advertisement for a local restaurant. "Eat at Joe's Cafe, best food in town" read the accompanying legend. The ad also carried a picture in full color of a plate of ham and eggs. The hen and the pig stopped to admire this outdoor art, and the hen said to her companion, "Doesn't it make you feel good to think that this very morning you and I have combined to bring nourishment and pleasure to many happy breakfast eaters?" The pig looked at his companion and again at the picture, shook his head, and said, "Well, yes, and then again no. You see, you have made a contribution, but mine is a total commitment."

By making a total commitment to the welfare of others and by firm adherence to belief in God I have learned to face advancing years with hard-won courage.

Ed Crabtree

Elizabeth Yates

B. *1905*

ЖЖ

Born in Buffalo, New York, where she spent much of her childhood on the family farm, the internationally known writer concluded early "that everything has a purpose and deserves respect . . . the rotation of crops, the rhythm of the seasons, the necessary hard work, together with the interrelationships of animals and land, were all meaningful to me as a child." This respect for "the years' orderly procedure," this undying faith in "the enduring nature of the good," is the principal hallmark of Elizabeth Yates's writings.

She has written many books, holds seven honorary degrees, and received many awards, among them the Newbery Medal in 1951 and the New Hampshire Governor's Award of Distinction in 1982. Throughout her long productive life she has stood aloof from literary fads and fashions in her choice and treatment of subjects. An inner independence and integrity are her characteristics.

Presently serving as a member of the board of the New Hampshire Association for the Blind, the Hearing Ear Dog Program, and White Pines College, Ms. Yates's pleasures are her friends, her garden, her dog, walking, and canoeing. "Shieling," the two-hundred-year-old farmhouse which she and her husband restored, is her home in Peterborough, New Hampshire. The forty-five acres of field and woodland, now known as Shieling Forest, have been given to the State of New Hampshire for use as a learning center and recreational activity under the care of the Division of Forests and Lands.

ALWAYS AHEAD

Always there had been something ahead, and always it would call upon something within to face it. At six that was too big a word to understand and impossible to spell, but on that first day of school it existed and was drawn from a recess within. Was it courage? She had been told she was a big girl now and she was excited about going to school, but she clutched hard the hand of the grown-up that held hers as they went up the steps of the big building, through the door, and to the entrance of the First Grade room; then she had to let go, had to face that room full of children, some few she knew but many she had never seen before.

As the tall teacher came toward her, she felt her hand slip from the familiar grasp and suddenly she was alone—only herself and that new experience. She couldn't turn around and run away, she couldn't cry out to the grown-up retreating, she could only go forward and in that moment of time she felt something take hold of her inwardly, a new something. It was courage. She said "Good morning" to the teacher as she had been told to do, said her name, then went toward the desk that had been pointed out as hers. Yes, she was a big girl now, ready to face what was ahead.

Time went by and it was her tenth birthday that was being celebrated; an important day for she was adding another digit to her count and that meant a big step forward. Even bigger was the day when she entered the teens. There were other great occasions. To be sixteen was one, and then to be twenty-one: a grown-up now who could vote, a young woman who could take her own stand. Each stage of growing had blended into the next effortlessly, inevitably. It was like the song in a play that she had been in—

> We see the seasons come
> But never see them go,
> And by this simple token
> Each one of us may know
> That the nature of things good
> Begins but never ends,
> No matter what it is
> From happy days to friends.

The year moves on in an ordered round
From beauty to beauty sublime,
And the joy of each day that was lost
Is found in the fullness of time.

She had studied Browning and could agree with him that "the best is yet to be." How could it be otherwise when already there had been so much good? And yet, in those thirty-two stanzas of "Rabbi Ben Ezra" there were words that said life would be hard. It wasn't until the last that the meaning of "best" became clear, and it was a prayer—

My times be in Thy hand!
Perfect the cup as planned!
Let age approve of youth, and death complete the same!

She had learned Wordsworth's "Ode on Intimations of Immortality" and cherished the thought that

Trailing clouds of glory do we come
From God, who is our home.

But it was Tennyson's "Ulysses" that challenged her as the years went on, especially the last lines—

Tho' much is taken, much abides; and tho'
We are not now that strength which in old days
Moved earth and heaven; that which we are, we are;
One equal temper of heroic hearts,
Made weak by time and fate, but strong in will
To strive, to seek, to find, and not to yield.

Yes. Always there would be something ahead. This was the learning that was life; and the savor, too.

From a vantage point of years I look back on her now: how eager she had been to do the work that she knew was hers to do, the work with words; how blest she had been to find one with whom she would share the greater part of her life through marriage with its delights and disciplines. As they grew to know each other they found out more about themselves and felt at home in life. It was not always easy, but sorrow was balanced by joy and hard times were offset by gains in understanding, and everything could be shared: books, travel, experiences, ideas, spiritual discoveries, and long, long talks about God.

They had climbed mountains, run rivers, slept under the stars by campfires, visited sophisticated cities, and stayed in small villages. Pictures had been taken so the times could be relived, and small treasures purchased that would remind them of places visited. It had all been good, even the hard times. Like a guiding thread she held to words ingrained early: "All things work together for good to them that love God." The key was in the first words—all things. Whatever happened could be turned to good.

It was difficult to assure herself that "the best is yet to be" when the time came that she was alone. He had gone ahead, that was all, and it was up to her now to find her own way. Alone but not lonely: that was the pact she made with herself. She was realistic enough to know that there would be deserts to cross, rivers to ford, mountains to climb. She would accept the challenge as on that first day in school when she had found what was needed to face the unknown. Courage. Years later her inner feeling was confirmed when she came upon the words of a medieval mystic, St. Isaac the Syrian: "The ladder that leads to the Kingdom of Heaven is hidden within you, and is found in your own soul. Dive into yourself and you will discover the rungs to ascend."

Actuarial statistics said she was old. Whatever that meant she would make it a way of life; a country to be explored.

Old was a beautiful word, but so misunderstood, so maligned. A house that had weathered and sheltered for centuries was honored; wine that had mellowed for years was respected; antiques had high prices placed on them; and there were few who could indulge themselves in an old car, so costly was it. People in fulfilling their years became antiques; appraisals of their value might vary, but they deserved honor and respect. She had some friends, a few years ahead of her, whom she held dear for their calm, their wisdom. They carried their years jauntily, like a packsack full of surprises. Though infirmity might have compelled them to live with limited activity, nothing had happened to their minds, their hearts.

There were others with whom time was an enemy to be fought, though secretly they knew the battle was a losing one. "I don't like what's happening to me!" "I don't want to be old." Such useless notions. She could remember when some childish petulance had been rebuked with the words "Act your age." Now it was "Be your age" and therein find what it had for you. Tennyson aside, yield was the word now, yield to the rhythm of life. Of what avail a pretense of youth? It was vitality that mattered. "How young you look" was a foolish comment, as if youth were the norm. "How well you look" was a tonic.

She felt no different in her inmost self, but outwardly there were changes. There was a lessening of energy so that things took longer to do. There was a tendency to withdraw, but of this she knew she must be watchful. However circumscribed life might become, it was essential to keep in stride though the pace might be slower. I am a saunterer now, she told herself, liking the word for its connotation, coming from Saint Terre, and implying the pace pilgrims went on their journeys to the Holy Land.

Her coterie of friends began to diminish, some to the comfort of retirement homes, some to the Unknown. There were stalwart ones who still thrived on travel and chided her because she now chose to stay at home. Through books and in her imagination she did travel. There were many places she had never been—up the longest river to its source or the highest mountain to its summit. She had not been where past civilizations had lived and disappeared, or gone below the ocean to discover what undersea life was like. She dreamed of possibilities like travel by satellite and observing from outer space what the Great Wall, the Rift Valley, the Barrier Reef looked like from above. Her imagination led her into fantastic adventures—a balloon ride over the pyramids, across Siberia, beyond the Arctic Arch to Lapland to see the northern lights or over Tasmania when the penguins make their run for the land. It was tempting to think of revisiting familiar places at special times—the opera season in Milan, Christmas in Vienna, the flower show in London; but she was content with the voyage she was on into the land of the eighties.

It required neither passport nor travelers' checks, and the itinerary she laid out herself. No new clothes were needed except as worn ones were replaced, no phrase books, no luggage. It would be all right, she persuaded herself, if she went into it with the enthusiasm and curiosity she had had for distant lands. So she began to make herself ready. She cut down on commitments and schooled herself to say no to many things she had done because she felt she should and settled on things she really wanted to do. Time that had once seemed so pressured was now an available commodity. There were others moving forward in the progression that was life who would take her place; they were younger with new ideas and a resource of strength. She began to find advantages that offset the relinquishments; and as her own senses became less sharp she discovered a deepening sensitivity for others. She gave herself little treats—breakfast in bed, a cup of tea to rest her, dinner out with a friend.

Things were coming to her more and one of the first lessons she had to learn was to accept them with grace. Love was more widely shared. Disappointments hurt less. Time seemed to be providing an immunity. She grew more selective as she willingly took on change as the pattern of life. And it required courage, for the new way meant taking a stand from the person she had long been to the one she was becoming. Often her thoughts went back to the guide on one of their Swiss climbs. With the peak still before them and a glacier to cross with several yawning crevasses, he had turned back to them with a smile lighting his sunbronzed face and said "Courage, mes amis," then turned to press on. The way he said the word gave it an intensity of meaning: challenge and response were one.

Letting go of the past with its habits, its set ways of doing things, she tightened her hold on the thread that had been guiding her and expected good. She would look for it and make it happen.

Now it seemed that it was not so much a journey she was making as a graduate course she was taking. She filled one notebook with her discoveries and bought another. Why bother being annoyed when she couldn't remember as well as she had when she learned Wordsworth? She had her own intimations and she would write them down for safekeeping. So she made lists—a plan for the day, books read or to be read, friends to telephone, shopping reminders, a Bible verse to keep her on course, directions to herself. Once done, her mind was free for activity. Why let mail pile up? Deal with it promptly and conclude that most of it could go in the round file. Clutter made inroads on energy, so reduce it. When a new thing came her way she endeavored to move along something old—clothing, equipment, whatever was not necessary. It would be easy to eat too much, but if she fed hunger not appetite she would be in control. There was much necessary decision making that need not be put off to others and a future day. There were some matters she could decide on and make it simpler for everyone. Finish small tasks the day they were begun and give the next day its own leeway. This was all part of growing; and achievement, however slight, made her feel competent to handle the present.

Simplify—that was another key word. Do things the easiest way. See friends often but, whether food is involved or not, know that conversation is the real nutrient. That may lead to reminiscence, a pleasant indulgence; but be careful for it goes back not forward and the journey is always ahead. Take nothing for granted: show your appreciation, express your gratitude, be generous with affection. The words "used to" could be a trap; better far was it to substitute "This is the way now." She found her summation in *moreso*: what she was now she would be moreso as the years advanced. Crotchety and critical? Large-hearted and loving? Withdrawn or outgoing? It was up to her.

There was always room in one of the notebooks for jottings from a library book or one borrowed from a friend that could not be kept to refer back to. In Daniel Callahan's *Setting Limits* she found reflections on the "status of the aged" that were significant to her. Of their needs, courage came first, then humility, patience, and "*simplicity* as a way of traveling light; *benignity* (a kind of purified benevolence) to offset tendencies to avarice, possessiveness, and manipulation; and *hilarity*—a celestial gaiety in those who have seen a lot, done a lot, grieved a lot, but now acquire the detachment of the fly on the ceiling looking down on the human scene." To this she would add vigor of spirit—the drive to keep going to carry out one's desire to serve to the very end . . . Across the miles she clasped hands with an unknown writer who spoke to her and for her.

A young friend said to her one day, "It must be awful to be old."

She had taken a long moment to reply. "Yes, it is awe-ful. So much is being done these days to keep people living longer, living well, that we who are old have a great responsibility to live our lives fully; to do what can be done and bring to it something of what we have learned; to show that life is still rich and good; to face reality and discover our strength. Look in the Psalms and find that line about those who love the Lord, 'They still bring forth fruit in old age, they are ever full of sap and green.' "

"I see what you mean," the young one said.

But did she? Didn't one have to be old before one could talk about what it was like?

"And the best is yet to be." So softly she said the words that they might have been inaudible.

Her wants had become almost nonexistent and her needs were few, except for the continuing one of quiet. Aloneness. Hours during which she might read, or listen to music, or just be. The world around her had so much for her to absorb. The trees in their leaf-leaving were glorious, not only in their color but in the ballet made by the leaves as they found their way to the ground. Always this beauty had been, but she felt more responsive to it than ever. There was a day, sitting in her garden, when she watched her beloved old dog chase an equally beloved old cat that belonged to a neighbor and they were both walking. The rigors of age were upon them but they were still doing what nature had conditioned them to do. There was a memorable moment when distantly she heard the sound of geese in their migration. Scanning the sky she saw them, just visible in the morning mist—a perfect V; yet even as she watched the leader fell back into the formation and another moved forward to take that place. This would go on and on, long after she could follow their flight across the sky: always one ready to draw back so another could come forward. These were not unusual happenings, but they gave her much to think about, to weave into her own life and where she was in time.

"Are you still writing?" she was asked.

"Am I still breathing?" she answered.

Her work and her life had been one for so long they could not be separated by a mere matter of years. The spring from which she had drawn had its source deep in the earth. It was unfailing, but she would go to it now with a cup instead of a bucket.

Always there was something ahead, perhaps only a small event like a concert or a friend coming to see her. Looking forward gave incentive to her days. Life had had great moments; looking back she could recall many of them as she thought her way through the decades. But there was no doubt in her mind that the greatest moment of all was ahead— the transition called death. It was no use speculating about the future, although there were some who had been brought back from the experience and whose words were of light that was encompassing, of love that was enveloping. Whatever; it would be a continuum of all that had been good here, only Moreso. She thought of Vaughn Williams, the composer, who when near his end was asked if he would be writing music in heaven. "I shall be music," he replied. She thought of an epitaph seen in a little country churchyard: "How friendly seems the vast unknown since you have entered there."

I know her well, that little girl growing through life's stages from childhood to old age, each one readying her for the next. I can remember her feeling when on that first day of school she let go of the hand that held hers, the feeling that came from within and that sent her forward, and with it uncertainty and trepidation had dissolved.

Barrie gave brave words to Peter Pan at a time when danger threatened: "To die will be an awfully big adventure."

Richard Barlow

Malcolm Muggeridge

B. *1903*

The British journalist, social critic, and theologian Malcolm Muggeridge is one of the most prolific and highly regarded prose writers of our time and surely one of the most paradoxical. In the 1930s he was a champion of the Soviet Union and later became one of its harshest critics. He served as a spy for British intelligence during World War II, as the editor of the British humor magazine *Punch*, as rector of Edinburgh University, as a TV film writer and panelist and, for the past thirty years, as a crusader for the virtues of nondenominational Christianity and the traditional values it upholds.

While serving as an interviewer for the BBC, Muggeridge repeatedly shocked his audiences with his willingness to put down just about anyone, from the Queen to Che Guevara. In the mid-1960s his caustic attacks on the Royal Family nearly ended his BBC career, and in 1969, after roasting Christiaan N. Barnard in an interview, he was banned from South Africa.

A vegetarian who neither drinks nor smokes, Muggeridge believes that abstemiousness and a degree of asceticism are necessary if one is to work past seventy. He admits readily that he has never "cared greatly for the world or felt particularly at home in it" and insists that "pessimism" is Christianity's greatest strength. In recent years, however, he has found that attending Mass near his home is "a wonderfully fulfilling thing . . . the church is packed with children, and I love to have Mass with all these little children around, and come away feeling enormously happy."

THE PROSPECT OF DEATH

The one sure thing about our mortal existence is that it will end; the moment we are born, we begin to die. The basic fact of death is today highly unpalatable, to the point that extraordinary efforts are made, linguistically and in every other way, to keep death out of sight and mind.

Mother Teresa, with characteristic audacity, calls the place where derelicts from the streets of Calcutta are brought by her Missionaries of Charity (actually a former Hindu temple), a home for dying destitutes, whereas the sanctuaries for the more affluent derelicts of the west are called rest homes. Even in the chillier world of hospitalization, terminal ward is preferred to death ward, termination being scientific and so anodyne, unlike death which is fearsome and mysterious.

Even those who for one reason or another advocate killing off unborn children and the debilitated old seek to clothe their murderous intentions in elusive terms such as: "retrospective fertility control" for abortion, and "mercy killing" for euthanasia. A month spent in Florida in the company of fellow-geriatrics gave me some idea of the lengths to which the old are induced to go in order to distract their thoughts from their impending demise. In, let us call it, Sunshine Haven, everything was done to make us feel that we were not really aged, but still full of youthful zest and expectations; if not teen-agers, then keen-agers, perfectly capable of disporting ourselves on the dance-floor, the beach, or even in bed. Withered bodies arrayed in dazzling summer-wear, hollow eyes glaring out of garish caps, skulls plastered with cosmetics, lean shanks tanned a rich brown, bony buttocks encased in scarlet trousers— it all served to make a Florida beach on a distant view a macabre version of Keat's Grecian Urn:

> *What men or gods are these? What maidens loath?*
> *What mad pursuit? What struggle to escape?*
> *What pipes and timbrels? What wild ecstasy?*

Nearer at hand, the impression was more in the vein of Evelyn Waugh's *The Loved One*. At Forest Lawn, the original of Waugh's Whispering Glades, the cadavers are scented and anointed and dressed for their obsequies in their exotic best, down to underclothes; in Sunset

255

Haven, pre-cadavers likewise array themselves for social occasions like young debutantes and their squires out on a spree, and behave accordingly, though sometimes with creaking joints and inward groans. Of all the amenities available in Sunset Haven—bingo, swimming pools, books, billiards and golf—the one never spoken of or advertised in any way is the crematorium, discreetly hidden away among trees and bushes, and unmentioned in the illustrated brochures. Yet evidently business is brisk through the winter months despite the sunshine and the geriatric *joie de vivre* so much in evidence. Death becomes the dirty little secret that sex once was; Eros comes out of hiding, and old Father Time tries to secrete his scythe.

Another method of, as it were, sweeping death under the carpet is to stow away the debilitated old in state institutions, where they live in a kind of limbo between life and death, heavily sedated and inert. Private institutions for the affluent old are naturally better equipped and staffed, but can be very desolating, too. Those under Christian auspices, especially when they are run by nuns, usually have long waiting lists, not so much because the prospective inmates are particularly pious, as because they want to be sure that some zealot for mercy-killing will not finish them off arbitrarily by administering excessive sedation or, if they happen to need to be in an iron lung or attached to a kidney machine, by pulling the plug, as it is put in today's rather disgusting medical jargon.

In any case, disposing of people who live inconveniently long, and of defectives of one sort and another, has, from the point of view of governments, the great advantage of saving money and personnel without raising a public hullabaloo—something governments are always on the lookout for. It is, of course, inevitable that, in a materialist society like ours, death should seem terrible, and even inadmissible. If Man is the very apex of creation, with nothing greater than himself in the universe; if his earthly life exhausts the whole content of his existence, then, clearly, his definitive end, his death, is too outrageous to be contemplated, and so is better ignored.

Simone de Beauvoir, in her book *A Very Easy Death*, describes her mother's death from cancer as being "as violent and unforeseen as an engine stopping in the middle of the sky." The image is significant; death is seen, not as the finale of a drama; nor as the end of an act, to be followed by a change of scene and the rest of the play; not even as an animal expiring; but as the breakdown of a machine which suddenly and maddeningly stops working. "There is no such thing as a natural death," Madame de Beauvoir concludes. "All men must die, but for every man his death is an accident, and, even if he knows it and consents to it, an unjustifiable violation." In the light of such an attitude, death becomes a monstrous injustice, an act of brutal oppression, like, say, the Vietnam War, or apartheid in South Africa. One imagines a demo led by Madame de Beauvoir, and all the demonstrators chanting in unison: "Death out! Death out!"

The slogan is not quite as preposterous as might at first glance be supposed; the crazy notion that some sort of drug might be developed which would make its takers immortal, a death-pill to match the birth-pill, has been seriously entertained. And how wonderfully ironical that *soma*, the drug in Aldous Huxley's *Brave New World* that was to make everyone happy for evermore, should have been the name originally chosen for thalidomide! Nor is it fanciful to detect in the mania for transplants of hearts, kidneys and other organs, perhaps even genitals, a hope that it may become possible to keep human beings going in-definitely, like vintage cars, by replacing their spare parts as they wear out.

Again, experimentation in the field of genetics would seem to hold out the prospect of being able in due course to produce forms of life not subject to death. Jonathan Swift, in *Gulliver's Travels*, showed a clearer sense of our true human condition when he made the immortal Struldbrugs, encountered by Gulliver on this third voyage to the flying island of Laputa, not, as Gulliver had supposed they would be, wise, serene and knowledgeable, but rather the most miserable of creatures, excruciatingly boring to themselves and to others. Whenever they see a funeral, Gulliver learns, they lament and repine that others are gone to a harbor of rest, to which they themselves never can hope to arrive.

Indeed, sanely regarded, death may be seen as an important factor in making life tolerable; I like very much the answer given by an oc-togenarian when asked how he accounted for his longevity—"Oh, just bad luck!" No doubt for this reason among others, death has often in the past been celebrated rather than abhorred; for instance, very ex-quisitely, by the Metaphysical Poets, among whom John Donne may be regarded as the very laureat of death. So alluring did he find the prospect of dying that when he was Dean of St. Paul's he had himself painted in his shroud so as to be reminded of the deliverance from life that lay ahead. Sleep, he points out, even just for a night, wonderfully refreshes us; how much more, then, will sleeping on into eternity be refreshing! And then:

> One short sleep past, we wake eternally,
> And Death shall be no more, Death thou shalt die.

In our own time, Dietrich Bonhoeffer manifested a similar attitude to death when, with his face shining in joyful expectation, he said to the two Nazi guards who had come to take him to be executed: "For you it is an end, for me a beginning." Likewise Blake when, on his deathbed, he told his wife Catherine that to him dying was no more than moving from one room to another. As his end approached he sang some particularly beautiful songs, which, he told Catherine, were not of his composition, but came directly from Heaven.

Alas, I cannot claim total certainty of this order, and fall back on Pascal's famous wager, which requires us to bet on eternal survival or eternal extinction. Confronted with such a choice, as Pascal points out in his *Pensées*, the obvious course must be to back the former possibility, since then, "if you win, you win everything; if you lose, you lose nothing." So, I back eternal survival, knowing full well that if eternal extinction should be my lot, I shall never know that I have lost my bet, and taking no account of exotic notions like Reincarnation, or of the so-called "evidence" provided by people who have been in a coma and imagined they were dead. The fact is that to know what being dead is like, you have to die, just as to know what being born is like you have to be born.

In support of my choice, I can say with truth that I have never, even in times of greatest preoccupation with carnal, worldly and egotistic pursuits, seriously doubted that our existence here is related in some mysterious way to a more comprehensive and lasting existence elsewhere; that somehow or other we belong to a larger scene than our earthly life provides, and to a wider reach of time than our earthly allotment of three score years and ten. Thus, death has seemed more alluring than terrible, even, perhaps especially, as a belligerent of sorts in the 1939–45 war; for instance, wandering about in the London Blitz, and finding a kind of exaltation in the spectacle of a bonfire being made of old haunts like Fleet Street, Paternoster Row, the Inner Temple, as though, not only might I expect to die myself, but the world I knew, the way of life to which I belonged, was likewise fated to be extinguished. Now, death seems more alluring than ever, when, in the nature of things, it must come soon, and transmits intimations of its imminence by the aches and pains and breathlessness which accompany old age.

It has never been possible for me to persuade myself that the universe could have been created, and we, *homo sapiens*, so-called, have, generation after generation, somehow made our appearance to sojourn briefly on our tiny earth, the same characters and situations endlessly recurring, that we call history. It would be like building a great stadium for a display of tiddly-winks, or a vast opera house for a mouth organ recital.

There must, in other words, be another reason for our existence and that of the universe than just getting through the days of our life as best we may; some other destiny than merely using up such physical, intellectual and spiritual creativity as has been vouchsafed us. This, anyway, has been the strongly held conviction of the greatest artists, saints, philosophers and, until quite recent times, scientists, through the Christian centuries, who have all assumed that the New Testament promise of eternal life is valid, and that the great drama of the Incarnation which embodies it is indeed the master-drama of our existence. To suppose that these distinguished believers were all credulous fools whose folly and credulity in holding such beliefs has now been finally exposed, would seem to me to be untenable; and anyway I'd rather be wrong with Dante and Shakespeare and Milton, with Augustine of Hippo and Francis of Assisi, with Dr. Johnson, Blake and Dostoevsky than right with Voltaire, Rousseau, the Huxleys, Herbert Spencer, H. G. Wells and Bernard Shaw.

It must be admitted that as the years pass—and how quickly they pass, their passing speeding up with the passage of time!—our world and living in it come to seem decidedly over-rated; as Saint Theresa of Avila put it, no more than a night in a second-class hotel. Even so, it is extraordinary how even in old age, when ambition is an absurdity, lechery a bad joke, cupidity an irrelevance—how even then I find myself, as the General Confession in the Book of Common Prayer puts it so beautifully, following too much the devices and desires of my own heart. Talking to the young I have noticed with wry amusement how they assume that round about the late sixties a kind of cut-off operates whereby the world, the flesh and the devil automatically lose their appeal. If only it were so!

The best I can hope for in my dotage is to emulate the state of mind of the Sage in Dr. Johnson's *Rasselas*, reflecting that of his creator:

> My retrospect of life recalls to my view many opportunities of good ne-
> glected, much time squandered upon trifles and more lost in idleness and
> vacancy. I leave many great designs unattempted, and many great at-
> tempts unfinished. My mind is burdened with no heavy crime, and there-
> fore I compose myself to tranquility; endeavour to abstract my thoughts
> from hopes and cares which, though reason knows them to be vain, still
> keep their old possession of the heart; expect with serene humility, that
> hour which nature cannot long delay; and hope to possess in a better
> stage, that happiness which here I could not find, and that virtue which
> here I have not attained.

Nonetheless, the mystery remains; and ever must. Some eight decades ago I came into the world, full of cries and wind and hiccups;
now I prepare to leave it, also full of cries and wind and hiccups.
Whence I came I cannot know, least of all in the light of contemporary
myths like Darwinian evolution, Freudian psychology, situational ethics, Marxist prophesy, and so on—surely the most absurd ever. Whither
I go, if anywhere, I can only surmise, helped thereto by the testimony
of true visionaries like the author of the *Cloud of Unknowing*, Blake,
Dostoevsky, and, of course, above all, Jesus Christ; by inspired works
of art like Chartres Cathedral and the *Missa Solemnis*, by the dedicated
lives of saints and mystics; above all, by the Incarnation and all its
consequences, in history, in what we still call western civilization, now
toppling into its final collapse, in providing infallible signposts in the
quest for God.

The hardest thing of all to explain is that death's nearness in some
mysterious way makes what is being left behind—I mean our earth
itself, its shapes and smells and colors and creatures, all that one has
known and loved and lived with—the more entrancing; as the end of
a bright June day somehow encapsulates all the beauty of the daylight
hours now drawing to a close; or as the last notes of a Beethoven
symphony manage to convey the splendor of the whole piece. Checking out of St. Theresa's second-class hotel, as the revolving doors take
one into the street outside, one casts a backward look at the old place,
overcome with affection for it, almost to the point of tears.

So, like a prisoner awaiting his release, like a schoolboy when the end of term is near, like a migrant bird ready to fly south, like a patient in hospital anxiously scanning the doctor's face to see whether a discharge may be expected, I long to be gone. Extricating myself from the flesh I have too long inhabited, hearing the key turn in the lock of Time so that the great doors of Eternity swing open, disengaging my tired mind from its interminable conundrums, and my tired ego from its wearisome insistencies. Such is the prospect of death.

© Mitch Eagan

Lawrence Treat

B. *1903*

Lawrence Treat, a cum laude graduate of Dartmouth College and a graduate of Columbia Law School, worked hard to overcome a conventional upper-middle-class background. He practiced law for six months and four days, at which time the firm he was working for broke up, not, he insists, "through any fault of my own." He immediately set sail for Paris, where he lived for more than a year, wrote poetry, and set up his first drive-it-yourself car rental agency. He had three cars, which broke down gradually, in sequence. After the third car's demise he turned to writing and specialized in the mystery genre.

He sold the first book he wrote and dedicated the rest of his life to literature, and lived happily ever after. His total output is about twenty-five books, several hundred stories, and one hundred and fifty pictorial mystery puzzles, a type he invented and most of which were published under the title of *Crime and Punishment 1, 2, 3*.

He originated the police procedural novel and was one of the founders of Mystery Writers of America, now 1,600 members strong. A past president, he has been active in it throughout its existence. He has been honored by various awards, including two Edgar Allan Poe Awards, a short story prize at the International Crime Writers Congress in Stockholm, and a special award for a TV story on the Alfred Hitchcock program.

Treat lives on Martha's Vineyard, where wild swans and egrets fly over the saltwater pond in front of his house. Now in his eighties, he admits that "some day I must act my age. But not yet. Not yet."

WITH A
LITTLE BIT OF LUCK

First of all, I take issue with the title of this book. It takes no courage to grow old. It happens when you're not looking, and there you are. Did it take courage for me to get born, to reach my forties or my seventies or any other age? Courage has nothing to do with it, and all in good time I'll die. It happens to everybody, and if millions before me could do it, so can I.

I'd love to live forever. I've rarely been bored for more than a few hours, and I never expect to be, for I love being alive. If my back hurts and I can't bend down, or if I get out of breath from merely leaning down and brushing my teeth, then I sit down, take a few deep breaths, and presto! I feel strong and potent, bright of mind and warm and loving of heart.

There are certain labels I reject, and one of them is that of senior citizen. The idea is thrust upon me almost every day. I wish not to think about age, either as a reason for respect or as a cause for pity. In earlier societies, largely agricultural ones, you were superannuated at forty or fifty. And although the age has been upped in recent years, the idea of old age as some peculiar form of life, probably useless, still lingers. And while I'm fully, and sometimes painfully, aware of my limitations, I try to accept them, although there are occasions when it hurts.

For instance, at the recent International Congress of Crime Writers, I was chatting with some friends at the hotel where we had our head-quarters. In the course of the conversation one of my friends looked at his watch and suggested that we'd better start for the reception at the public library. It would be a long walk, but a nice one, he suggested. I can still walk a mile, I thought, but not on New York City pavements. And when I get to the library I'll have to stand at the cocktail party for at least an hour or two. So I declined to go with the others, and my wife and I took a taxi and held hands all the way. Real tight.

Frustration?

It bothers me at times, but on the whole I'm used to frustration. It started at birth, and one of my earliest experiences in life was being circumcised, with nobody bothering to ask for my consent.

To be sure, my early days had many pleasures. I was cuddled and

265

fussed over, but it all stopped when my elders got tired of me. Every infant learns that the world is unfair. I'm still trying to accept the fact, but I do so grudgingly, if at all.

As I grew up and reached my teens, the frustration was even sharper. Adults pushed me around to suit their convenience. They had private jokes and conversations from which they excluded me. They stayed up as late at night as they pleased, and had all sorts of rights. I had none, save the few they granted me. And I wasn't even told what sex was all about.

So much for childhood, or at least my taste of it.

If old age is a second childhood, it's the best childhood that I could want. I admit I can't play tennis or go clamming or ice skating, but what of it? In the local library I have all the books I can possibly read, and I have the leisure to read them. I can watch baseball or ballet or listen to my favorite symphony, and all this with the companionship of the one person I'd rather be with than anybody else in the entire world.

But far more important, I'm still writing, which is what I'm made for and which I either love to do or have to do, I'm not sure which. Once I started my career as a writer, I set up the habit of getting to my desk as soon as possible after I was up, and then working all morning (I'm a morning worker, and whatever I do after lunch comes out of the wrong typewriter) and maintaining the regime seven days a week, every week in the year, except when interrupted by guests or other acts of god. There are times when I sit at my desk, or in the easy chair alongside it, and bamboozle myself into thinking I'm at work. Sometimes I fool myself and sometimes not, but I still honor the custom.

As I write this, it's 8 A.M., the galleys of my next book are on the shelf above my desk, notes of a story that I've been mulling over are piled on the other side of my desk, scribblings from another project or two are tacked up on the wall, and somewhere else is the correspondence that I meant to answer last week. And I'm supposed to be going downhill?

I live my career, which is something like a good marriage—it starts with euphoria, and while it has its ups and downs, it becomes the very fabric of life. I can't live without it. I practice it, dream it, take it to bed with me every night, work on it at breakfast, and embroider it throughout everything I do all day long. I am a vehicle for the production of words, and I never get old. I may slow up, I may have to use a thesaurus, and my sales may decline, but I am a writer and I write. In concrete terms, I work hard, words flow easily, and I do what I want to do.

I tend to think more about maturity than I do about old age; about developing a commitment to life; about developing an awareness of the awesome importance of life and its consequent responsibilities. I've been an atheist ever since my early teens, and I still am. I'm strongly moralistic and inclined to idealism, and the passage of years has given me confidence not only in myself, but in the principles by which I live. I believe that whatever has happened has been my own doing. I glory in being me, despite all the blunders and mistakes. Stupid or not, they're mine, and I accept them.

Oh, sure, I realize that I'm a product of many forces over which I have no control and that it's silly to think that I govern my own destiny, but I believe it nevertheless. I've made mistakes, some of them very serious indeed, but they were made with the best of motives, so let me keep on blundering along.

I've done nothing to deserve all that I have—and I do have a lot. I never bothered about my health or exercise. I swam and played tennis for the fun of it. I drank, sometimes too much, and I still have a cocktail every night, and sometimes two. I'm known as the best martini maker in the neighborhood, and I sit down before dinner with my drink next to me, a pad and pencil on my lap, and with my favorite Beethoven on repeat. I think and dream and get ideas and start stories.

I belong to the confraternity of writers, and the least of my worries is the problem of age, since I have no control over it. All I know is that I've survived thus far, and for one reason only.

I'm lucky.

Shannon OCork

Phyllis A. Whitney

B. *1903*

❧ ❧

With over thirty-five million copies of her thirty-three romantic suspense novels in print in paperback alone, Phyllis Whitney is one of the best-selling writers in the world. First published at the age of fifteen in *St. Nicholas*, a magazine for young people, she then followed the course of most beginning writers, producing hundreds of short stories, many of which did not sell. Since 1941, when she attained her first hardcover publication, Miss Whitney has become an international success. Writing first for young people, she later moved into the adult field, where her novels have become bestsellers, here and abroad. Among recent titles are *Flaming Tree* (1986), *Silversword* (1987), *Feather on the Moon* (1988), and *Rainbow in the Mist* (1989).

In 1988 Miss Whitney wrote her seventieth book in her eighty-fifth year. In the same year she received the Grand Master award from Mystery Writers of America for lifetime achievement.

Miss Whitney, who was born in Yokohama, Japan, of American parents, has also lived in the Philippines and China. After the death of her father, she and her mother returned to the U.S., which she saw for the first time at the age of fifteen. This early travel has exerted a strong influence on her work; many of her books are set in areas she has visited in Europe, Africa, and the Orient.

Most of her life Miss Whitney has spent working with books in one field or another. She was children's book editor for the *Chicago Sun* and for the *Philadelphia Inquirer*, and instructor in juvenile fiction at Northwestern University and, for eleven years, at New York University. In addition to her many novels, she is also the author of the well-known texts, *Writing Juvenile Stories and Novels* (1947) and *Guide to Fiction Writing* (1982).

Since the death of her husband in 1973, Miss Whitney has lived near her daughter, first on Long Island, then more recently in Virginia. She has not remarried.

HIGHER MOUNTAINS
YET TO CLIMB

When I was in my forties and had to have a serious operation, the surgeon told me that the "mending" would probably last for no more than twenty years. Looking ahead blithely to that distant future, I assured myself that by that time it wouldn't matter. When I was that old I wouldn't care. Now that I've reached my eighty-fifth year, I have discovered how much everything "matters," and that I care more than ever about a great many things. Perhaps some of what I've learned along the way to this "enlightenment" is worth sharing.

Fortunately, I discovered early that my driving life force lay in putting words on paper; I had no choice but to become a storyteller. This has been a way of life for me—not a goal. I didn't think about fame and fortune—I just wanted to be published and perhaps read. It would be pleasant to earn my living by writing, I thought, but this would have to take care of itself. I wrote because I had to write. After all the usual rejections and struggle, I began to be published in the book field, though financial returns were very small for thirty years and more. I kept on trying to learn my craft, and eventually remarkable rewards came my way.

None of this would have been possible if I hadn't given attention to the three motors that run any life: body, mind, and spirit. These are the aspects I must still nurture if I am to have a sense of well-being and enough energy for all the things I still want to accomplish. In my early years I knew none of this and had to learn the hard way that these three were of equal importance and not one must be neglected. Though they are intertwined and need to work together, the body is the one that begins to plague us most with advancing years, so I'll deal with the physical first.

All my life I have fought ill health, having started off rather badly as an American child growing up in the Orient, where I lived mostly in hotels. Good nutrition was not part of my childhood, so I was sick a great deal of the time. I lost both my parents while I was still in my teens, so I had little guidance when it came to my health, or anything else. I simply took my ailments for granted, never realizing that I was causing them, or that I was traveling a disastrous road.

There is a saying that when one is ready the teacher will appear. I've found this to be true many times in my life. Sometimes it has been a book that changed my course. Or perhaps a friend or mentor opened a new way for me. On one occasion it was only a voice—but it came at a time of need when I was ready to listen.

Some thirty years ago, when I was suffering from an extreme fatigue that doctors told me was all in my mind, and when neither spirit, mind, nor body was working properly, I began to listen to a voice on the radio in New York. Carlton Fredericks was a pioneer in the field of nutrition, and on that day he appeared to be describing my symptoms exactly. What was more, he didn't believe it was necessary to suffer from mysterious tiredness, headaches, near-blackouts, depression, confusion, and other assorted ills. He didn't even think I was ready for a psychiatrist—not if my trouble was hypoglycemia. At that time doctors considered this an "imaginary disease." Carlton knew better. He knew that a good part of the population suffered in one way or another from these or related symptoms, and his voice came over the air when I was desperate enough to listen.

Sugar addiction was the main cause of what was wrong with me. A very real addiction. Doggedly, painfully, I emptied the sugar bowl, banished confections from my house, and began to eat the six small meals a day that would keep my blood sugar from its debilitating swings. In a few weeks, astonishingly, I could notice improvement, with my symptoms lessening and disappearing altogether. Today I am a fervent "health nut," and the study of nutrition and its application has helped to keep me feeling younger than my years, to say nothing of keeping my brain working. For me, prevention has become the key word—not waiting until I am sick, but learning how to set up the barricades against disease. In many ways I am in better health now than when I was young, and I have of course become a missionary!

Medical nutrition, or complementary medicine, as Dr. Robert Atkins calls it, is surely the medicine of the future, since it can accomplish without drugs and side effects what doctors are not always able to cure. It is "complementary" because it can be used to work together with treatment in the orthodox field. Certainly our goal should be maximum health, instead of struggling along on the minimum, as I used to do.

Exercise is part of the body picture. However, until more recent years there was little advice available on how to exercise safely. So I was enthusiastic, but not very sensible. Damaged knee cartilage has set a pattern of difficulty that I still struggle against. No more bicycle riding, no more rowing, or hiking, so that I sometimes look wistfully at people older than I am who can bend their knees. Nevertheless, I walk eight or ten times around the decks of my house every day, as well as doing limbering and stretching exercises indoors.

Contentment in these years, satisfaction in my work, and that sense of well-being that I value, depends in part on acceptance of what can't be helped, and a willingness to supplant the old with something new. When I was ten I loved to play with paper dolls. I cut out families from fashion magazines, named each member, and made up endless stories about them. Often I looked at unfortunate grown-ups who no longer played with paper dolls and felt unhappy. Not for them, but for me. How awful it would be when I was old and must give up my paper friends.

At that early age I hadn't learned that something new and interesting always comes along to take the place of the old, raising us to the next level of growth and maturity. Not to look back with regret, but to savor today is a pretty good rule to live by.

The mind, of course, is the director of all that happens to us. To stay young as we all know we really are inside, our minds must be constantly challenged and taught new ways, kept open to ideas we may have rejected yesterday, but which prove worth looking at now. It is well recognized that the brain that isn't worked hard enough deteriorates.

My writing has taken care of this automatically, so I am fortunate in that respect. Each new book demands new research, new learning, so that my mind must stay active and excited. If I am to succeed with my fiction, I must retain the wonder of a child as I look out my window, wherever that window may be.

Weariness can set in as we grow older—a tiredness of spirit as well as body—and this may defeat us if we allow it to. Here the study of nutrition can continue to help. The right nutrients can lift depression, raise the energy level, get us going again at any age. This is a complex subject, and if there is no expert in our vicinity, we can visit the library (or health food store) and start reading. The experts have written hundreds of books, and we need to find out what works for us. Help is there.

When restricting walls crowd us in and narrow our field of vision, it's up to us to break them down and let in the light. With each new reaching-out to learn, new hope can bring a surge of energy we didn't know we possessed. Walls are only there to be pushed down. And muscles grow stronger with the effort.

Discouragement is always the enemy. How can all these terrible things be happening to me? I can't fight anymore! But like the Little Engine in those baby books, we always can. It's unfortunate that from early on we are programmed toward old age and death. We are taught to expect infirmity; taught that illness is inevitable. This dark outlook can color our thoughts and bring on exactly what it promises. We each have our own handicaps—that's part of being alive—but we also have free choice and it is up to us in mind, body, and spirit to work past limits others have set for us, and move ahead. One of my favorite axioms comes from the Chinese: "Man who says it can't be done should not interrupt man who is doing it."

I have recently built a house of my own for the first time, a house planned for me. (All those level decks outside!) I am sure that some heads have wagged gloomily over such foolishness. At my age how long can I possibly hope to enjoy my new workroom? But I am enjoying it, for whatever time, and I am learning new methods of working that enable me to be more creative in my writing. One satisfying aspect of my life in these years is the knowledge that I am writing better books than when I was ten and twenty years younger. The mind—that second motor on my list—never needs to stop at previous boundaries, but can always learn new ways and furnish its own special energy and motivation.

As someone has said: "Dying is not dangerous." If there is nothing afterwards, then I won't know the difference and I'll have no regrets. But if, as I have come to believe in these later years, there are some interesting adventures ahead, that's fine. In the meantime I'll try to have my best possible years in this world as it is for me at present.

Not long ago an interviewer asked me the question, "What was the best time of your life?" I answered her truthfully when I said, "Right now." There is so much pain and struggle and grief behind me that I'll never have to face again. I know I am far stronger for having made the journey. If there are new tests ahead (and there always are), I will know better how to meet and deal with them.

My husband's attitude when he was dying of cancer is something I will never forget. He went right on planning for the future, his future, though he knew what lay ahead. Listening to him I realized that this was not denial, but a way to live the time left to him. To go on as though he would live forever, and thus keep busy with plans and doings, even from his bed, was something to give everyone else courage. A pox on death—that would be dealt with when the time came.

There wasn't much that was amusing during those long months, but we still found happenings we could laugh about. I can remember my mother and father laughing together, even after they had both developed that same disease and knew it. I'm grateful to them for the gift of a sense of humor. It's no news that laughter keeps our bodies going and our spirits light.

In the past, friends have sometimes said to me, "How lucky you are! Of course you can be happy." Lucky? Is it lucky to lose one's parents when young, to have no money, no formal education (I used to mind that—I don't anymore) and only very modest talent that needed a lot of work to develop? There was a record behind me of marriage, divorce, remarriage and the loss of a second husband, death of a brother, death of a granddaughter, the near suicide of a grandson—are these what is called being "lucky"? Yes, I am lucky indeed because I have a daughter who is my best friend and adviser, a beautiful granddaughter, and now a new great-grandson. I am fortunate—but not because everything fell into my lap. One has to work at being happy.

Which brings me to the third part of the trio—spirit. This is more difficult to talk about, being made of mist and smoke, instead of flesh and blood and cell tissue like the other two. Yet perhaps it is the most important element of all because it can rise above body and mind and take us wherever we want to go. The mind can be the cautious critic and hold us to what is sensible, practical, realistic—all those left-brain qualities. The spirit can throw all that aside and soar. It can mend the ailing body and raise the depression that besets the mind. It can free us to move into creative right-brain territory. All of us are on our own here. We must find our own different ways, and we can learn from one another.

I have never been a religious person. As a child I was sent to whatever Sunday school was offered in whatever country I was living. Denominations blurred for me, just as races have always blurred. Several lifetimes later when I moved to Long Island to be near my daughter, I joined the Unitarian group she belonged to. It was reassuring to be among those who held a broad view toward all religions and races. This was where I could stay happily for a time. I had always been an agnostic—not knowing the answers, but questing. I admired and re-

spected those who had the faith to be true believers—in whatever—
but I went on questing. A search, I am sure, that will never end, and
which has taken me in chance directions that fill me with surprise and
wonder. Though, of course, there are those who claim that nothing
happens by chance.

These days, words that I might have shrugged off ten years ago intrigue and tantalize me: reincarnation, channeling, spirit guides, one's
Higher Self. Well!

Do I believe in the claims for these words? I don't know. At least
they make my imagination grow new wings, even though I still lack
the faith of those who are certain. I know I will find out in good time.
I don't really care whether I was a temple maiden in Egypt centuries
ago, though I believe that how we live in this life may bring us to
something better (or worse) later on. I am not yet a full convert, but
neither do I deny. I am doubtful about the mind that narrows in old
age. I listen with interest, and I watch the unexplained that goes on
happening all around me. I am learning about the power of "spirit" as
it affects my everyday life and my writing.

There is so much that I have tapped into that I can't explain, and
which may come under the heading of the mystical. What is this energy
that comes to me in my storytelling? Very early as a writer, I learned
that I could lie down, relax, close my eyes—and watch the next scene
of my story happen. In color! Though sometimes it might take days,
or weeks, for what I was seeking to come clear. The pattern seemed to
be that I must feed information into my mind—bits and pieces of whatever puzzle I needed to solve in my novel. I would then ask my question
and put the matter away for a time. When I took it out later and looked
at the problem, a solution would often have attached itself. This is an
experience we all have in problem solving.

Now, however, I have been able to speed up this mysterious process.
Today I live (in my new house) in the beautiful foothills of the Blue
Ridge Mountains in Virginia, near the Monroe Institute. Robert Monroe
has written fascinating books about his out-of-body experiences. There
is a laboratory at the institute that studies the human brain, human
consciousness, in an unusual way. The concentration tape developed
by the institute has proved miraculously valuable to me as a writer. It
uses a method of getting the two hemispheres of the brain to work
together. Sounds begin on the tape with the recorded rush of waves
on a beach—soothing, relaxing. Then a synthetic wave sound takes

over, a steadier sound that I can't quite describe. Concentration in this state comes easily. Where in the past I had to give the process of finding my scenes, or answering my story problems, a space of time—and the answers didn't always come—now when I lie back in a reclining chair with my earphones and tape, everything comes in a flash, often only in moments. What's more, the ideas are far better than I could have thought up consciously. I have used this method through the writing of three books, and as my confidence grows, I am startled by the inventiveness and the creative ideas that are presented to me so quickly. From where?

Is all this coming from some Higher Self? Or from my "Guides"—those guardian angels that some religions tell us are assigned to every soul at birth? Or perhaps answers come from some vast bank of thought out there in the ether that holds all the ideas that ever were or are to be. This is a concept held by many, from Plato on down, and it might explain why a "new" idea can appear simultaneously from different thinkers, all in different parts of the world. Writers often have the dismaying experience of coming up with a "fresh" idea, only to have it appear in the work of another writer who is on the same course at the same time. Perhaps there is some sort of ESP going on that we haven't yet begun to understand. In any case, the process seems to free the right brain to travel beyond our usual limits.

If I can use it, I don't really need to know how it works. I am willing to grant that in my lifetime a great many miracles have occurred. I have moved from riding in rickshaws to jet planes, and from the first little crystal radio to satellites that feed television programs all over the world. Who knows how many more "scientific" miracles are to come?

I only know that I have made contact with something that is helping and counseling me through the medium of my own mind. I am respectfully grateful that it is there and that I can turn to it in so many ways.

Another phase of my life that has grown out of all this is a period of meditation every day. Not the sort of meditation that empties the mind—that isn't for me. This is a period during which I focus on what I need for the day and ask for help. Before breakfast I take a few moments to relax. Perhaps I even hold a crystal in my hands (I will use any "magic" I can) and talk to myself quietly about the day ahead. I send a message to my recalcitrant knees and to any other part of my body that needs attention. I build up hope and optimism for the day.

And, above all, I ask for help. The source is there for me to tap, and it appears to be a benevolent "higher power" that comes to my aid. Have I become a true believer, after all? In any case, I always say, "Thank you," to whatever, or whoever, has helped me. These matters are all part of that remarkable third element—spirit.

There is one more aspect of growing older that I haven't touched upon. It is a fourth element that probably involves all three, body, mind, and spirit. If there is to be any joy and satisfaction in life, this additional element must be present. Three words define it—sharing, helping, giving, and thus leaving one's mark on life for the good of others. When I can help someone because of what I have in me, this is one of my "highs" in life. I don't believe there is any one of us who can't reach out in some way to help the person who needs the special gift we have to share.

One of the wonderful things about being alive is that it is never too late. It's not too late to write a book, to learn a new language, to travel, to build a house, or to make a new friend. I've seen writing careers begin when the person was seventy and more, and I am still making new friends.

The interviewer who asked about the best time of my life also asked if I thought I'd reached my peak as a writer. That shook me up for a minute, but I knew the answer. How could I arrive at a "peak" with all those higher mountains out there to climb? I'm not all that far up on my present slope, but the climb is still exhilarating.

Just so I can get up in the morning and look forward to my day, always realizing that what I do with it is up to me. I didn't really believe in old age when I was young—and I'm quite sure I don't believe in it now.

Fritz Eichenberg

B. *1901*

❡ ❡

Deeply sensitive, courtly, and soft-spoken, Fritz Eichenberg is one of the greatest living wood-engraving artists in the world. Over a long and prolific career
he has illustrated over a hundred books, most of which are recognized literary
classics. From Swift's *Gulliver's Travels* to Dostoevsky's *Crime and Punishment*,
from Bronte's *Wuthering Heights* to the *Tales of Edgar Allan Poe*, readers have
been enriched by his subtle artistry for more than sixty years.

Born in Cologne, educated there and in Leipzig, Eichenberg grew disgusted
with Hitler—whom he frequently lampooned in cartoons—and emigrated to
the United States in 1933. He became a Quaker in 1940, and it has been said
that "the pacific strain in both the man and his work can be felt not only
instantly upon meeting him but in his more renowned single prints such as
'Gandhi, Great Soul,' 'Black Crucifixion,' and 'Lao-Tse,' whose tao-chi teach-
ings he venerates."

In spite of the fact that he has received six honorary doctorates, has been
named one of the "Outstanding Educators of America," and has had an archive

279

created for his work at the Yale University Library, he is, according to one critic, "never more nor less than himself—a visionary living in Thoreauvian simplicity only for his craft, a xylophile daily facing in his woodblocks 'an emptiness,' as Wallace Stevens puts it, 'that would be filled.' "

IMAGE-MAKING AS IMMORTALITY

Having our active span of life laid out more or less on our own initiative, we rarely spend time or thought on the years when the tools of our efforts will be taken out of our hands. Image-making has been my lifelong passion, and it has served me devotedly for almost a century. Whatever courage I can muster to face my remaining life span will be based on the impact my work may prove to have had on those who have seen and responded to it. Even when my hands refuse to obey the dictates of my wood and graver, I relish the thought that my spirit, the essence of my existence, will survive in the lives of those with similar concerns and in our common work.

I could not conceive of old age without the many friends I conjure up from a section of my brain. Engraved in my memory are the thousands of God's creatures I have met in my long life, saints and sinners, popes and commissars, the possessed and the dispossessed, the whole and the injured. I see faces that cling to me, faces I garnered on voyages around the world. These vast numbers of faces, gathered day by day, are kept alive in my memory by the fire of a compassion and a love for drama and humor, tragedy and irony, which I learned long ago.

The vast, seemingly inexhaustible panorama of the human face has sustained and inspired me all my life. The lines reflecting drama as well as comedy become deeply etched in the human countenance, a rich harvest for the artist to reap at any stage of his life. Having worked in almost every medium, I was always enticed back to the beauty and intimacy and the inner strength of the woodblock, its readiness to yield graciously to the sharp point of the graver, the gouge, and the knife. With these tools, each assuming a character and a patina of its own, I could conjure out of the dark surface, like a spotlight thrown on the stage, the images forming in my mind, give substance, light, and shape to ideas defined by authors I admired, and in them express my own.

The flow of my graphic interpretation induced a literary public to develop a more active interest in reading the Russian classics. This was my main effort over the past half century. I believe it bore fruit and it has caused me to look back with a certain pride from my vantage point of old age.

My interest in Dostoevsky started when I was a student in Leipzig more than fifty years ago, and it was sustained over the years as an active influence on my thinking. I actually made lithographs illustrating *Crime and Punishment* and the beginning of *The House of the Dead* when I was twenty. But my experience of life, at that time, was not enough to do it justice. After a number of years of being an artist-reporter for many German publications, and then adjusting to a new country and a new life, I was commissioned to do another *Crime and Punishment*, illustrated with wood engravings. After this came other works by Dostoevsky, and by Tolstoy, and Turgenev, and Pushkin. These established me as a kind of specialist in the graphic interpretation of the Russian classics. The philosophy of total commitment so movingly expressed in the work of these great Russian writers influenced my own work ever afterwards.

As I age, I continue to be sustained in body and spirit by the endless procession of human feelings, elation and agony, pride and frustration, that has flown into my work—I hardly know how—and which has touched other people. As an artist devoted to literature, I have always seen the world as a stage peopled by mankind, where no favorites are played, where heroines and villains come and go, where each performs according to his ability. I am trying to slip into the skin of an actor, Heathcliff, or one of the brothers Karamazov, and to feel and to see as they do. By a quirk of destiny, I have been given the special gift of identifying myself almost completely with the character I must depict, hero or minor player, in a story, play, or drama.

The human mind, despite its preoccupation with the daily load of facts that demand decision, desperately needs the relaxation that only the spiritual world can provide. To watch the trees throw themselves with the passion of a dancer into an approaching storm is sheer poetry. The breeze, carrying the scent of the first spring flowers to our nostrils, intoxicates our minds. We discover Pegasus in the fleeting clouds of an autumn sky. Continual rebirth, seasonal change, an ever breath-taking and breath-giving drama: the mystery of giving birth to yet another living creature on this planet. It does not take a connoisseur to appreciate the beauty of the humble sunflower or of the feather from a peacock's tail. All life is art if we only learn to venerate and respect it as such, wherever we find and nourish it. This perception only grows with age.

Fritz Eichenberg, ''Heathcliff Under the Tree'' from *Wuthering Heights* by Emily Brontë (wood engraving 10¼″ × 7″) © 1943

The artist, eager to show the accessibility of nature, goes for a stroll along his favorite beach. At random, he picks up sticks and stones swept ashore by the restless ocean. Some, waiting since time began, will be resurrected in his hands, to start a life of their own. With an eye or a mouth, added with the help of a small brush, he creates his own Peaceable Kingdom of strange creatures, never seen before, imps and goblins, demons and angels, to be shared with others. These missiles from the ocean find their place in the hearts and minds of friends all over the world. These gifts of love are returned over the years, even into old age.

In every living man's soul, there is likely to exist a large-sized yearning for immortality. In my many decades of making images, I flatter myself that a few may have attained the rank of "icons." One of them may be "Heathcliff Under the Tree," or the image of Raskolnikov in one of Dostoevsky's most powerful novels. I admit to deriving pleasure and satisfaction from this thought. I feel that I was blessed with a gift, and I have tried to put it to use. When my hand can no longer hold the wood and the graver, I can still look back with a feeling that I did not waste it, or neglect such talent as I had.

It takes courage to confront an enemy; it gives strength to be in the company of friends. I found this out in my early school days when I innocently picked out Alfred Rethel's print, *Der Tod als Freund*, as the subject of a class essay. At home, my father was dying a slow death from Parkinson's disease, and World War I was raging on the western front. In the print, a church bell is being rung by death while an ancient bellringer is peacefully expiring in his easy chair. The sun is setting, and a little bird sits on the windowsill, promising that he will free the old man's spirit. I had great fear of losing my father, and this image reassured me that there was peace at the end. It was an image of redemption then, and it is now. I believe that the spiritual life will continue.

In his frightening novel, *1984*, George Orwell describes the shadowy world of the future peopled by faceless robots. I confess that I would lack the courage to live in such a world. I will fight to the finish to maintain my own face, and to keep alive the memory of all the expressive faces I have seen and of some that I have been privileged to create.

Leslie A. Marchand

B. 1900

In the world of letters few need to be told that Leslie Marchand is the greatest Byron scholar of this century, if not the most distinguished and important who has ever lived. This shy, wry scholar, known for his careful manner, has visited almost every place where his hero is recorded to have set foot and has examined, copied, and classified every scrap of paper from his pen.

Marchand's romantic voyage of scholarship began in 1946, while he was a professor of English at Rutgers University, teaching a course on the romantics. He soon discovered that there was no good modern biography of Byron and that a growing quantity of previously unknown material was rapidly becoming available. It was then that he set to work collecting Byron's letters, which led to several of his books on the poet, among them the highly praised *Byron: A Biography* (1957). His most important work, however, is his twelve-volume series, *Byron's Letters and Journals*, published by John Murray and the Harvard University Press between 1973 and 1982. Citing his four-decade involvement in researching Byronia, James Atlas of the *New York Times* said that Marchand's work is "more than a matter of diligent library research. [The author] belongs

285

among those intrepid literary historians portrayed in Richard Altick's *The Scholar Adventurers* . . . Marchand was convinced from the start that a great many of Byron's papers remained at large and he set off to Europe in the summer of 1947 determined to recover them."

Now living in Florida, the Rutgers professor emeritus has been a Guggenheim fellow, a National Endowment for the Humanities fellow, and is the recipient of the James Russell Lowell Prize from the Modern Language Association of America (1974) and the Ivan Sandrof Award from the National Book Critics Circle (1982).

Marchand believes that "Byron has a certain 'desperate integrity.' With all his persiflage he was constant to two beliefs that are just as relevant today: a love of liberty and a hatred of cant. Byron has helped me to see the humor in a mad world and the incongruities of self-deception."

THE LIFE FORCE

In *The Almond Tree*, Robert Liddell's first novel, published in 1938, when he was thirty, one of the characters says: "It is very easy to be wonderful if one can only manage to remain in this world for eighty years or so; an octogenerian need do little more than blow his nose to win applause." This is perhaps a wholesome deflation of the popular notion that old age brings wisdom.

What does an old man think? If he has kept his health and is not obsessed with contemplating his illnesses, his thoughts will not be significantly different from what he has thought through most of his mature life.

Here are a few things which have occupied my thoughts. I have no illusion that they will bring me applause.

First of all, I believe it takes little courage to grow old. The life force takes care of it. Hazlitt wrote that no young man thinks he will ever die. Even with a full knowledge of the facts of human existence and the relative shortness of it in terms of the countless lives before him and the infinity to come, it is hard for any normal healthy young person to be philosophical and face the facts rationally for the same reason that the eighteenth-century gentleman could not be a philosopher because his cheerfulness was always intruding. For the young the years pass slowly—a year is an eon and it is hard to see beyond it.

The more remarkable phenomenon is that healthy old people are hardly more concerned with the end of life, though rationally they know that it is much nearer, and for them time passes faster. Robert Louis Stevenson has observed this remarkable fact clearly and commented upon it brilliantly in an essay called "Aes Triplex." Generally, he argued, the hedonist and the unbeliever has an easier time of it and is less obsessed with life's ending than the Calvinist concerned with his soul hereafter. He lives for the day and its pleasures and satisfactions and is less troubled by thoughts of its end. For him, death is certain and final, but he doesn't dwell upon it constantly. If he has any solid interests in life, they, in combination with the life force, drive out thoughts of the inevitable termination. Nature has taken as good care of the old as of the young. If healthy in mind and body, old people think as little about death as the young, and, as Stevenson said, read the obituaries with as little concern as the young, only congratulating themselves that they have outlived their contemporaries.

Those who are obsessed with the uncertainties of immortality are in a worse state, and for all their faith are inclined to think of the end of life with some dread and to think of it too much. As Byron says, "The stupidest, and dullest, and wickedest of human bipeds is still persuaded that he is immortal." Once freed from that obsession one can live pleasantly until the end, only hoping that it comes painlessly and quickly.

Of course, those who insist on being philosophical, or logical, and who can keep cheerfulness (which is driven by the life force) from creeping in, can see the whole pageant of life and death as a tragedy for the individual—born with an irrevocable death sentence—whatever the purposes of nature may be. But if we extend logic to viewing the whole show from nature's point of view, it is easy to see the tragedy of eternal life on earth—even discounting the horror of contemplating Swift's Struldbrugs, those senile immortals. If no creatures died a natural death, the planet, already overpopulated by the prolongation of life through advances in medical science and a neglect of birth control, would soon become unlivable. Not even the life force could make life bearable, and untold suffering and unnatural death—starvation, war, pestilence, and all the ills that Malthus foresaw—would inevitably thin the ranks of mankind. The struggle for survival would be the sole instinct spurred by the life force, and greed, rivalry, and mean self-interest would drive out all human kindness and embitter what we know as the pleasantness of life while it lasts. To ask for more than the normal span of life is to ask for a worse tragedy than death. "Our little life is rounded with a sleep."

With hundreds of thousands of people living into their eighties and nineties, the tragedy of growing older is retirement. I have long considered retirement a dirty word. After I left university teaching I was fortunate to settle on a project that occupied my energies fruitfully for more than a dozen years, into my eighties. The editing of the complete letters and journals of Lord Byron took me to important libraries in America and abroad, introduced me to interesting people, and gave me a worldwide correspondence. But after I published the final, one-volume selection of the letters and journals my work on that project was finished and I felt a letdown. It did not strike me with full force until I had to undergo a serious operation. I came out emaciated in body and spirit and with a feeling of emptiness. What lay ahead? I had no grand project. I was eighty-four (middle age by Florida standards). Should I write my memoirs? Most people of literary inclinations turn to that at my age. My life had been interesting enough, but could I make it appear so to others? I had little stomach for it. What to do?

In time, I began to see that what concerns me most as I grow older is the illogicality of human affairs. I do not know whether this is due to the increase of years or to the fact that human irrationality seems increasingly to overwhelm the world at the very time in the atomic age when rational thinking is so essential to our survival. My study of Byron alerted me to the constant presence of the mask of pretense that often hides the plain or ugly face of reality in our world. Byron wrote in Don Juan:

> *"But now I'm going to be immoral; now*
> *I mean to show things as they are,*
> *Not as they ought to be . . ."*

Urged on by the Byronic hatred of cant, I began writing "letters to the editor." But I soon discovered that most editors consider my views of the world too outlandish and too radical for publication, so I resorted to writing letters to myself. After accumulating a barrel full of these I sat back and relaxed. Why should I concern myself with such ironies of unreason that fill our daily newspapers? Why not live the best life I can and accept people for what they are? Is the final wisdom of age the discovery that I cannot change the world? Must I in the end "accept the universe" whether I wish to or not? Must I "accept the pleasures of life leisurely, and its inconveniences with a shrug"?

Then came another mood. This strong urge to accept life as it is is not the only choice open to me, nor is it necessarily the best one. No, the urge to accept life as it is is countered by an impulse even stronger in me not to compromise by taking things as they are on too easy terms, but to speak out whenever opportunity offers against irrationality in human affairs. I need not throw in the towel. I can do myself and the world as much good as I can by living my life to the fullest that my opportunities and talents permit. The best I can do is to try to make life less unhappy for those about me and within the possibilities and limited reach of my political influence, small as that may be. With realistic eyes I still need never retire from the struggle to make a better world of an imperfect one. Even though I recognize that the battle can only be successful imperfectly and in a limited sense, it sustains me.

Ralph Pyle

D. Elton Trueblood

B. 1900

Born in the last month of the nineteenth century near Pleasantville, Iowa, D. Elton Trueblood is an eighth-generation Quaker in direct line. After living a childhood filled with "wholesome fun and manual work on the family farm," he entered into academic life with zest, earning degrees from William Penn College (A.B.), Harvard University (S.T.B.), and Johns Hopkins University (Ph.D.). He is the recipient of fourteen honorary doctorates.

Working to fulfill a ministry that would enable him to apply his Quaker faith to every activity of his life, Trueblood has had a varied and extremely influential career. He has taught philosophy at Haverford College, Garrett Theological Seminary, Harvard University, Stanford University, and, for over twenty years, at Earlham College, where he remains a professor-at-large. In 1954 the United States Information Agency asked him to fill the newly created post of chief of religious policy. Upon accepting the post, he declared that the U.S. needs "the three P's the Communists have: a philosophy, a program, and a passion." Determined to demonstrate to the world the spiritual values the West had to offer, he embarked on a number of ambitious projects, including his exhibition, "The Church in America," which showed by picture and text the richness, variety, and vitality of religious life in America.

After leaving the agency in 1956, Trueblood returned to Earlham College, where he helped to found the Earlham School of Religion and the Yokefellows International, whose members voluntarily accept the disciplines of the Bible. Soon thereafter followed a steady stream of books, most of which were published by Harper & Row, among them *The Yoke of Christ* (1958), *Confronting Christ* (1960), *The Company of the Committed* (1961), and *The People Called Quakers* (1966).

Now living alone at Meadowood, near Valley Forge, Pa., since the death of his wife in 1984, Professor Trueblood continues to speak, think, and write, and remains one of the world's most influential theologians.

THE BLESSINGS OF
MATURITY

In Plato's *Republic*, we are told of a conversation which occurred between Socrates and Cephalus, in which Socrates is reported as saying, "There is nothing which for my part I like better, Cephalus, than conversing with aged men; for I regard them as travelers who have gone on a journey which I too may have to go, and of whom I ought to inquire whether the way is smooth and easy, or rugged and difficult . . . Is life harder towards the end?" The essence of the old man's reply was that "old age has a great sense of calm and freedom."

Being now older than Socrates was when he died, I am in a position similar to that of the old man in the greatest of Plato's works. Like him, I am pleased to be able to share anything which I have been able to learn on life's journey, by telling what I can about the condition of the road which we are all destined to travel.

Never ignoring or denying the physical hardships of old age, I nevertheless affirm that the joys of my maturity have been very great indeed. The calmness and freedom of which Cephalus spoke are real! The fact that autumn is, in many ways, the most beautiful season of the year is a parable of human life, as well as a fact of nature. The slower pace is itself a remarkable blessing. I rejoice each morning, as I face the day, that, in contrast to all of my former life, I do not have more insistent responsibilities than I am able to accomplish. If I wish to do so, I can just sit and be grateful. Fortunately, I can do this without infringing upon some duty which is necessary, either for my own survival or for the welfare of others.

It came to me as something of a surprise to discover that the last chapter of life could be so enjoyable. Of course, I should not have been surprised, for I had been told; but we tend to be slow of understanding. That wise man, Dr. Samuel Johnson, made the point unmistakenly when he said that "vernal flowers, however beautiful and gay, are only intended by nature as preparatives to autumn fruits." It has amazed me to realize that these profound words were written by the famous sage when he was only forty years old. I have now lived longer than did the scholar from whom I have gladly learned for many years, and this I recognize as an unearned blessing.

We may wish that Dr. Johnson had been allowed more years in which to enjoy the fruits of a life so strenuously spent, but perhaps it was better that he should die when he did. At least he was relieved of some excruciating pain. It is moving to us to remember that, at the end, the brave man refused to take any more sedatives for the alleviation of his agony. When told by his attending physician that he could not recover without a miracle, Johnson replied, "Then I will take no more physic, not even opiates; for I have prayed that I may render my soul to God unclouded."

I am certainly grateful for the fact that I have lived as long as I have, partly because the time allotted to me permits me to assemble my memories in some semblance of order. The outcome is that time never seems to drag. Each added day affords me an opportunity to remember some event or some person, already partly forgotten, but now recovered with vividness. This is what we mean by the gathering of the autumn fruits without the sense of urgency which was inevitable when the plants, destined to produce fruits, were being watered, nurtured, and tended. The more I contemplate, the more accurate the agricultural figure seems to be; in a sense I have been a farmer all of my life.

In thinking what Plato intended by stressing the freedom which old age may provide, I begin to understand. In what sense am I more free than I was in earlier years? Part of my freedom is freedom from hurry. Of course I have not totally abandoned travel, and am, as I write these words, planning another trip to England; but my good fortune is that I can now make my plans without being hectic. Because I am not trying to do too much, I can savor each step of the journey.

It would be ridiculous for me to claim that I shall give no more public addresses because I cannot now know what are the particular opportunities that will arise, but I *can* affirm that my addresses will be comparatively few. I shall not travel long distances to speak, except under circumstances which give reasonable promise that a real difference can be made. Realizing the limits of my energy, I propose to use what remains as wisely as possible and, in any case, not to waste it. The upshot is that I mean to stay home as much as I can, to tend my garden, to nurture my flowers, and to enjoy leisured thinking. Sitting in the corner of my bedroom, with the volumes of Addison and Johnson at arm's reach, seems to me so delightful that it would be foolish of me to give up such an opportunity except for some adequate reason. I may travel a little, but I shall go by train when I can arrange to do so; and, if I fly, I shall try to avoid close connections. Running through an airport to catch a departing plane seems to me a foolish act, especially for a person more than eighty years of age.

At home, there are books to be reread, and other books to be read for the first time. Here they are in my library, waiting patiently for my attention; and now, at last, I have the time. I realize that we tend to read the great books too early, before we have enough experience to understand them, and sometimes we never open them again. Such neglect is a serious mistake, which may be corrected if we continue to live. In my own case I have the blessing of the possession of a great many notebooks which go back to college days. By good fortune I discovered, very early, the value of using bound notebooks for separate courses. While loose leaves tend to become lost or scattered, the bound notebook can be retained intact and placed upon a shelf, like a published volume. I am glad that I bought my notebooks long ago in Harvard Square because they can be enjoyed over and over in my present life. Though the sentences remain exactly as I put them down nearly sixty years ago, the experience is improved by being renewed.

Every old person is a poet, at least in Wordsworth's sense of the term. We are poets because we can experience "emotion recollected in tranquility." The gratefully remembered experiences, far from being diminished by the lapse of time, may actually increase in value. Memories seem to be more enjoyable when they are put in order. If any person has lived even a moderately full life, the accumulation of his memories is literally inexhaustible. When I try to put my memories within the covers of a book, I soon realize that it would be possible for almost any person to fill thousands of pages. Recorded memories are therefore necessarily *selective*. Though many of our memories are pleasant, this is by no means true of all. If a person is honest with himself, he will recognize, in contemplation, various wrong turnings which he has made. Though these cannot be undone, they can be faced without evasion, and forgiveness can always be sought. Since not all of the fruits come to maturity in perfect condition, every person is bound to think, with Whittier, of what "might have been."

No one can write honestly about the final chapter of life without a frank facing of its problems. Not all are as fortunate as Cicero said that he was, for there are some who lose even the power to remember. Great numbers of older people suffer from arthritis and other diseases, thereby requiring constant medication, if pain is to be rendered endurable. I want always to recognize the problems of maturity even while I mention blessings.

Perhaps the best thing we can do is to encourage people to look upon the life of maturity without a debilitating sense of foreboding. What, unfortunately, is often demonstrated is a self-fulfilling prophecy of disaster. Though physical ailments are, of course, real, it is important to remember that attitude has a great deal to do with human well-being. Some ailments are suffered because they are expected, loss of mental power being a case in point. Though physical disabilities are sometimes inevitable, it is important to remember that there is more than one way of facing them. Here is where the dying scene of Dr. Johnson is such an antidote to despair. Though we cannot stop the pain, we can nevertheless determine, in some measure, the way in which it is encountered.

The worst evils that sometimes occur in old age are not physical, but spiritual. In some cases older people, possibly in reaction to frustration, develop the habit of indulging in continual complaints about other people, including those who serve them most unselfishly. When this occurs it is always an occasion for sorrow because what might have been a period of peace becomes one of constant turmoil. One of the best solutions of this problem is the advance recognition of the danger, along with the conscious effort to avoid it.

Freedom from the necessity of setting everyone else straight can come at any time of life, but the conscious development of this particular freedom is especially important in declining years. It is even possible to develop the habit of deliberate silence, when pointing out the mistakes of others may do more harm than good. Though composing a letter of criticism may be therapeutic for the writer, there is no necessity of actually posting it. Instead of showing others where they are wrong, we can nurture the habit of thankfulness for what is right, being especially thankful that things are no worse than they are. In any case it helps to know that querulousness serves no useful purpose, and that, furthermore, the complaining mood is intrinsically self-defeating. When I am tempted to complain about the world situation, I find it helpful to start enumerating the things for which I have reason to be grateful.

The primary blessing of maturity is that, as Plato taught, it makes possible various forms of liberation. Many older people are liberated from the hectic struggle to get ahead in life, to build a reputation, and to establish a home. Suddenly I realize that, for the first time in my life, I do not have too many duties. Last evening I looked at my date book, in order to prepare my mind for the morning, and experienced the exquisite pleasure of observing a blank page. That does not mean that I shall do nothing today, but it does mean that whatever I do will be free from temporal pressures. I do not know, of course, what demands either the daily mail or the telephone will bring; but, right now, the space in the date book is gloriously empty. I am enjoying the clock, rather than fighting it. For many men and women in middle life this kind of freedom is never experienced. It is a particular joy of maturity to be able to produce, but to produce without strain.

The paradox of time in maturity is that we can be vividly conscious of our inevitable temporal finitude and yet enjoy its abundance, because we are in no great hurry. To know that "the night cometh" may actually be to sense a liberation from worry about lack of accomplishment, rather than the sadness which we usually associate with those sacred words. If I have only a few years in which to live, as is certainly the case, then the intelligent thing to do is to enjoy each day as though it were the last.

Another freedom of maturity is financial. For millions of people in the contemporary world, old age is the period marked by liberation from the necessity of earning. While some find it necessary to seek paid employment after the age of seventy, numbers of women and men can, because of Social Security, pensions, and personal savings, avoid entirely any search for an earned income. Even when inflation has diminished the value of savings, the older person can, in many instances, survive without financial worry, partly because the need of buying is radically reduced. In my own case, much of the freedom from financial pressure arises because I need fewer things than I once required. I am free from paying tuition, and I certainly do not need an extra car. My clothing is such that there is almost nothing in that line that I now desire. Actually I have entered a period of conscious distribution rather than of accumulation. I do not have to save for old age, for I am there already. Best of all, the freedom from earning can become liberation for service, especially, in my case, an opportunity to help people to secure proper employment, and to assist new authors in their own writing.

One of the most common misconceptions about old age is the supposition that it is always a period of intellectual decline. While, for some, decline undoubtedly occurs, this is by no means universal. When we are expressing our debt to Plato, it is good to remind ourselves that he wrote *The Laws* when he was eighty. In this magnificent final work of a brilliant mind we are far removed from the discourses which are purely Socratic, the author having achieved genuine maturity.

Many people are unaware of the numerous examples of intellectual achievements on the part of persons of advanced age and might be encouraged if told about them. Cato, the first Latin prose writer of any importance, learned Greek when he was eighty. In modern history, a brilliant example of late achievement is that of Verdi, who produced *Falstaff* on February 9, 1893, when the composer was in his eightieth year. It is a fair assumption that many persons fail to keep alert and productive because of a lack of expectancy. What is potential may be lost, not because of some physical ailment, but primarily because of lack of use. It is literally true that what we do not use, we lose.

Dr. Johnson's well-known example is a source of encouragement to many who know his story, chiefly because of Boswell's famous *Life*. Of the one hundred known prayers of Johnson, the one which has the greatest appeal for many of his loyal readers is his "Last Prayer," composed shortly before he died. With the *Dictionary*, *The Rambler*, and *The Lives of the Poets* far behind him, the reverent man had not lost his ability to create memorable phrases. In my own judgment, Johnson never created a more felicitous combination of words than when he wrote, "Make this commemoration available to the confirmation of my faith, the establishment of my hope, and the enlargement of my charity." Even to the very end, in spite of constant sickness and excruciating pain, Johnson was producing what, years earlier, he had termed "autumn fruits." Even in 1752 the brave man had already written, "To faint or loiter, when only the last efforts are required, is to steer the ship through tempests, and abandon it to the winds in sight of land; it is to break the ground and scatter the seeds and at last to neglect the harvest."

I boldly affirm that, after eighty, I can memorize either poetry or prose as rapidly as I ever could. Part of this is because I have so much uninterrupted time to devote to a valuable task. I can also affirm that the daily disciplines of prayer and Scripture grow more valuable with the added years. If I needed spiritual resources earlier, I need them even more now; and fortunately, my time for them is abundant. Part of the reason for the possibility of productivity in old age is the accumulation of resources. In this sense, I am richer than I was in any earlier period of my life. When I speak or write today, I speak and write out of the overflow.

In my own experiences, the gift of temporal freedom provides me with the opportunity of using each added day in the fashion which is most productive in my particular situation. For example, I now understand that the most productive part of any day, for me, is that from 7:30 A.M. to 9:00 A.M. In this hour and a half I feel as strong as I felt in my younger years and seem to think more clearly than at any other time of my life. The intelligent procedure, then, is to guard the time and to employ it creatively. When my prime time is over, I often need to rest or to change my pace. A valued contemporary once helped me by saying, "I'm a pretty good man, up to eleven A.M." Of course, I recognized that the remark was intended to be humorous; but, as is often the case with humor, my friend was expressing something profoundly true.

One of the blessings of maturity which is seldom sufficiently recognized is that of genuine humility. In early life there is a strong tendency to suppose that we have all of the answers, but some experience of life can cure this malady. One mark of intellectual growth is the recognition that there *are* no simple answers. The simple answers, we finally realize, are always wrong, because the world is not simple! The mystery of life, far from being dispelled by added years, actually increases with experience. On the whole, the wisest people are also the most humble because, in the heritage of Socrates, they have discovered that advancement involves the recognition of ignorance. A few years of real living can make any person realize that what we do not know far exceeds what we know.

Frequently, these days, I turn to the words of John Stuart Mill, who said that the world cannot too often remember that Socrates existed. This is one reason why I have installed a bust of the humble Athenian in my personal library. We do not know much about the early life of Socrates, except that he was a brave soldier. Possibly he was not always as humble as he showed himself to be at the end, when he saw clearly that the essence of wisdom is to know that we do not know.

Long after Socrates, it became essential to the Christian message to recognize that real freedom comes at the end of a process rather than at the beginning. "If you continue in my word, you are truly my disciples, and you will know the truth, and the truth will make you free" (John 8:31–32, RSV). Plato had some intimation of this profound idea when, near the end of his final book, he wrote: "The learners themselves do not know what is learned to advantage until the knowledge which is the result of learning has found a place in the soul of each." Real freedom is something to be achieved, but it cannot be achieved cheaply. It comes at a price, and it is more a consequence than an antecedent. Only when the learning process is ended, or is ending, do we know what is learned. This is why authors often admit that they do not know what they are trying to say until they come to the end of the writing process. Because prefaces are usually written last, it is foolish for readers to omit them.

In the logic of living, gratitude is the normal result of humility. The more we realize that we are unworthy of our friends, the more grateful we tend to become. By a happy development of publishing, Cicero's famous essays on "Old Age" and "Friendship" are now bound together in one volume, as they should be. In earlier years we may not appreciate friendship, and sometimes we do not really value it until we have lost it. It is not a mere coincidence that makes us place our Thanksgiving celebration in the late autumn.

One of the noblest words in our language is *grace*, defined as "unearned blessing." We live by grace far more than by anything else. Accordingly, I find that one thing which I want to put into practice in my own life is the conscious and deliberate habit of finding somebody to thank. The person to thank may be the driver of the bus, the teller at the bank window, the church janitor, the policeman on the beat, the mail carrier, the clerk in the grocery store, the telephone operator, and many more. In this fashion, gratitude can become a way of life. The greatest blessing of maturity is that gratitude may transcend the single occasion, to become both habitual and continuous.

Leland Stowe

B. 1899

❧ ❧

The veteran journalist and author who wrote the ablest, most sensationally far-reaching reports on the events that led to World War II was awarded the Pulitzer Prize for foreign correspondence in 1930. Ten years later he achieved world celebrity status with the most important scoops of the war: his exposé of the "Trojan-horse" treason which enabled Germany to invade Norway with lightning speed, and his reports of the British blundering and inefficiency that lost the Norway campaign. His story of the Nazi invasion put other European nations on guard against Fifth Column attacks in their own territory, while his revelations of the unprepared British expedition led to a shake-up in the British cabinet and, it is said, to the ultimate ousting of Chamberlain as prime minister.

Stowe's achievements are even more interesting in light of the fact that, in the fall of 1939, the *New York Herald Tribune* told him he was "too old to report another war." (Not quite forty at the time, but youthful and physically energetic, he had served his paper admirably for thirteen years.) Three hours later he was hired by the *Chicago Daily News* and went off to Europe. A colleague of Stowe's said that when he "couldn't get a plane, a car, or a horse, he'd start out to walk." He hiked ten miles through mud and snow over a mountain range near Trondheim, Norway, to reach the Swedish border and file three exclusive reports on the British disaster. After the war he not only warned the Allied powers about the danger of spreading Communist regimes in Europe and China, but of the inevitable Soviet nuclear menace to the United States and the arms race it would precipitate.

In addition to his work as a newspaper correspondent, Stowe has authored eight books, served as a roving staff writer for *Reader's Digest*, and has contributed scores of articles to national magazines, among them *Life, Look, The Nation, New Republic, Atlantic Monthly*, and *Harper's*. From 1956 to 1969 he was a professor of journalism at the University of Michigan. He has received honorary degrees from Harvard, Wesleyan, and Hobart College, and was awarded the French Legion of Honor and the Military Cross of Greece.

A REPORTER LOOKS BACK

Courage to grow old? Well, honestly, I've never had much fear of the approaching unknown. I can't recall needing that courage. I've simply come to accept the fact that eventually one *does* grow old . . . but better to cross that bridge when you come to it; when you feel you are aging—not before. By then you should be strong enough inside to face it and, hopefully, strong enough physically to handle it. But the hows and whys of growing old do intrigue me, especially now that I've reached the age where I'm on that last-lap acceleration, fast-nearing ninety. Stay your scimitar, old reaper! At least long enough for me to figure out how I got this far.

If it doesn't take courage to grow old, what does it take? Faith in living, I believe, faith that its compensations will multiply with time. I suppose Goethe pinpointed my attitude best of all when he said that "the main thing is to have great desire and skill—and perseverance to accomplish it." Beyond a doubt, a firm belief in these principles has made it possible for me to grow old without undue perturbations. It all adds up to this equation: Attitudes + Habits = Motivations; Motivations + Goals + Dreams = Character—all cindered into solid bricks for the passageway into growing old.

How so? Because our attitudes, habits, motivations, goals, and character are welded by a variety of factors. Notably, early parental influences (plus or minus), family and community relationships, geographic and environmental exposures, employment and educational experiences; by personal goals and dreams, and by the obstacles we encountered and how we confronted them. Under the impact of ingredients such as these our habits and character gradually coalesce as the shape and features of a granite statue emerge, chrysalis freed, from a sculptor's chip-chippings, scrapings, smoothings, and polishings.

The sculptor who provided the basic character-forming materials in my life was my farmer-woodsman father. Dad began his sculpting by giving me chores to do as soon as I could stagger into the kitchen with a nightly basket of firewood. At age eight he assigned me to milking Daisy, our Jersey cow, every night. Precariously perched on a rickety stool, I could barely encompass her bulging udder with both hands, then squeezing with all my might extract mere dribblings into the pail in my lap. That's where Dad's ever-pertinent maxims became unfor-

gettable: "Where there's a will there's a way." "Persistence pays off."
Night after night these verities were driven into my attitudinal clay to
the stinging swishes of Daisy's wiry, heavy-plumed tail across my face—
and an occasional propellant of tears of frustration. But even a half-
milked pail rippled a degree of achievement. And when at last, weeks
later, I lugged a near-brimming mammary harvest up to our kitchen I
was triumphantly aglow. Of course, at the time I'd never heard of that
ancient Roman Publius Syrus, but his pre-B.C. adage proved true: "His
own character is the arbiter of everyone's fortune." And mine was
sprouting its minuscule roots on a milking stool!

Hard work, however, was just one aspect of Dad's preconditioning
for my growing up properly equipped. "You are going to college, Lee,
if I have to borrow money to get you there," he repeatedly told me.
That launched me into goals and dreams, although they seemed at the
time close to unattainable. But Dad often admonished: "Think big, and
you'll go farther—maybe much farther than you can imagine." Compelled to drop out of a country school's eighth grade to support his
widowed mother and her five smaller children, Dad's goal for us became
immutable. So for four years he scrabbled and scraped to provide half
of my college expenses while I earned the remainder—by waiting ta-
bles, washing dishes, tending local residents' furnaces, clerking in a
downtown grocery, and whatnot.

Much earlier than college, however, I had gestated another dream
far more unlikely of materialization. One sunny day when I was eleven,
I lay on the hillside behind our rented farmhouse, my dog Prince cuddled beside me. Gazing across the mile-long reservoir below and over
its dense bordering treetops, I suddenly ruminated: Beyond those
woods stretches Long Island Sound . . . and beyond that the Atlantic
Ocean . . . and beyond it, EUROPE. If only I could go there someday!
Then spouted the ice cold squelcher: But that's impossible . . . Dad and
Mom can never afford to send you to Europe, and how could you ever
earn enough to pay your own way?

The go-to-Europe virus hibernated all through college but was temporarily numbed by my vastly exciting "real life" discoveries as a cub
reporter in Worcester, Massachusetts, and particularly when I entrained
for New York without a job or the assurance of finding one. But that
was where real life beckoned in Neon-Flashing Capital Letters. With
rare luck I promptly found a chance for freelance reporting at the City
News Agency; part-time assignments at $3 each, waiting for possible

summons from 9:00 A.M. to 8:00 P.M. Some days I got two and earned all of $6. By tight scrimping I could just cover cheap cafeteria food and a cubicle room at Brooklyn's YMCA. Within three weeks, however, the *New York Herald* assigned me to its reportorial staff.

Early on, a chance discovery led me down from the *Herald* building on City Park Plaza's southern edge to harbor-skirting Battery Park. There on a sunny May day, while munching a hot dog sandwich on an inviting bench, my boyhood dream was rekindled. Out of the Hudson River steamed ship after ship, and as they churned into the Atlantic swells, they resurrected that voice first awakened on that hillside slope of my boyhood. You must sail to Europe! Somehow, you MUST get to Europe!

Week after week those Atlantic furrowers haunted and taunted me. Then, months later, the city editor handed me several pages of telegraph copy for decoding. This long dispatch, datelined Riga, U.S.S.R., had been filed by the *Herald's* correspondent. The moment I scanned his opening paragraph I was overwhelmed, even transfixed. Here was a reporter seated in a far distant foreign courtroom, recording the Bolsheviks' trial of a foredoomed group of Russian priests. On the very spot! An eyewitness to history! What work or profession could be more exciting? What profession more challenging and rewarding? . . . This is it, Stowe. You must become a foreign correspondent! As I typed on and on, the keys branded that conviction on my mind and soul.

Over the ensuing four years that most alluring goal remained an unsmotherable urge. By 1926, then reporting for a merged *New York Herald Tribune*, I learned that Arthur Draper, its veteran London correspondent, now occupied a desk next to the managing editor's. Why not ask his advice about becoming a foreign correspondent? So, one June day I did just that. And after encouraging receptivity, Mr. Draper astonished me by asking: "If you had a choice between our London or Paris bureaus, which would you prefer?" I gulped as if swallowing an orange, thinking fast and hard. "I'd go anywhere in the world where I could be useful to the *Herald Tribune*," I managed to state. "But to be absolutely honest, I'd choose Paris." Plainly quite surprised, my London-loving mentor demanded: "Why Paris?" "I'd like to go where the traditions, customs, and culture are completely different—and where I'd learn a foreign language as well." There it was . . . "Nothing ventured, nothing gained." The following week Draper flabbergasted me with a twinkling smile: "Could you sail for France on July tenth?"

The next twelve years burgeoned into the richest growing-maturing chapter in my career: an eyewitness to history at last. They propelled me from London to Madrid, into the Balkans, to Istanbul; into direct associations with premiers, foreign ministers, dictators, kings, princes, and other global headline makers—such myriad impacts they're impossible to encapsulate. As a war correspondent, I observed, firsthand, Hitler's rise to power and Germany's seizure of Norway and the stunning rout of half-trained, half-armed British battalions to the north. Every event or interview deepened inner awareness of political and social responsibilities, of intellectual and cultural enrichments; of exuberant adventures while greedily garnering life's opulences. In short, treasurable memories for that sundown passageway.

Memories are contingent on what you chose: like picking wild flowers for their beauty and perfume, or selecting thistles and stinkweeds. If it's predominantly the latter, a masochist's penalties inevitably ensue. But if we will, most of us have happy memories for nostalgic recourse—my own so many that the thorny few become misty phantoms; equally suppressible by anyone so motivated. For the aging, memories are cheering tonic, ever at one's beck and call.

Skipping countless unforgettable memories, what did I learn from reporting the Great War? Among the verities that reporting the war drilled into me was this: one can keep going on sheer willpower. When once asked, "What makes a champion?," Jack Dempsey replied: "You have to be able to keep on going when you can't." Countless mortally ill elderly do the same, a stirring example to us all. But why keep going? In my case, because I had an important mission to fulfill, public responsibilities to meet, just as others have domestic, communal, or civic responsibilities. It's part of aging with a purpose (the French call it a "reason for being"). The extent to which one has determined what his responsibilities are, and the extent to which he has upheld them, largely determines the quality of his retirement. If there is a reason for being, and if the challenges are met, life is almost always worthwhile.

But concerning war reporting, what about the chances of being killed? Did I ever fear death? Not while my combat-zone mission endured. I believed my mission was so imperative that somehow I'd survive—and I did, unscathed, though not without a quota of almost hairbreadth close calls. Yet I somehow fully expected to survive. Fear of dying is a disease I've never really known, and I have none now. But those with strong religious convictions do possess a peerless advantage. Being an agnostic myself, an unknown Deity has had to suffice, and I've repeatedly prayed to this unknown supreme power as fervently as any Fundamentalist bishop. Whatever its foundation, faith conquers fear of death. During the Greek-Italian war I asked the dictator-premier Metaxas what made the underdog Greeks fight with such incredible valor. "For us, who are Greek Orthodox," he said, "death is only an episode." Three weeks later he died in transcendent serenity.

What do all these experiences have to do with handling those declining years? They revert to the attitudes and habits and character and goals and dreams—tools for aging affectively. These molding instruments indelibly crystallized how I would face retirement without qualms. This is why, despite nearing ninety, I've never felt or acted retired—or old!

Everyone knows—or should know—that keeping occupied is one necessity in growing old; either physically or mentally, or both. Predictably, my boyhood environment created my lifelong physical hobbies: planting trees, shrubs, and flowers, and gardening vigorously from the first purchase of a home in 1926, averaging close to 130 tallied hours each gardening season. I'm down to 80 hours a season now, here in my eighty-eighth year, but I'm still out there cutting, pruning, and churning up dirt whenever possible. And I always take walks for exercise therapy and read good books for mental pleasure.

All depends on health conditions and hobbies, but especially on intellectual interests. For creative persons, including writers like myself—as for Titian at eighty-two and Pablo Casals past one hundred—there's no problem. One can't help doing what one loves. "Live all you can," urged William James. "It's a mistake not to." And Peter Ustinov's counsel is an infallible guidepost well meriting emulation: "Since we live out our lives in the prison of our minds, our duty is to furnish them well."

Dr. Paul Arthur Schilpp

B. *1897*

❧❧

At sixteen, Paul Arthur Schilpp, the son of a pioneer German Methodist minister, came to the U.S. to enter Baldwin Wallace College in Berea, Ohio, in 1913. In 1916 he graduated from Berea with honors and subsequently earned an M.A. from Northwestern University, a B.D. in divinity from Garrett Theological Seminary, and a Ph.D. in philosophy from Stanford University. Now one of America's most distinguished living philosophers, he is best known as the creator and editor of the widely acclaimed *Library of Living Philosophers* series, considered by many to be the most outstanding work of contemporary philosophy in the twentieth century. Starting in 1939, with his first book on the philosophy of John Dewey, Schilpp went on to edit eighteen more volumes examining such thinkers as George Santayana, Martin Buber, Alfred North Whitehead, Karl Popper, Jean-Paul Sartre, and his friend Albert Einstein, among others.

Professor Schilpp has said that "all my life I have believed that no man is greater than the causes he espouses and to which he is dedicated and no cause is greater than the improvement of humanity in all areas. Humanity is in danger of succumbing to thoughtless emotionalism, unwilling to pay the price of serious thinking. Love, I believe, is more powerful than hate, and ideas are still the most effective weapons."

The recipient of several awards and honorary doctorates, Schilpp has been associated with liberal causes throughout his lifetime, especially the movement for pacifism, world government, and social justice. Still actively lecturing and teaching, he currently holds the title of Distinguished Research Professor of Philosophy Emeritus at Southern Illinois University, after having previously taught for twenty-nine years in Northwestern University's philosophy department.

AT 92

As I write this essay at past ninety-one years of age, I have just returned from Madras, India, where I gave the keynote address at an international seminar celebrating the centennial of the birth of philosopher-king Sarvepalli Radhakrishnan. And although it was a long journey, especially at my age, I wanted to participate in honoring my late friend and colleague, the subject of one of my volumes, *The Philosophy of Sarvepalli Radhakrishnan* (1952) in my *Library of Living Philosophers* series. This is because, like other things I do, I believe it important to engage in worthwhile activities within the limits of my capacities. Although I can no longer walk as fast or read as well as I did ten years ago, due to visual impairment and cardiac difficulties, I still support, as best I can, the causes to which I have long been committed: global peace, world government, social justice, human rights, and democracy. Old age has slowed me down, but it hasn't stopped me.

It is true that I spend more time in contemplation now, reading by the fire in winters, or out on the patio listening to music on my earphones in spring and summer. The extraordinary vitality for which I was once enviably noted has escaped me; but I have more hours now to enjoy my second family, Erich, now thirty, and Margot, twenty-five, growing up, and completing their educations, taking the challenge as they "debate" with me. I even enjoy our cat, whom I named Sasha, a beautiful long-haired calico. Once the children had to beg for our first cat, the Siamese Suki (who reached seventeen before she died). I always thought I liked only dogs and hated cats. But Suki and Sasha conquered me in old age with their affectionate ways and brought a change of heart in my seventies!

As to exercise, I am afraid I am and always have been lazy. Where once I played tennis with a vengeance, I gave that up years ago on doctor's orders due to angina pectoris. Despite my wife's urging to walk, I fear that is mostly to the campus and back to my car; I am too sedentary. I no longer sit up all night playing chess anymore either. I am too much like the late great chancellor of the University of Chicago, Robert M. Hutchins, who said, "Whenever I feel the urge to exercise I lie down until it goes away." Whereas I once smoked cigarettes and a pipe and drank very rarely, I now have a jolly drink almost every

night, but stopped smoking the day of the surgeon general's announcement of the health risks. But my diet of food is optional, except that I
avoid too much cholesterol, salt, and sweets. My parents both almost
reached ninety and so I have that best secret of old age: "Be choosy
when you pick your parents!"

Still, even if you have been blessed with good genes, the difficulties
of old age are legion. "Grow old along with me/The best is yet to be."
Well, for Browning that may be the case, but for most of us it's not.
Somewhere after our sixty-fifth birthdays, if not before, the problems
of aging creep up on us. Likely we have known lens implants, hip or
knee replacements, ear surgery, arthritis, or bypass operations. Increasingly the kitchen counter accumulates a rainbow of pills—orange for
the heart, green for rheumatic joints, pink for stomach, yellow for blood,
etc. In time, we have pillboxes divided into four-or five-hour spans for
two, three, four, or more certain hours of the day! And don't forget
eardrops, hearing aids, dentures, and high-powered eyeglasses. And
then, too, there is that car in the garage—those free and independent
wings which once flew me so easily and without a thought hither and
yon. I've surrendered my driving. It hurts my pride, but the truth is
that too many senior citizens stay behind the wheel beyond the limits
of safety for themselves or others.

All-around good health is slipping for all but a few of the more
fortunate who are "graying" in America. Their "get up and go has got
up and went" as the adage has it. Whom can we count over seventy-
five who claims to have the youthful vitality of a fifty-year-old? And
while TV's "Golden Girls" and George Burns's jovial movies paint a
rosy view of later life, the frolic is not there for many. The bounce is
gone. Perhaps Katharine Hepburn and Henry Fonda conveyed a little
more realism in *On Golden Pond*. Aging can be frightening and depressing, although it is lessened greatly when a good marriage finds two
clinging loyally together.

And indeed, even if one has had the luck to retain good health, as
have I, the Ogre of Death is awaiting in the wings as the years move
along. Inevitable as birth, so comes death, a natural process that claims
us all. It is the ending that most of us dread. Some find comfort in
religions, believing that their mortal flesh will be shed, leaving the way
for their eternal spirit to linger in perpetuity. Personally, I can't buy it.
I join those who believe that our lives are here and now. Heaven and
hell are in this earthly life, although I am willing to concede that our

influence may live on in the deeds and creations of those whom we have influenced. I do not fear death. Whenever it comes, I shall welcome it.

Worse than the fear of death is the fear of being left alone. If you live long enough you will experience the awful silence of an empty house when your long-time companion, husband or wife, is suddenly no more. And more loneliness comes as your old friends disappear. Although my wife of some thirty years is alive, nearly ninety-five percent of my contemporaries are dead. Some young enough to be my children died in their sixties and seventies. Then, too, some of my friends lived on, only to endure drawn-out bad health and financial misfortunes in their ripe old age.

My experiences have led me to believe in euthanasia when an illness is terminal. As for myself, I have filed a living will with our doctor and hospital. I do not want to be kept alive hooked to life supports.

As for the financial catastrophes facing senior citizens that we read about daily, what choice does a compassionate, thinking person have but to support Medicare and the creation of a national medical health bill? I believe strongly that adequate medical and dental services should be available and affordable equally to all in our democracy. (Of course, I am an old-fashioned Norman Thomas Socialist and a liberal Democrat.)

With the depressing news behind us, what can we do then to make old age as enjoyable as possible? First, of course, I believe strongly that finding our life work, our employment, or our profession is the most powerful factor. At sixty-five I could not understand why anyone so young would want to retire. Even at age seventy I was puzzled to see so many of my colleagues crave retirement. I have reached the conclusion that my attitude results from the fact that I truly enjoyed my work and could never seriously contemplate stopping it.

Whether one is working or retired, a homemaker, a stamp collector, or a scientist, meaningful work is crucial. The world, I've noticed, is full of round pegs in square holes. If you are in misery at the task you perform eight hours a day—whether that's watching TV in retirement, or punching a clock at a factory—life isn't worthwhile. And it's no secret that unhappy souls usually exit sooner than happy ones. "Get out and do something else" is the counsel I gave my college students.

Just as important, we need to enjoy and care for other people and to contribute as best we can to their well-being. This means not only our close circle of friends, but the wide interdependent world that surrounds us. Such caring does not mean that we should expect too much of our children and grandchildren. Don't expect them to attend to you out of gratitude. Rather, let love come to you free of guilt and lead your own life. Make your own new friends and go about your business.

When I reflect upon what essentially has meant most to me in life, I think more of my teaching than of the celebrated *Library of Living Philosophers*. I hope to be remembered as a teacher. What a joy it was to me to receive countless letters on the occasion of my ninetieth birthday from students over the years who told me that I had influenced their lives, one way or another, for the better. Nevertheless, it certainly is not for me to say to what extent my teaching has ultimately "taken." Certainly I did not make enough converts to make a real difference in the goal of world peace.

Essentially I am sure I would live my life much the same if I had to live it over. Indeed, I would be a teacher again, because I can think of no profession more satisfying or fulfilling. I miss teaching. I miss the classroom and the students. Although I go to the campus occasionally, I spend less and less time in my office there. A new generation of students and faculty have come and gone since I retired six years ago, and my contacts are limited. That is the cold fact. I am no longer an active teacher.

Looking back, I wish I had given more time to my family—written more faithfully to my old parents in Germany, and spent more time with all six of my children. But like many career-oriented men, I found myself enveloped too much by my professional life.

I do not seem to recall a time in my life when I resented "growing older"—and I still don't. It is the quality of life that is far more meaningful than the number of years. Human existence is whatever we make it. Happiness, I grant, is important. But to pursue it as conscious end is self-defeating. I am in harmony with what Einstein once said: "Man is here for the sake of other men—above all for those upon whose smile and well-being our own happiness depends, and also for the countless unknown souls with whose fate we are connected by a bond of sympathy. Many times a day I realize how much my own inner and outer life is built upon the labors of my fellowmen, both living and dead, and how earnestly I must exert myself in order to return to give as much as I have received."

Grateful acknowledgment is made to the following for permission to reprint previously published material:

Associated University Presses, Inc.: "The Bright Plain" from *New and Selected Poems* 1942–1987 by Charles Edward Eaton. Copyright © 1987 by Associated University Presses, Inc. Reprinted by permission of the publisher, Associated University Presses, Inc.

Dragon's Teeth Press: "Nota Bene" and "The Lost Garden" from *Late News from Adam's Acres*. Copyright © 1983 by Cornel Lengyel. Published by Dragon's Teeth Press, El Dorado National Forest, Georgetown, California 95634. Library of Congress Catalog Card Number 82:71821. ISBN: 0-934218-25-0.

Dramatists Play Service, Inc.: Excerpts from *The Crocodile Smile*. Copyright © 1972 by Jerome Lawrence and Robert E. Lee. Reprinted by permission of the authors and the Dramatists Play Service, Inc.

Harcourt Brace Jovanovich, Inc.: Excerpt from "The Love Song of J. Alfred Prufrock" in *Collected Poems* 1909–1962 by T. S. Eliot. Copyright 1936 by Harcourt Brace Jovanovich, Inc. Copyright © 1963, 1964 by T. S. Eliot. Rights in the USA administered by Harcourt Brace Jovanovich, Inc. Rights in all other territories administered by Faber & Faber Ltd. Reprinted by permission of the publishers, Harcourt Brace Jovanovich, Inc. and Faber and Faber Ltd.

Macmillan Publishing Company: Excerpts from "Sailing to Byzantium" in *The Poems of W. B. Yeats: A New Edition* edited by Richard J. Finneran. Copyright 1928 by Macmillan Publishing Company. Renewed 1956 by Georgie Yeats. Rights in the USA administered by Macmillan Publishing Company. Rights in all other territories administered by AP Watt Ltd. Reprinted by permission of Macmillan Publishing Company and AP Watt Ltd. on behalf of Michael B. Yeats and Macmillan London Ltd.

The Sunday School Board of the Southern Baptist Convention: Excerpts from chapter one of *Essays In Gratitude* by D. Elton Trueblood. (Nashville: Broadman 1982). All rights reserved. Used by permission.

ABOUT THE EDITOR

Phillip Berman was educated at the University of California at Santa Barbara, where he received his B.A., and at Harvard, where he received a master's degree in comparative religions. He is founder and president of the Center for the Study of Contemporary Belief and the author of over twelve books, among them the highly regarded *The Courage of Conviction*. His forthcoming book will be the first extensive oral history of American beliefs and values.

The Center for the Study of Contemporary Belief is a nonprofit public interest organization dedicated to the promotion of tolerance and intellectual and spiritual growth in society at large. To further these aims, the Center publishes books, sponsors national lecture programs, and is currently developing a seminar and retreat facility in northern New Mexico.

If you would like to learn more about the Center's programs on spiritual growth, life-long learning, or aging, please fill out the following form and send it to:

THE CENTER FOR THE STUDY OF CONTEMPORARY BELIEF
Postal Box 300553
Denver, Colorado 80203

Name _____

Address _____

_____

_____

Phone Number _____